Vairāgyaśataka of Bhartṛhari

Vairāgyaśataka of Bhartṛhari

With Hindi and English Translations and Purport

A Critical Edition based on
Śāradā Manuscripts

Sugyan Kumar Mahanty

PRINTWORLD
Publishers of Indian Traditions

Cataloging in Publication Data — DK
[Courtesy: D.K. Agencies (P) Ltd. <docinfo@dkagencies.com>]

Bhartṛhari, author.
Vairāgyaśataka of Bhartṛhari : with Hindi and English translations and purport : a critical edition based on Śāradā manuscripts / Sugyan Kumar Mahanty.
pages cm
English, Hindi and Sanskrit (Sanskrit in Devanagari and roman).
Includes bibliographical references and index.
ISBN 9788124612996 (PB)

1. Renunciation (Philosophy) – Poetry. 2. Sanskrit poetry. 3. Sanskrit poetry – Translations into Hindi. 4. Sanskrit poetry – Translations into English. 5. Bhartṛhari. Vairāgyaśataka. I. Māhānti, Sujñānakumāra, 1968- translator, writer of added commentary. II. Bhartṛhari. Vairāgyaśataka. III. Bhartṛhari. Vairāgyaśataka. Hindi. IV. Bhartṛhari. Vairāgyaśataka. English. V. Title.

LCC PK3791.B28V35 2025 | DDC 891.21 23

ISBN: 978-81-246-1299-6 (Pb)
First published in India, in 2025

Printed and published by:
D.K. Printworld (P) Ltd.
Regd. Office : "Vedaśrī", F-395, Sudarshan Park
ESI Hospital Metro Station, New Delhi - 110015
Phones : (011) 4172 2626, 98713 94815
e-mail : indology@dkprintworld.com
Web : www.dkprintworld.com

।। नमो राघवाय ।।

श्रीतुलसीपीठ सेवा न्यास, चित्रकूट

सस्थापकाध्यक्ष : पद्मविभूषण श्रीचित्रकूटतुलसीपीठाधीश्वर जगद्गुरु रामानन्दाचार्य

स्वामिश्री रामभद्राचार्य जी महाराज

पञ्जी. क. 30/96-97

मङ्गलवाक्

ॐ भद्रं कर्णेभिः शृणुयाम देवाः। भद्रं पश्येमाक्षभिर्यजत्राः।
स्थिरैरङ्गैस्तुष्टुवाꣳसस्तनूभिर्व्यशेम देवहितं यदायुः।
(श्री) रामपादाब्जभृङ्गस्य स्वाचार्यस्य जगद्गुरोः।
(श्री) रामानन्दस्य वन्देऽहं श्रीपदाम्भोजपादुके॥

विदितमेव तत्रभवतां भवतां परिकलितमङ्गलमयमनीषाणां महानुभावानां विद्वद्भिमृग्य-यशसां यत् महाकालचरणारविन्दपूतायाः क्षिप्रापरमपावनतरलतरलितसौन्दर्यभाजः श्रीमहाकालनगर्या उज्जयिन्याः राजाधिराजस्य महाराजस्य भर्तृहरेः संस्कृतभाषासमर्पितं मङ्गलमयं किञ्चिदवदानम्। महाराजो भर्तृहरिः भवन्नपि सार्वभौमशासकः तिष्ठन्नपि महाराजपरमपावनसमलङ्करणमण्डितपदे कश्चनासीद् अदूष्यवैदुष्यसम्पन्नः प्रतिभासम्पन्नश्च। सतीष्वपि बह्वीषु रचनासु महाराजस्य भर्तृहरेः रचनात्रयं संस्कृतसाहित्ये तीर्थराजत्रिवेणीव शोभामाधत्ते इति मामकीनः कश्चन निरत्ययः प्रत्ययः। तत्रभवतो भगवतः महाराजाधिराजस्य श्रीभर्तृहरेः शतकत्रयं यस्मिन् शृङ्गारशतकं, नीतिशतकं, वैराग्यशतकञ्चेति। अन्ययोः शतकयोः का घटनेत्यत्र नैव विमर्शस्य मम पार्श्वे कश्चनानेहाः। किन्तु अहं साम्प्रतिकशतकघटनायाः समवलोके तत्रभवतां भवतां दृष्टिमावर्जयितुं चेष्टे। श्रूयते यन्महाराजभर्तृहरेः काचिदासीत् प्रेमानुबन्धिनी वल्लभा, साम्राज्ञी सा, तस्यां महाराजो भर्तृहरिः प्रकामं स्नेहानुबन्धनं करोति स्मेति वर्तते किञ्चिदपूर्वमैतिह्यकम्। तत्र वर्धमानेऽपि भर्तृहरेः प्रेमानुबन्धने तस्यां का द्रुहिणनिर्मिता घटना इति विचार्यैव चेतश्चमत्कारितां भजते।

सा महाराजे न स्निह्यति स्म, यं च स्निह्यति स्म सा, सोऽप्यन्यत्र स्नेहं करोति स्म। संयोगत एकया घटनया साकम् एतस्याः द्रुहिणनिर्मितवैचित्र्यमण्डितायाः सम्मोदितपण्डितायाः समखण्डितायाः घटनायाः पटाक्षेपोऽजायतेति दृढं नियतुं प्रभवामि। तत्र एकं सुन्दरं फलं यन्महाराजो भर्तृहरिः स्वकीयपत्न्यै समर्पयति। सा च यस्मै स्निह्यति स्म तस्मै समर्पयति। स च पुनः कस्यैचित् समर्पयति, या महाराजे स्नेहं करोति स्म। अन्ततोगत्वा फलं पुनः महाराजपार्श्वे आगतम्। महाराजो विचारितवान् – कुत इदम्? कथमिदम्? कीदृशमिदम्? यदा वास्तविकता ज्ञाता तदा संसारस्य निःसारतायाः कामस्य च कुटिलकलायाः वासनायाश्च कस्याश्चित् दुर्दान्तलीलायाः स्मरणं कारं कारं सञ्जातनिर्वेदः परिकलितसमस्तसंशयच्छेदः समवाप्तदारुणमनोभावनाविदारणखेदः कारुण्यमुपयातो महाराजः प्रावोचद् वैराग्यशतकस्य द्वितीये श्लोके। स च श्लोक एवंविधः –

पत्राचार - श्रीतुलसीपीठ (काँच मन्दिर) आमोदवन, चित्रकूट, सतना - म.प्र. (485334)

सम्पर्क सूत्र : +91 8085607376, +91 9151491008 | tulsipeethchitrakoot@gmail.com | jagadgururambhadracharya.org

यां चिन्तयाम्यनुदिनं मयि सा विरक्ता
साऽप्यन्यमिच्छति नरं स नरोऽन्यसक्तः ।
अस्मत्कृतेऽपि परितुष्यति काचिदन्या
धिक्तां च तं च कुसुमेषुमिमां च मां च ॥

पञ्चानां धिक्कारमूलकमिदं – धिक्कृतिपञ्चतयं सामान्यस्यापि जनस्य हृदये विदारणाय कल्पत इति नात्र कश्चन सन्देहः। स कथयति – यां प्रियतमामहं निरन्तरं चिन्तयामि सा उज्जयिन्याः साम्राज्ञी मयि विरक्ता, मयि विरक्ता सत्यप्यन्यस्मिन्ननुरक्ता। यस्मिन् साऽनुरक्ता स जनोऽन्यत्रानुरक्तः। अस्मत्कृते च काचिदन्या परितुष्यति। एवं विध्वस्त-सकलविश्वासं परिकलितहृदयविदारकनिःश्वासं समवलोकित – महापुरुषवैराग्याश्वासं सङ्केदकल्पितभयङ्करतमोच्छ्वासं वैराग्यशतकीयं द्वितीयं पद्यं परमात्मनः पादपङ्केरुहयोः प्रपत्तये प्रकामं सामग्रीमाधत्ते इत्यहं विविक्ततया निगदितुं प्रभवामि। एतया दुर्घटनया परिकल्पित-परमेश्वरपदपद्मप्रपत्तिसङ्घटनया घटनया महाराजस्य चित्तमेव एतावद् आन्दोलितम्, अत एव स पञ्च व्यक्तीर्धिक्करोति। तां, तं, कामम्, इमां महाराज्ञीं, मां स्वकमपि। किमेतस्मिन् भग्नविश्वासे परिकलितशोकोच्छ्वासे सर्वथैवाविश्वस्तान्तरङ्गे परिकलितकरुणातरङ्गे भग्नसमस्तसङ्गे समुच्छलितविरक्तिगङ्गे कोऽपि स्थातुं प्रभवेदिति? इयं घटना महाराजस्य वैराग्यस्य कारणं जाता। अत एव महाराजेन भर्तृहरिणा सम्पूर्णराज्यं त्यक्त्वा वैराग्यं स्वीकृत्य परिव्राजकता स्वीचक्रे। स च गुहां सेवितुं गतः। अद्याप्युज्जयिन्यां भर्तृहरिगुहा जागर्ति चर्कर्ति च महाराजस्य विशुद्धवैराग्यवैभवम्।

अस्यैव कारुण्योत्तरङ्गितस्य काव्यबीजस्य नवाङ्कुरोऽयं वैराग्यशतकाख्यः। किं नाम वैराग्यशतकमिति? सत्स्वपि बहुषु प्रकाशितेषु एतत्प्रतिभूतेषु ग्रन्थरत्नेषु महाराजस्य वैराग्यशतकस्य इदं शतकं विद्वन्मनोरमम्। अनुसन्धित्सु पाथेयभूतं परमपूतम् इत्यत्राहं सविश्वस्ति निगदितुं चेष्टे। शारदापाण्डुलिपौ प्राप्तमिदं रत्नं महत्कौशलपूर्णं कलापूर्णं कुतूहलपूर्णं चेति। संयोगतः सौभाग्यतश्च अस्मदनुजकल्पेन उत्कलनिवासिना जगन्नाथचरणारविन्दोपासिना सुज्ञानकुमारमाहान्तिमहाभागेन प्रकाश्यमानं ग्रन्थललाममैतद् अनुसन्धातृणाम् अनुसन्धित्सूनाञ्च परमपाथेयं भवितेति महदविस्मरणीयमवदानं सुरभारत्याः कृते। एतेन विदुषा महता यत्नेन समुपलब्धानामनेकासां प्रतीनां सङ्कलनमाश्रित्य सङ्कलय्य च तत्तत्पाठभेदान् प्रदर्श्य च भिन्नभिन्नटिप्पणीः, यद्विद्वन्मनोरञ्जनं समाचरितं तत्कृते सम्पूर्णं विद्वज्जगद् आधमर्ण्यमाकलयिष्यति एतद्विद्वन्मचर्चिकाभूतस्य परमपूतस्य पण्डितप्रकाण्डस्य। तत्र स्ववक्तव्यस्पष्टीकरणार्थमहमेकं पद्यमुद्धर्तुं समीहे यद्वैराग्यशतकस्य द्वितीयम्। अत्र द्वौ पाठभेदौ दिदर्शयिषाम्यहम्। प्राचीनप्रतिषु "यां चिन्तयामि सततम्" इति लिखितमस्ति। अस्यां प्रतौ माहान्तिमहाभागः लिखति "यां चिन्तयाम्यनुदिनम्"। सर्वत्र "सततम्" अत्र "अनुदिनम्"। द्वयोर्मध्ये कश्चन भेदः समवलोक्यते न वेति तत्र स्पष्टम्। सतताऽनुदिनयोः अर्थभेदं विचारयिष्यामः तदा नूनमेव कश्चनानन्दोऽनुभविष्यते। सातत्ये आनुदिन्ये च कश्चन भेदो वर्तते। दिने दिने इत्यनुदिनम्, सातत्येऽपि दिनानां व्यतिक्रमो नास्ति, सातत्यं वर्तते, कदापि कदापि प्रहराणां दिनानां घटिकानां पलानां व्यतिक्रमो जायते। अनुदिनमिति कथने कश्चन व्यतिक्रमो नास्ति। यामहम् एकमपि क्षणं विस्मर्तुं न प्रभवामि सैव मद्विषये विरक्ता, भवतु नाम विरक्ता, अन्यत्र

नानुरज्येत, साऽन्यत्राप्यनुरक्ता, साऽप्यन्यमिच्छति नरं, यं च प्रति अनुरागविषयवती सा, सोऽपि तस्यां नानुरक्तः। स नरोऽन्यसक्तः। अस्मत्कृते च, अहम् इमां चिन्तयामि, इयं न चिन्तयति, किन्तु अन्या काचन मां चिन्तयति, अस्मत्कृते च परितुष्यति काचिदन्या। अत एव एवंविधे विश्वासहीने दीने संसारे निःसारे निराधारे परिकृतशोकपारावारे काऽऽवश्यकता मादृशस्य जनस्य? तां धिक्, तं धिक्, कुसुमेषुं = कुसुमसायकं कामदेवं धिक्, इमां साम्राज्ञीं धिक्, मां मादृशं लम्पटमपि धिक्। अत्र पञ्चानां धिक्कृतौ प्राचीनप्रत्यां धिक्तां च तं च मदनं च इमां च मां च इति पाठः यदि स्वीक्रियेत तदा कश्चन भयङ्करतमो दोष आगच्छति, स च स्वीकृते पूर्वपाठे मदनञ्च इमां च मां च इत्यत्र सन्धिरपेक्ष्यते। सन्धिः कथं वार्यताम्? यदि वैयाकरणसम्बन्धिदोषः काव्ये तर्हि महाननर्थः। पुण्यजनकतावच्छेदकता न स्यात् अत एव वयं पतञ्जलिं प्राञ्जलयः प्रार्थयामहे यत् कथमेतस्य दोषस्य परिहारः स्यात्? तदा पतञ्जलेः कारिकां शरणीकुर्मः।

> संहितैकपदे नित्या नित्या धातूपसर्गयोः।
> नित्या समासे वाक्ये तु सा विवक्षामपेक्षते॥

वाक्ये तु सा विवक्षामपेक्षते, अत इदं वाक्यम्। सन्धेः अनिवार्यतानिवारणाय वाक्यकल्पना, कल्पनायां च वाक्यद्वयात्मिकायां पुनर्महाननर्थः। "सम्भवत्येकवाक्यत्वे वाक्यभेदो न युज्यते"। अत एव पूर्वपाठे भीषणमिदं दूषणम्। श्रीसुज्ञानकुमारमाहान्तिमहाभागानां पाठे एतस्य परिहारः। शारदापाण्डुलिप्यां मदनं च इमां च इति नास्ति। "कुसुमेषुमिमां च मां च", कुसुमेषुः = कुसुमसायकः कामः। एवं बहुषु स्थलेषु मयाऽनुभूयते यद् अर्द्धशतकेऽपि पाठभेदे या रमणीयताऽनेन विदुषा प्रादर्शि, यत् कौशलं समुद्घाटितं, यच्च पाटवम् अनुसन्धातुरेतस्य नूनमेव तत् प्रशंसापात्रतामाटीकते।

राष्ट्रियसंस्कृतसंस्थानभूतं केन्द्रीयसंस्कृतविश्वविद्यालयम् एतत्कुलपतिम् एतत्कार्य-कारिणीम् एतन्मन्त्रालयं च वर्धापये। यत्र श्रीसुज्ञानकुमारमाहान्तिमहाभागसदृशा विद्वन्मणयः केन्द्रीयसंस्कृत-विश्वविद्यालयरत्नाकरस्याभां विभावयन्तः एतादृशानि ग्रन्थरत्नानि प्रकाशयन्ति। एतद्ग्रन्थस्य प्रकाशकाय डी०के० प्रिण्टवर्ल्ड इत्यस्य प्रमुखाय श्रीसुशीलमित्तलमहोदयाय अपि साधुवादान् वच्मि।

श्रीसुज्ञानकुमारमाहान्तिमहाभागायापि अनेकाः शुभाः मङ्गलाशंसाः व्याहरामि। एवंविधान्यनेकानि कार्याणि कारं कारं विदुषां हर्षपारावारं वर्धयमानोऽसौ विद्वान् चिरं जीवतु। भद्राणि पश्यतु। अभिरामं रामं च भजताम् इति –

> मन्दाकिनीपयःपूरसिक्तपादाम्बुजाय च।
> रामाय पूर्णकामाय जानकीजानये नमः॥

स्वस्ति। इति मङ्गलमाचरते।

जगद्गुरुरामानन्दाचार्यस्वामिरामभद्राचार्यः
पद्मविभूषणो ज्ञानपीठपुरस्कारभाक्
श्रीचित्रकूटतुलसीपीठाधीश्वरः।

प्रो॰ श्रीनिवास वरखेड़ी
कुलपतिः
केन्द्रीयसंस्कृतविश्वविद्यालयः
संसदः अधिनियमेन स्थापितः
(प्राक्तनं राष्ट्रियसंस्कृतसंस्थानम्,
भारतसर्वकारस्य शिक्षामन्त्रालयाधीनम्)

Prof. Shrinivasa Varakhedi
Vice-Chancellor
Central Sanskrit University
Established by an Act of Parliament
(Formerly Rashtriya Sanskrit Sansthan,
Under Ministry of Education, Govt of India)

पुरोवाक्

उज्जयिन्या राजा भर्तृहरिणा स्वरचितैस्त्रिभिः नीति-वैराग्य-शृङ्गारशतकैः संस्कृतसाहित्योद्यानं संसिच्याभिनव-काव्यसुमभिस्तदाभा संवर्धिता। संस्कृतसाहित्ये सन्ति यद्यप्यसंख्यानि तादृग्विधासंवलितानि काव्यान्यपरिमेयानि तथापि भर्तृहरिशतकानि विगतसहस्राब्दद्वये विश्वस्मिन्विश्वे नैतिकतां, भौतिकसुख-भोगवादगतनश्वरताम्, आध्यात्मिकचेतनानुप्राणितविरागताञ्च जने जने उन्मेषयितुं यथा प्राभवन् न तथा तादृशानि काव्यान्तराणि।

भर्तृहरेरन्वर्थनामान्यतमं काव्यं वैराग्यशतकं त्याग-वितृष्णावैराग्याणामुपदेशपरम् उत्कृष्टं काव्यं, यद्धि पारमार्थिकजीवनाय आसक्ति-कामना-वासनाऽसन्तोष-भौतिकतावादादीनपाकर्तुं प्रेरयति। काव्येऽस्मिन् भौतिकेच्छानां व्यर्थता, विषयासक्तेस्तुच्छता, याचनाभ्यो दूरता, दासत्वस्य नीचता, नारीविषयककामुकतायाः निन्द्यता चेत्यादिभिः सह संन्यासत्यागानासक्त्यादयोऽपि समर्थिताः सन्ति। जीवनस्य रहस्यमध्यात्मभावजागरणद्वारा परमतत्त्वव्यासङ्गाध्यवसाय एव इति भर्तृहरेर्दर्शनमत्र प्रतिबिम्बितमस्ति।

सम्प्रति भर्तृहरिकृतीनां शतोत्तराणि संस्करणानि अनुवादाश्चोपलभ्यन्ते, परं तेष्वेकतरममपि शारदापाण्डुलिप्याधारेण न विहितं, परिणामत उपलब्धानि प्रायः सर्वाण्यपि संस्करणानि मूलकृतिभिः भेदं बिभ्रति। ऐदम्प्राथम्येन केन्द्रीय-संस्कृतविश्वविद्यालयस्याचार्यः प्रो॰ सुज्ञानकुमारमाहान्तिमहोदयो भर्तृहरिरचितानामेतासां तिसृणां कृतीनां दुर्लभ-शारदापाण्डुलिप्यन्वेषणे आत्मानं विनियुज्य तदाविष्कारे साफल्यमवापेति प्रथमः कल्पः। अथ चानेन 2023तमे वर्षे हिन्दी-आङ्ग्लानुवादैः सह तदीयनीतिशतकस्य शारदापाठसहितं समीक्षात्मकं संस्करणं प्रकाशितमित्यैतिहासिकी उपलब्धिः। तस्याञ्च शृङ्खलायां प्रो॰ सुज्ञानकुमारमाहान्तिमहोदयसम्पादितं भर्तृहरिरचितवैराग्यशतकस्य शारदापाठमूलं समालोचनात्मकं संस्करणं हिन्दी-आङ्ग्लानुवादैः सह प्राकाश्यमेतीति निश्चयेन मोदप्रदम्। तदीयेयं कृतिः छात्रेषु, अनुसन्धातृषु, विद्वत्सु, सामाजिकेषु च सुग्राह्या स्यादिति विश्वसिमि।

वैशाखशुक्ल (अक्षय) तृतीया, संवत् 2081
10 May 2024

प्रो॰ श्रीनिवासः वरखेडी
कुलपतिः
केन्द्रीयसंस्कृतविश्वविद्यालयः, नवदेहली

56-57, संस्थानिकक्षेत्रम्, जनकपुरी, नवदेहली - 110058
56-57, Institutional Area, Janakpuri, New Delhi - 110058 (INDIA)
Ph. No.; (0) 011-28523949, **EPABX**: 28524993, 28521994, 28524995
EMAIL : vivechancellorcsu@gmal.com / vc@csu.co.in, **WEBSITE** : www.sanskrit.in

Prof. Banamali Biswal
Professor & Dean (Academic Affairs,
Yogic Science & Holistic Health Practices)
Central Sanskrit University
Established by an Act of Parliament
(Formerly Rashtriya Sanskrit Sansthan, Deemed to be University)
56-57, Institutional Area, Janakpuri, New Delhi - 110058
Mobile : 9450781742 / Email : banamali7@gmail.com

Prelude

I FEEL honoured to write a few words to this critical edition of the *Vairāgyaśataka of Bhartṛhari* based on the Śāradā manuscripts (भर्तृहरिकृतं वैराग्यशतकम् – शारदामातृकाधारितं समालोचनात्मकपाठसहितम्) by Professor Sugyan Kumar Mahanty. I perceive this work as a novel and valuable addition to the realm of education and scholarly inquiry. Bhartṛhari, the king of Ujjain, has nurtured and enriched the garden of Sanskrit literature with his immortal opus *Śatakatrayī* (comprising the *Nītiśataka*, *Vairāgyaśataka* and *Śṛṅgāraśataka*). His works have been revered and admired worldwide as they have imparted the finest moral principles for over two millennia. Numerous editions and translations of Bhartṛhari's works are available, but none of them is based on the Śāradā manuscripts, thereby lacking proximity to the original text.

For the first time, Professor Sugyan Kumar Mahanty has discovered these rare manuscripts in the Śāradā script and has undertaken the task of preparing a critical edition of these three masterpieces by Bhartṛhari. As part of this endeavour, he has already published a critical edition of Bhartṛhari's *Nītiśataka* based on the Śāradā manuscript in 2023, accompanied by Hindi and English translations. I hope, in future, he will provide us similar work on the *Śṛṅgāraśataka* in this series.

The *Vairāgyaśataka*, as indicated by its title, extols the significance of seclusion. It refutes the value of addiction, attachments, desire, lust, dissatisfaction and exclusive dominion over materialism in order to attain a peaceful existence. It exposes the futility of desire, condemns infatuation, advocates detachment from entreaties, highlights the ignobility of servitude and underscores the repulsiveness of lasciviousness towards women. It advocates for renunciation, detachment from action and liberation from sensual objects. It also reveals the realities such as the irreconcilability of sensual desires, the pervasiveness of lust, the timeless nature of desire, the boundless nature of craving and the inevitability of death. Ultimately, Bhartṛhari unveils the secret of the significance of life, which is to experience transcendental reality through spiritualism.

According to Bhartṛhari, how can living beings find happiness in this fleeting and mortal life, which is as transient as waves and bubbles in water? In old age, with a decrepit and wrinkled body, a person must leave everything behind and plunge into the abyss of time. The pursuit of pleasures may continue, but the individual's existence comes to an end. The poet has expressed such profound feelings in the following lines:

भोगा न भुक्ता वयमेव भुक्ताः तपो न तप्तं वयमेव तप्ताः।
कालो न यातो वयमेव याताः तृष्णा न जीर्णा वयमेव जीर्णाः॥ – *वैराग्यशतकम्* 7

We were not the ones enjoying the pleasures, but rather the pleasures themselves were enjoying us. We were not the ones doing penance, but rather we ourselves were the ones doing penance. Time did not go anywhere, but rather we ourselves went away. The desire did not fade away, but rather we ourselves became old.

In this manner, Bhartṛhari has emphasized the significance of impermanence and renunciation of the world. This Śataka has witnessed a remarkable fusion of poetic talent and philosophy. It portrays the growing apathy towards worldly attractions and pleasures. The poet's sole desire is to spend his time chanting "Śiva-Śiva" in a sacred forest. The human attraction to the opposite sex is not constant. The person whom (he or she) one desires or loves may be involved with someone else. In fact, the king himself had a bitter experience coming to his wife Queen Piṅgalā as she was in love with another person. The poet expresses this sentiment aptly in the following renowned verse:

यां चिन्तयाम्यनुदिनं मयि सा विरक्ता
साऽप्यन्यमिच्छति नरं स नरोऽन्यसक्तः ।
अस्मत्कृतेऽपि परितुष्यति काचिदन्या
धिक्तां च तं च कुसुमेषुमिमां च मां च ॥

– *वैराग्यशतकम्* 2

The woman (Piṅgalā), I mull over whom, shows no interest in me. The person (*Aśvapāla*) whom (Piṅgalā) loves is infatuated with another woman (*rājanartakī*). The *rājanartakī* has affection for me (King Bhartṛhari). How shameful it is for Piṅgalā! How shameful it is for Aśvapāla! How shameful it is for *rājanartakī*! How shameful it is for the Cupid and even for me Bhartṛhari!

The above inconsistency in love forces the poet to think the following way which has become an example of disgust sentiment (Bībhatsa Rasa):

स्तनौ मांसग्रन्थी कनककलशावित्युपमितौ
मुखं श्लेष्मागारं तदपि च शशाङ्केन तुलितम् ।
स्रवन्मूत्रक्लिन्नं करिवरकरस्पर्धि जघनं
मुहुर्निन्द्यं रूपं कविवरविशेषैर्गुरुकृतम् ॥

– *वैराग्यशतकम्* 20

> The poets give such metaphors as golden vessels to the breasts which are but two lumps of flesh; the mouths, seat of phlegm and mucus, are compared to the moon; the loins, outlet for wet urine, are likened to the forehead of an elephant; thus glorifying the human form is always contemptible.

The poet is sometimes astonished that in spite of the following universal fact related to different stages of human life, people do not think of the welfare of the self:

> व्याघ्रीव तिष्ठति जरा परितर्जयन्ती रोगाश्च दस्यव इव प्रहरन्ति गात्रे ।
> आयुः परिस्रवति भिन्नघटादिवाम्भो लोको न चात्महितमाचरतीति कष्टम् ॥
>
> – *वैराग्यशतकम्* 108

> Like a tigress, fearsome is old age. Illnesses attack the body like enemies. Life flows like water from a leaky vessel. Is it not a wonder yet that man engages in actions not conducive to well-being?

In another significant verse, he describes an inter-conflict (*antardvandva*) of a person who is forced to beg for his family due to extreme poverty with a fear to denial of his entreaty. Sometimes such a situation forces a man towards renunciation or relinquishment:

> दीनां दीनमुखैः सहैव शिशुकैराकृष्टजीर्णाम्बरां
> क्रोशद्भिर्विधुरैः क्षुधातिविधुरां पश्येन्न चेद्गेहिनीम् ।
> याच्ञाभङ्गभयेन गद्गदगलत्त्रुट्यद्विलीनाक्षरं
> को देहीति वदेत्स्वदग्धजठरस्यार्थे मनस्वी जनः ॥
>
> – *वैराग्यशतकम्* 8

> Distressed, misery written on her face, constantly tugged at her worn-out clothes by hungry, crying children – if one were not to see such a wife, who is that wise person, smitten with hunger, with a choked and faltering voice, would say "Give me", fearing refusal of his entreaty?

Even staying in a precarious condition, men never get rid of the worldly matters. In poet's words:

भिक्षाशनं तदपि नीरसमेकवारं शय्या च भूः परिजनो निजदेहमात्रम् ।
वस्त्रं च जीर्णशतखण्डमयी च कन्था हा हा तथापि विषया न परित्यजन्ति ॥

– *वैराग्यशतकम्* 19

For eating I have tasteless food once a day, after begging of alms; the earth for a bed, and my own body as a servant; for dress, a blanket made from hundreds of rags; and yet alas! sensual desires do not leave!

In this short span of changing life a man well understands the transiency of enjoyment due to inner body and outer-body changes:

क्षणं बालो भूत्वा क्षणमपि युवा कामरसिकः
क्षणं वित्तैर्हीनः क्षणमपि च सम्पूर्णविभवः ।
जराजीर्णैरङ्गैर्नट इव वलीमण्डिततनु-
नरः संसाराङ्के विशति यमधानीजवनिकाम् ॥

– *वैराग्यशतकम्* 111

For a moment like a child, for another moment a lascivious youth; one moment a pauper, another a wealthy person; at the end of life, the body worn out by age and covered with wrinkles, man enters the abode of Death like an actor exiting the stage.

From the above observation of mine, it is clear that there are certain factors which push a man towards renunciation, the prominent of which are failure in love, unfaithfulness or cheating of paramour, uncertainty of life, transiency of enjoyment, adverse bodily effects, diseases, poverty, etc. I would like to brief these facts with my couple of *anuṣṭubh*s:

प्रेमगतमसाफल्यं प्रेमिणामविश्वस्तता । जीवने क्षणिकत्वं च वैराग्ये मूलकारणम् ॥
क्षणभंगुरता भोगे रोगाः शरीरमध्यगाः । चरमं चापि दारिद्र्यं सन्ति वैराग्यहेतवः ॥

Professor Sugyan Kumar Mahanty has taken on the task of not only providing a critical edition of the text but also explaining the philosophies and ideas of Bhartṛhari regarding the transient nature of materialism and the eternal nature of consciousness.

The contents of this book are of great significance. It begins with a Foreword and Preface, followed by an Introduction in English by the author. The Introduction covers topics such as the life and contributions of Bhartṛhari, the text of *Vairāgyaśataka* and its editions, and information about the newly discovered Śāradā manuscripts of the *Vairāgyaśataka*. The main body of the book includes the original text and translations in both Hindi and English, along with explanations for each of the 111 verses of the *Vairāgyaśataka*. The author has provided a heading for each verse, making it easier for readers to navigate. The book concludes with Appendices, which contain critical notes on variant readings in the Śāradā manuscript, an alphabetical index to the verses, an index to special words and the original Śāradā manuscript of the *Vairāgyaśataka* in Devanāgarī transliteration. The book is being published by D.K. Printworld, New Delhi and I am confident that it will be well-received and appreciated by its readers.

I would like to conclude my Prelude with the following *anuṣṭubh*s of mine:

सुज्ञानस्य महज्ज्ञानमुभयोः शास्त्रकाव्ययोः ।
महान्ति तस्य कार्याणि प्रकाशनप्रसङ्गतः ॥
संस्कृतवाङ्मये ये च महान्तः कवयस्समे ।
भर्तृहरिश्च तेष्वेव महकविः प्रसिद्ध्यति ॥
तस्य महाकवेः ख्यातं काव्यत्रयं विशेषतः ।
नीति-शृङ्गार-वैराग्यान्याधृत्य शतकं पृथक् ॥

सम्पादनं समीक्षाभिर्वैराग्यशतकस्य वै।
कृतं सुज्ञानवर्येण शारदामातृकाधृतम्॥
अत्रास्त्याङ्ग्लानुवादेन हिन्दीभाषान्तरो नवः।
शीर्षकाणि च पद्यानां दत्तान्याशयपूर्वकम्॥
एवं पुस्तकमेतच्च च्छात्राणामुपकारकम्।
विदुषां शिक्षकाणाञ्च भवेद्वा मार्गदर्शकम्॥
अस्यैव लेखकस्यापि कार्यमेतादृशं पृथक्।
नीतिशतकसम्बद्धं पूर्वमस्ति प्रकाशितम्॥
प्रस्तुत-पुस्तकस्यास्ति महत्त्वं व्यापकं यतः।
तस्य विद्वत्समाजे स्यात् स्वागतमभिनन्दनम्॥

Before I stop, I extend my best wishes for the success of this publication and thank the learned author Professor Sugyan Kumar Mahanty for this valuable contribution.

Banamali Biswal

Preface

I FEEL extremely delighted to present this critical edition of *Vairāgyaśataka of Bhartṛhari* based on Kāśmīrī Śāradā manuscripts along with translations and purports of each stanza, both in Hindi and English. Present edition owes its inception to Shri Susheel Mittal, director of D.K. Printworld, New Delhi, who assigned me to prepare a flawless edition of all the three Śatakas of Bhartṛhari along with reliable Hindi and English translations. Considering the nature of assignment relating to the area of my study as well as my interest, I accepted the task with a nod of consent. I started to collect the different printed editions of all the Śatakas, where I noticed multitude variations in readings of the text and in the number of verses. I did not find any agreement among those printed editions in matter of their number, order and text. Consequently, I got a havoc of trust and reliability on the available text of those editions and felt it difficult to decipher the primary text on the foundation of these available editions. Then, I started searching the oldest manuscripts of these Śatakas, and as a result of my search, I found a single manuscript of the *Nītiśataka* in Śāradā script, which I transcribed into Devanāgarī. Then I collated the text of Śāradā along with that of other major printed editions. I noticed relevance and significance of the text of Śāradā that is close to the primary text, which I have established with supportive arguments in the *Nītiśataka of Bhartṛhari* (a critical edition supplemented with Kāśmīrī Śāradā text having Hindi and English translation and purport), published by D.K. Printworld, New Delhi in 2023.

Next, in the process of my search of Śāradā manuscripts, I procured five manuscripts of the *Vairāgyaśataka*, on the base of which this edition has been prepared with critical notes on variant readings. In the last four centuries many printed editions have been published in India and abroad, but none of those has been based on the Śāradā manuscripts. D.D. Kosambi had collected 377 manuscripts but no manuscript had been found in Kāśmīrī Śāradā out of those as he mentions in his *The Epigrams Attributed to Bhartṛhari*.[1]

As far as social aspects are concerned, the *Vairāgyaśataka* is as important as the other two works of Bhartṛhari, i.e. the *Nītiśataka* and *Śṛṅgāraśataka*. the *Vairāgyaśataka* advises an individual to remain detached from addiction, absurdity and desires. It arouses a repercussion of prurient propensities and establishes the fallout of indulgence in sensual pleasures. It inspires to attain supreme bliss following renunciation and spiritual pursuit.

I pay my homage to almighty, by whose grace this work has been completed without any obstacles. I must utilize this occasion to announce my obeisance from the depth of my heart to the immortal soul of my parents and departed Gurus whose blessings have always been the foundation of my courage to undertake the literary recreation and to adhere to dedicate myself for the cause of Sanskrit and Indological Research.

I express my deep sense of gratitude to Professor Shrinivas Varakhedi, honourable Vice-Chancellor of Central Sanskrit University, New Delhi, who blessed me with his gracious foreword. My thanks are also due to Professor Banamali Biswal, Dean of the Academic Affairs, Central

[1] Kosambi, 1948, Introduction, p. 57.

Sanskrit University, New Delhi for his blessings in the form of an enriched Prelude.

I also extend my thanks to my beloved wife Sipra, daughter Prachi and son Prameya who continuously render their support to me to carry on and uphold the service to Sanskrit.

I am ever grateful to Shri Susheel Mittal, the director of D.K. Printworld, New Delhi and render my appreciation with great applause to him not only for publishing my manuscript but also inspiring me to pursue critical and creative literary activities on Indology.

I shall think of my endeavours a success if this edition of the *Vairāgyaśataka* will be meaningful to the scholars, resourceful to the researchers and useful to the public in general. Finally, I would like to cite Mallinātha:

इहान्वयमुखेनैव सर्वं व्याख्यायते मया।
नामूलं लिख्यते किञ्चिन्नानपेक्षितमुच्यते॥

ihānvayamukhenaiva sarvaṁ vyākhyāyate mayā ।
nāmūlaṁ likhyate kiñcinnānapekṣitamucyate ॥
– *Sañjīvanī, Kumārasambhavam,* canto 1

Chaitra Śuklapratipadā,
Vikrama Saṁvat 2081
9 April 2024

Sugyan Kumar Mahanty
(सुज्ञानकुमारमाहान्तिः)

Abbreviations

Ms eG-1	Śāradā Manuscript No. 4145, Recovered from Digital Resource – UPSS Lucknow, digitized by EE Gangotri
Ms eG-2	Śāradā Manuscript, Baramulla 5, digitized by E-Gangotri Digital Preservation Trust
Ms ORLS-3	Śāradā Manuscript No. 2276, Recovered from Oriental Research Library, University Campus, Srinagar, India
JKM.1911	Joglekar, K.M. (ed.), 1911, *Bhartrihari's Niti and Vairagya Shataka*, Bombay: Oriental Publishing Company
GAV.1954	Gopalachariar, A.V. (ed.), 1954, *Bhartihari's Sringara Sataka and Vairagya Sataka*, Madras: V. Ramaswamy Satrulu & Sons
VŚ	*Vairāgyaśataka* (present edition)

Contents

1

Introduction

The Life and Contributions of Bhartṛhari

THE widely known personal history of Bhartṛhari, the author of three Śatakas, has little reliability. The authorship of three distinct treatises — the *Śatakatrayī, Vākyapadīya* and *Bhaṭṭikāvya* — is traditionally attributed to Bhartṛhari. *Śataka* is an anthology with 100 poems. The *Śatakatrayī* of Bhartṛhari is comprised of three Śatakas, i.e. the *Nītiśataka, Śṛṅgāraśataka* and *Vairāgyaśataka.* The *Vākyapadīya,* a treatise on grammar, is also ascribed to Bhartṛhari. The *Bhaṭṭikāvya,* a grammatical poem, is the third work attributed to Bhartṛhari. The question arises here: whether Bhartṛhari is the same person to whom all these three distinct treatises are ascribed to? The tradition also claims that Bhartṛhari was a scion of a royal family of great celebrity, deserved to wear the kingly crown.

There is a folklore about him that once upon a time King Bhartṛhari got a fruit that would render immortality to anyone who ate it. Bhartṛhari gave it to his beloved wife, his wife to her paramour, and he in his turn to his darling, and she offered the same to King Bhartṛhari, the most beloved of her heart. Thus turning back of the immortal fruit brought a great change in his mind. This is the plot, what the verse 2 of *Vairāgyaśataka* indicates:

yāṁ cintayāmyanudinaṁ mayi sā viraktā
sā 'pyanyamicchati naraṁ sa naro 'nyasaktaḥ ।
asmatkṛtepi parituṣyati kācidanyā
dhiktāṁ ca taṁ ca kusumeṣumimāṁ ca māṁ ca ॥

This incidence made him so thoroughly disgusted with the pleasures of this world, renouncing the worldly pleasures and leisure, and he undertook *saṁnyāsa,* resigning his crown in favour of his younger brother Vikramāditya.

Now let us enter to the threshold of inquiry: Who is the real author of these Śatakas? Although there are some who are doubtful to ascribe the authorship of these three Śatakas to the legendary Bhartṛhari, there are ample and strong evidences which cannot refute to assign the authorship of these three Śatakas to Bhartṛhari. We had already discussed this topic elaborately in the introduction to the *Nītiśataka*. Following are some to support this:

- In the colophons of a large number of manuscripts, the three Śatakas, are ascribed to none other than Bhartṛhari. Therefore, it could be set down that three Śatakas are the works of a single authorship, i.e. Bhartṛhari only.
- We have considerable evidences to refute the statement in favour of the anthological character of these three Śatakas.

There are some scholars who have attempted to establish the identification of Bhartṛhari with the authors of the *Bhaṭṭikāvya* and *Vākyapadīya*. But there are neither sufficient literary evidences nor legendary lore to support their view.

I-tsang, the Chinese traveller to India in seventh century CE, states in his report that the author of the *Vākyapadīya*, the famous grammarian Bhartṛhari, died forty years before his visit to India. He also states that the same Bhartṛhari was a Buddhist who believed deeply in the three jewels and meditated in the twofold voidness (*śūnyatā*). Even Vācaspati Miśra, a scholar of the eleventh century CE, admits that Bhartṛhari, the author of the *Vākyapadīya* was a Buddhist. Kumārila Bhaṭṭa, a philosopher of the Mīmāṁsā school, also fiercely criticizes the Buddhistic approaches of Bhartṛhari. Therefore, the author of Śatakas who was an ardent follower of Vedāntic philosophy, cannot be identified with the author of *Vākyapadīya*, who was a dogmatic Buddhist.

In *Dhvanyāloka* (v. 4), Ānandavardhana extracts a verse from the *Śṛṅgāraśataka* (v. 6) of Bhartṛhari as:

smitaṁ kiñcinmugdhaṁ taralamadhuro dṛṣṭivibhavaḥ
parispando vācāmabhinavavilāsormisarasaḥ ।
gatānāmārambhaḥ kisalayitalīlāparimalaḥ
spṛśantyāstāruṇyaṁ kimiva hi na ramyaṁ mṛgadṛśaḥ ॥
— Tripathi 1963a: 1313

Abhinavagupta mentions Bhartṛhari in his *Locana* in two different instances (vv. 1 and 4) as under:

yathāha bhagavān bhartṛhariḥ –
yaḥ saṁyogaviyogābhyāṁ karaṇairupajanyate ।
sa sphoṭaḥ śabdajāśśabdā dhvanayo 'nyairudāhṛtāḥ ॥
— Tripathi 1963b: 270

tathāhi bhartṛhariṇedaṁ kṛtaṁ yasyāyamaudāryamahimā yasyāsmiñchāstre । *evaṁvidhassāro dṛśyate tasyāyaṁ ślokaprabandhastasmādādaraṇīyametadita lokaḥ pravartamāno dṛśyate* । — Tripathi 1963b: 1410

While differentiating two authors, Abhinavagupta cites Bhartṛhari saying "भगवान् भर्तृहरिः (*bhagavān bhartṛhariḥ*)" as the author of the *Vākyapadīya* and in the 4th *udyota*, he refers him differently saying "भर्तृहरिणेदं कृतं … (*bhartṛhariṇedaṁ kṛtaṁ …*)" as the author of the *Śṛṅgāraśataka* in his *Locana*.

The above citations evidently affirm that both Bhartṛharis are different and were existed before ninth century CE. Now let us discuss; if the later limit of the period of Bhartṛhari, the author of the *Vākyapadīya*, is ninth century CE, what is the prior limit of his age?

Some scholars like Colebrooke identify Bhartṛhari, the author of the *Vākyapadīya*, with that of the *Bhaṭṭikāvya*. But this identification seems to have no reliable evidences, as both the authors had different philosophical convictions, the former was a follower of Buddhism and the later was a Vaiṣṇava, as he glorifies the character of Rāma in his *Bhaṭṭikāvya*. The *Bhaṭṭikāvya* had been composed in Vallabhī during the reign of Śrīdharasena in the middle of the seventh century CE. A text colophon of the *Bhaṭṭikāvya* (22.1625) also supports this concept as hereunder:

kāvyamidaṁ vihitaṁ mayā vallabhyāṁ
śrīdharasenanarendrapālitāyām ।
kīrtirato bhavatānnṛpasya tasya
kṣemakaraḥ kṣitipo yataḥ prajānām ॥

Vallabhī mentioned here appears to have been the next capital after the old Dwārakā of the country Saurāṣṭra.

Throughout the *kāvya*, the grammatical formations of Pāṇini have been applied in. Even the author of the *Siddhāntakaumudī* had extracted the illustrations and examples from the *Bhaṭṭikāvya*. A author of a commentary *Jayamaṅgalā* (p. 1) mentions the author's name as:

lakṣyaṁ lakṣaṇaṁ cobhayamekatra viduṣaḥ pradarśayituṁ śrīsvāmisūnuḥ bhaṭṭināmā rāmakathāśrayamahākāvyaṁ cakāra ।

Thus, there is a strong disagreement about the identification of these two, the author of the *Śatakatrayī* and that of the *Bhaṭṭikāvya*.

The Editions of the Vairāgyaśataka

The New Catalogus Catalogorum, vol. XXXII, ed. Shiniruddha Dash, University of Madras, 2013 mentions about the following printed editions of the *Vairāgyaśataka*:

1. Kāvyāmalā Series, I.N.S. Press, Bombay, 1886.
2. Trivandrum, 1886.
3. *Laghukāvyāni*, Vanivilasa Press, Srirangam, 1911.
4. *Bālamanoramā*, Ser. 35, pp. 34-44, Madras, 1942.
5. *Oeuvres Poetiques de Nilakantha Diksita*, vol. I, P.S. Filliozat, Pondicherry, 1967.
6. Nirnayasagar Press, Bombay, 1891.
7. With commentary, Bombay, 1896.
8. English translation, Lahore, 1892.
9. Bombay, 1898, with commentary, 1902 & 1911, Hindi & English translations, 1914.
10. With Bengali metrical version, Calcutta, 1916.
11. With Gujarati exposition, Bulsar, Ahmedabad, 1916-17.
12. Calcutta, 1916.
13. With Kannada commentary by D. Narayana Sastri, Bangalore, Candasvari Press, 1925.
14. With Introduction in English and Kannada translation by S. Rangacara, Mysore, Sanskrit Sahitya Sadana, 1960.
15. With Hindi metrical and prose translation by Radhelala Trivedi and Jagannatha Sastri, Varanasi, Chowkhamba Vidyabhavan, 1961.
16. With translation by Svami Dhiresananda, Calcutta, 1966.

Other than the above printed editions mentioned in *The New Catalogus Catalogorum*, vol. XXXII, the following major editions of the *Vairāgyaśataka* have also been published in India and outside:

1. Bhagavan Panda (ed.), 1989, *Vairagyashataka*, 1st edn, Granthamandia, Vinodvihari, Cuttack, Odisha.
2. Bhartrihari, 1916, *Vairagya-Satakam*, Almora: Advaita Ashrama.
3. Bhartrihari, 2012, *Niti and Vairagya Shatakas with Notes, Translation*, a Critical Introduction and Bombay University question papers, Rarebooksclub.com.
4. *Die Sprüche des Bhartriharis*, by Peter von Bohlen August Campe, German verse translation of all three Śatakas.
5. Dixon Scott, 1941, *Bhartrihari Says*, 2nd edn, London: Frederic Muller.
6. A.V. Gopalachariar (ed.), 1954, *Bhartrihari's Sringara Sataka and Vairagya Sataka*, Madras: V. Ramaswamy Satrulu & Sons.
7. P. Gopinath, 2023, *Bhartrihari's Three Shatakam*, New Delhi: Central Sanskrit University.
8. K.M. Joglekar (ed.), 1911, *Bhartrihari's Niti and Vairagya Shatak*, Bombay: Oriental Publishing Company.
9. M.R. Kale and M.B. Gurjar (eds), 1898, *Nîtiśataka and Vairâgyaśataka*, Bombay: Gopal Narayan & Company.
10. J.M. Kennedy (ed.), 1913, *The Satakas; or, Wise Sayings of Bhartrihari* (Prose Translation of All Three *Śatakas*), London: T. Werner Laurie.
11. J.M. Kennedy (ed.), n.d., *The Satakas of Bhartrihari* (1st edn), London: T. Werner Laurie.
12. D.D. Kosambi (ed.), 1948, *Epigrams Attributed to Bhartrhari*, 1st edn, Bombay: Shinghi Jain Shastra Shiksha Pitha and Bharatiya Vidya Bhavan.
13. *Les stances érotiques, morales et religieuses de Bhartrihari*, French prose translation of all three Śatakas (n.d.). *In Les classiques de l'Inde ancienne*, Paul Regnaud, E. Leroux.

14. Narasimha Mishra (ed.), 2014, *Bhartriharishatakatrayi*, 1st edn, Bhubaneswar: Saraswati Prakashani.

15. *Nīti-Sṛṅgāra-Vairāgyaśatakatrayam*, Bombay: Khemaraj Shrikrishnadas, 1906.

16. *Śatakatrayam*, edited with Sanskrit commentary by Kṛṣṇa Śāstrī Mahabala, Bombay: Nirnayasagar Press, 1888.

17. K.T. Telang (ed.), 1874, *Nitishataka and Vairagyashataka of Bhartrihari*, Bombay: Government Central Book Depot.

18. *The Nîtiśataka Śringāraśataka and Vairāgyaśataka*, Hindi and English translation, Khemraj Shrikrishnadass, Bombay (n.d.).

19. *Two Centuries of Bhartrihari* (*Rhyming Translation of the Nīti and Vairāgya Śatakas*), tr. Charles Henry Tawney, Calcutta: Thacker, Spink and Co., 1877.

20. P. von Bohlen (ed.), 1833, *Bhartriharis sententiae et carmen quod Chauri nomine circumfertur eroticum*, Sanskrit text with Introduction, Translation and Notes in Latin.

Manuscripts of the Vairāgyaśataka

The New Catalogus Catalogorum, vol. XXXII, ed. Shiniruddha Dash, University of Madras, 2013 mentions copious number of manuscripts of the *Vairāgyaśataka*, available in various manuscript libraries as well as private collections in India and abroad.

D.D. Kosambi (1948: 10) says that there would be not less than 3,000 manuscripts of the *Bhartṛhariśatakatrayam*, most of which are hidden away in private collections. Kosambi, in his *The Epigrams Attributed to Bhartṛhari*, mentions that he has procured as many as 377 manuscripts of the *Bhartṛhariśatakatrayam* in various forms, i.e. original, photostat, microfilm, direct copy and in *Pratīka Index* (ibid.: 2). He mentions that no manuscript was in Kāśmīrī Śāradā out of 377 accessible manuscripts, from those he had procured (ibid.: 57).

Kāśmīrī Śāradā Manuscripts of the Vairāgyaśataka

In my recent research, I have procured five Kāśmīrī Śāradā manuscripts of the *Vairāgyaśataka*, the details of which are furnished as under:

1. MS No. 4145, recovered from Digital Resource — UPSS Lucknow, digitized by E-Gangotri in Śāradā script having 9 folios in 16 pages. In this manuscript, there are 111 verses along with a brief commentary on the text and with a colophon as "इति श्री तत्रभगवद्भर्तृहरिविरचितं वैराग्यशतकं समाप्तम् ॥". The abbreviation assigned here to this manuscript is: *Ms eG-1*. Following verse is mentioned in the beginning of the manuscript as the benediction (*maṅgalācaraṇa*):

   दिक्कालाद्यनवच्छिन्नानन्तचिन्मात्रमूर्तये
   स्वानुभूत्येकमानाय नमः शान्ताय तेजसे ॥

2. Another incomplete manuscript with no number recovered from E-Gangotri digitized source, under the series of "Baramulla 5 — Vairāgyaśataka (वैराग्यशतकम्) (by Bhartṛhari) digitized by e-Gangotri Digital Preservation Trust" in Śāradā script having 18 folios in 36 pages. In this manuscript there are 64 verses only with no colophon and no benediction (*maṅgalācaraṇa*). The abbreviation assigned here to this manuscript is: *Ms eG-2*.

3. MS No. 2276, recovered from Oriental Research Library, University Campus, Srinagar, India in Śāradā script having 44 folios in 86 pages. In this manuscript, there are 111 verses with a colophon as "इति श्री तत्रभवद्भर्तृहरिविरचितं वैराग्यशतकं समाप्तम् ॥". The abbreviation assigned here to this manuscript is: *Ms ORLS*. The following verse is mentioned in the beginning of the manuscript as the benediction (*maṅgalācaraṇa*):

   दिक्कालाद्यनवच्छिन्नानन्तचिन्मात्रमूर्तये ।
   स्वानुभूत्येकमानाय नमः शान्ताय तेजसे ॥

4. MS No. 1401, recovered from Dharmarth Trust, digitized by E-Gangotri in Śāradā script having 4 folios in 8 pages. The beginning folios of this manuscript are not available. This manuscript has a colophon as "इति श्री तत्रभवद्भर्तृहरिविरचितं वैराग्यशतकं समाप्तम् ॥". The abbreviation assigned here to this manuscript is: *Ms eG-3*.
5. Another manuscript with no number assigned has been recovered from Digital Resource, digitized by E-Gangotri in Śāradā script having 32 folios in 62 pages. In this manuscript there are 107 verses along with a brief commentary over the text and with a colophon as "इति श्रीभर्तृहरिणा कृतं वैराग्यशतकं सम्पूर्णम् ॥". The abbreviation assigned here to this manuscript is: *Ms eG-4*. The following verse is mentioned in the beginning of the manuscript as the benediction (*maṅgalācaraṇa*): "ॐ श्रीगणाधिपतये नमोनमः ।".

The Text of the Vairāgyaśataka

Sometimes, the determination of the text from the manuscripts is as complex and as intricate as to determine the meaning of a clung word (*śliṣṭa śabda*) without any context. In early days, in the manuscripts, there had been a trend of scribing without gaps between the words. Actually, in Sanskrit, if we join two or more words together, then all are considered to be compounded to a single word and, consequently, the meaning gets altered. Let us take an example: "मधुपात्रे" (*madhupātre*) and "मधु पात्रे" (*madhu pātre*), here the meaning gets changed only by joining and separating the two words मधु and पात्रे "मधुपात्रे" means in the vessel of honey and "मधु पात्रे" honey is in the vessel. Not only the determining the text, but compiling and editing the text from the manuscripts are more complex and perplex. The compiler and editor of the text has a crucial role not only to decide the meaning of the words, but also to retain the primary context and content of the author. There have always been possibilities of scribal errors and damaged texts in the manuscripts. To fix the errors and to restore the texts to their original form is the technique called textual criticism. Texts, in this connection, are defined as writings other than formal documents, inscribed or printed on paper, parchment, papyrus, or similar materials. Textual criticism, properly speaking, is an ancillary academic discipline designed to lay the foundations for the higher criticism, which deals with questions of authenticity and attribution of interpretation, as well as of literary and historical evaluation.

In tradition, it is revealed that, the literary editors and the exponents of epigrams used to attribute one's credit to another, may be unknowingly without searching the original and primary source. I must cite some evidences here to this fact. For example:

bhoge rogabhayaṁ kule cyutibhayaṁ vitte nṛpālādbhayaṁ
māne dainyabhayaṁ bale ripubhayaṁ rūpe jarāyā bhayam ।
śāstre vādibhayaṁ guṇe khalabhayaṁ kāye kṛtāntādbhayaṁ
sarvaṁ vastu bhayānvitaṁ bhuvi nṛṇāṁ vairāgyame-
vābhayam ॥

This verse primarily belongs to Kṣemendra's *Caturvargasaṁgraha*. As he mentions in his *Aucityavicāracarcā* —

śānte yathā mama caturvargasaṁgrahe — "bhoge rogabhayaṁ sukhe kṣayabhayaṁ … vairāgyamevābhayam".

But considering *vairāgya* its theme, the editors have interpolated this verse in the *Vairāgyaśataka*, ascribing to Bhartṛhari. This has been a major cause of interpolated texts available in our ancient treatises. The practice of misattribution had caused many interpolated texts and credited to different persons other than their authors. This practice was so deeply rooted that we can easily discover the evidences even in the treatises of the great authors and established exponents of historic treatises. Kṣemendra in his *Aucityavicāracarcā* has attributed the following verse to Śrīmadutpalarāja:

ahau vā hāre vā kusumaśayane vā dṛṣadi vā
maṇau vā loṣṭhe vā balavati ripau vā suhṛdi vā ।
tṛṇe vā straiṇe vā mama samadṛśo yāntu divasāḥ
kadā puṇyeraṇye śiva śiva śiveti pralapataḥ ॥ — *VŚ* 42

He, in his *Aucityavicāracarcā*, has also attributed the following verse to Candraka:

kṛśaḥ kāṇaḥ khañjaḥ śravaṇarahitaḥ pucchavikalo
vraṇī pūyaklinnaḥ kṛmikulaśatairāvṛtatanuḥ ।
kṣudhākṣāmo jīrṇaḥ piṭhirakakapālārpitagalaḥ
śunīmanveti śvā hatamapi nihantyeva madanaḥ ॥ 18 ॥

Thus, due to misattributions and interpolations, the unanimous texts and the texts of others have transmitted in many ancient treatises.

We have already discussed the crucial and subtle nature of the textual criticism in the Introduction to the *Nītiśataka* (p. 22), that:

> Texts have been transmitted in an almost limitless varieties of ways, and the criteria employed by the textual critic — technical, philological, literary or aesthetic — are valid only if applied in awareness of the particular set of historical circumstances governing each case. Sometimes, transmitted texts have been mutilated and defaced by the laxity or ignorance of scribes or editors. The technique of textual criticism helps to get behind this corruption in the endeavour to recover the autograph, i.e. the text as originally written by the author. It is clear, therefore, that, before the textual critic approaches the work of recension (i.e. the critical examination of all the documents in which a text is preserved) and emendation (i.e. the attempt to restore the corrupt passages which remain in a text after the work of recension is complete), is bound to consider the history of the text upon which he is working. He must diagnose the disease or else he may be attempting to correct errors which are of such ancient standing as to be incurable by modern methods,

> or he may be questioning a text which can be traced back to the original author. In the process of emendation, the text is restored with more or less probability. It is a crucial task that how to estimate the degree of probability that an emendation possesses, and how to decide between rival suggestions. There are two ways, by invoking (i) Transcriptional Probability, and (ii) Intrinsic Probability, the primary text is decided among variant readings of apparently equal authority. The emendation must be intrinsically probable, i.e. it must be something that the author is likely to have written. It must suit the context, the author's style and vocabulary, and any general laws, which have been proved to apply to his work.

There are many apparent examples of such transmitted texts, which have been mutilated and defaced due to the laxity and ignorance of the editors. Most of the available printed editions of the Śatakas of Bhartṛhari are seized with such irreconcilabilities. I must cite some examples of such irrelevances and irreconcilabilities, in view of *Vairāgyaśataka* 64 here:

mohaṁ [1]*mārjayatāmupārjaya ratiṁ candrārdhacūḍāmaṇau*
cetaḥ svargataraṅgiṇītaṭabhuvāmāsaṅgamaṅgīkuru ।

In this verse, the Śāradā reading *mārjayatāmupārjaya/mārjayatām umupārjaya* is replaced by the reading *mārjaya tām upārjaya* in both *JKM.1911* and *GAV.1954* editions. However, in both these editions, the word *tāṁ* seems to be meaningless, because the word *tāṁ* is an adjective to *ratiṁ*, arising a question to which *rati*, and finally leads to a fault named want of correlation (*sākāṁkṣatā*). As per the Śāradā text, however, the meaning of the poet's intention is to wipe away the earthly delusion on the banks of the River Gaṅgā. Therefore, the reading *mārjayatāmupārjaya* in the Śāradā text is apparently primary and original.

Most of the editors have the practice to replace the words with their synonyms if the meter is not disturbed. But, there

---

1 मार्जय तां — *JKM.1911, GAV.1954.*

is a rule in the *Jainakoṣa*: *śabdabhede dhruvo'rthabhedaḥ* (if the words are different, then meanings must also be different). In *Vākyapadīya* 1.123, Bhartr̥hari says that *na so'sti pratyayo loke yaḥ śabdānugamādr̥te* (there is no cognition in the world in which the word does not figure). Therefore, if the word is changed, the meaning also gets changed. An example of altered words must be cited here:

> *boddhāro matsaragrastā vibhavaḥ*[2] *smayadūṣitāḥ* ।
> *abodhopahatāścānye jīrṇamaṅge subhāṣitam* ॥ — *VŚ* 3

Here in *JKM.1911* edition, a variant reading प्रभवः (*prabhavaḥ*) is available in the place of विभवः (*vibhavaḥ*), found in the Śāradā manuscripts. A विभु (*vibhu* — an opulent and powerful individual) is often slurred with jealousy and hence should be advised with moral values. But a प्रभु (*prabhu*), meaning a Lord, is generally not a recipient of the precepts. Therefore, the reading विभवः (*vibhavaḥ*) that is found in the Śāradā manuscript follows the context.

An example of laxity and ignorance of the editors must be cited here:

> *sphuratsphārajyautsni dhavalitatale kvāpi puline*
> *sukhāsīnāḥ śāntadhvaniṣu rajanīṣu dyusaritaḥ* ।
> *bhavābhogodvignāḥ śiva śiva śivetyāttavacasaḥ*
> *kadā syāmo*[3] *harṣodgatabahalabāṣpākuladr̥śaḥ* ॥ — *VŚ* 44

In the fourth stanza of the verse, the Śāradā text of *syāmo* is replaced by the editor of *JKM.1911* edition as *syāma* (the form of the root *as* with the suffix *mas* in the potential mood) and by the editor of *GAV.1954* version as *yāsyāma* (in the form of the root *yā* with the suffix *mas* in the future tense). It seems that the text-editors, due to their laxity and ignorance, have considered *syāmo* as grammatically incorrect. In fact, the word *syāmo* is derived

---

[2] प्रभवः — *JKM.1911.*

[3] स्यामानन्दोद्गतबहुलबाष्पाप्लुतदृशः — *JKM.1911*
यास्यामोन्तर्गतबहुलबाष्पाकुलदशाम् — *GAV.1954.*

from the root √so — to bring into an end with the suffix *mas* in present tense, which means "to die". Therefore, considering the text *syāmo* to be incorrect is inappropriate and hence the altered text *syāma* destroys the poet's intention. Thus, the contextual appropriateness, antiquity and originality of the Śāradā text *syāmo* here is justified.

The Teachings in the Vairāgyaśataka

The great Bhartṛhari had composed three Śatakas, i.e. the *Nītiśataka, Śṛṅgāraśataka* and *Vairāgyaśataka,* when after abandoning the majestic power and royal splendour. These three Śatakas belong to that class of composition, which have retained their supreme position in didactic literature for the last 2,000 years and above. Scholars, not only in India, but in other countries also, have estimated these compositions to an unparalleled genus of didactic literature. Considering their pervasive importance, Abraham Roger translated these Śatakas into Dutch so far back in the middle of seventeenth century.

The *Nītiśataka* manifests thoughts, arising from a deeper insights, in the worldly affairs and their limitations; the *Śṛṅgāraśataka* also, as assumed, is not that to deal with erotic sentiment describing highly attainable pleasure out of the beloved company of youthful blossoms of beautiful women, but, in contrary, after careful study of the whole of the *Śṛṅgāraśataka,* one can easily grasp the turning point of the poet's concept to arouse a repercussion of prurient propensities. It has established the fallout of indulgence in sensual pleasures leading to turn one's life as the slave of passion. the *Vairāgyaśataka* is the outcome of repugnance with the havoc of mundane material world, prompting to repose in renunciation, tranquillity and quietude.

It advocates disapproval of addiction[4] and absurdity of desire.[5] It censures infatuation[6] and instructs to refrain from entreaty.[7] It also exposes the realities of the mortal world like irreconcilability of sensual desires, ubiquity of lust, agelessness of desire, endlessness of craving and inevitability of death. Bhartṛhari professes insignificance of livelihood by servitude[8] and adheres to disassociate with *karma*.[9] Extrication from sensual objects,[10] refraining from worldly attachments,[11] spiritual experience[12] and

---

4 *dhiktāṁ ca taṁ ca kusumeṣumimāṁ ca māṁ ca* । — *VŚ* 2
kṣāntaṁ na kṣamayā ... munibhistaistaiḥ phalairvañcitam । — *VŚ* 14
yenaivāmbarakhaṇḍena ... aho daurgatyametayo । — *VŚ* 16

5 *bhrāntvā deśamanekadurgaviṣamaṁ ... nādyāpi viśrāmyasi* । — *VŚ* 4
utkhātaṁ nidhiśaṅkayā ... tṛṣṇe sakāmā bhava । — *VŚ* 5
khalollāpāḥ soḍhāḥ ... tvamāśe moghāśe kimaparamato nartayasi mām । — *VŚ* 6
bhogā na bhuktā ... stṛṣṇā na jīrṇā vayameva jīrṇāḥ । — *VŚ* 13
valibhirmukhamākrāntaṁ ... tṛṣṇaikā taruṇāyate । — *VŚ* 15

6 *ādityasya gatāgatair ... pramādamadirāmunmattabhūtaṁ jagat* । — *VŚ* 7

7 *dīnāṁ dīnamukhaiḥ ... ko dehīti vadetsvadagdhajaṭharasyārthe manasvī janaḥ* । — *VŚ* 8

8 *svādiṣṭaṁ madhuno ... tāvaddāsyakṛtārjanairna hi dhanairvṛttiṁ samīhāmahe* । — *VŚ* 9
hiṁsāśūnyamayatnalabhyamaśanaṁ ... yāmanveṣayatāṁ prayānti sahasā sarve samāptiṁ guṇāḥ । — *VŚ* 11

9 *kṣāntaṁ na kṣamayā ... tattatkarma kṛtaṁ yadeva munibhistaistaiḥ phalairvañcitam* । — *VŚ* 14

10 *avaśyaṁ yātāra ... svayaṁ tyaktā hyete śamasukhamanantaṁ vidadhate* । — *VŚ* 17

11 *etasmādviramendriyārthagahanād ... mā bhūyo bhaja bhaṅgurāṁ bhavaratiṁ cetaḥ prasīdādhunā* । — *VŚ* 62

12 *tapasyantaḥ santaḥ ... na vidmaḥ kiṁ kurmaḥ katipayanimeṣāyuṣi janau* । — *VŚ* 41

renunciation[13] are the ways to achieve happiness and supreme bliss, as established by Bhartṛhari. The happiness, derived out of the knowledge of Self (*Brahman*), is superior to any other mundane pleasure,[14] as disclosed by him. Bhartṛhari unfolds that the secret of the significance of life lies in the pursuit of *puruṣārtha*[15] by diverging the mind from worldly pleasures[16] to the eternal entity and by devotion to God.[17] He wipes out the delusion of happiness in the worldly pleasures. He discloses that worldly pleasures are just remedies to the diseases like thirst, hunger and, lust, and yet people mistakenly take these remedies as happiness! As he tells:

tṛṣāśuṣyatyāsye pibati salilaṁ śītasurabhi
kṣudhārtaḥ śacchālīnkavalayati sāṁspākavalitān ।
pradīpte rāgāgnau ghananiviḍamāśliṣyati vadhūṁ
pratīkāre vyādheḥ sukhamiti viparyasyati janaḥ ॥ — *VŚ* 95

He warns that every material existence has the fear of destruction and the individual should not remain trapped in the false illusion of the perishable world. Let us quote him here:

---

13 *mahī śayyāśāyī ... sukhaṁ śāntaḥ śete muniratanubhūtirnṛpa iva* । — *VŚ* 82

14 *trailokyādhipatitvameva ... yatsvādādvirasā bhavanti vibhavāstrailokyarājyādayaḥ* । — *VŚ* 83

kiṁ vedaiḥ smṛtibhiḥ ... svātmānandapadaṁ praveśakaṭhinaṁ śeṣairvaṇigvṛttibhiḥ । — *VŚ* 84

15 *nābhyastā bhuvi ... śūnyālaye dīpavat* । — *VŚ* 92

na dhyātaṁ padamīśvarasya ... mātuḥ kevalameva yauvanavanacchede kuṭhārā vayam । — *VŚ* 12

16 *bhogā bhaṅguravṛttayo ... kvāpyātyantikasaukhyadhāmani yadi śraddheyamasmadvacaḥ* । — *VŚ* 101

17 *jīrṇā eva manorathāḥ ... na jñātaṁ madhusūdanāṅghriyugalaṁ muktvāsti nānyā gatiḥ* । — *VŚ* 93

āghrātaṁ maraṇena janma jarayā vidyuccalaṁ jīvitaṁ
santoṣo dhanalipsayā śamasukhaṁ prauḍhāṅganāvibhramaiḥ ।
lokairmatsaribhirguṇā vanabhuvo vyālairnṛpā durjanai-
rasthairyeṇa vibhūtirapyupahatā grastaṁ na kiṁ kena vā ॥
— *VŚ* 103

He reveals the secret of happiness that lies within the Self. He addresses that: Oh mind! Why are you troubling your own heart to please the minds of others? You can become pure-minded as well as free-spirited and attain the *cintāmaṇi* qualities within yourself, only when you are happy with yourself. And if you are happy independently, then which of your wishes will be unfulfilled? He must be quoted here:

pareṣāṁ cetāṁsi pratidivasamārādhya bahudhā
prasādaṁ kiṁ netuṁ viśasi hṛdayakleśakalilam ।
prasanne tvayyeva svayamuditacintāmaṇiguṇo
viviktaḥ saṅkalpaḥ kimabhilaṣitaṁ puṣyati na te ॥ — *VŚ* 35

2

The Vairāgyaśataka
A Critical Edition

मंगलाचरण

दिक्कालाद्यनवच्छिन्नानन्तचिन्मात्रमूर्तये
स्वानुभूत्येकमानाय नमः शान्ताय तेजसे ॥ 1 ॥

अन्वय — दिक्कालाद्यनवच्छिन्नानन्तचिन्मात्रमूर्तये स्वानुभूत्येकमानाय शान्ताय तेजसे नमः।

जो (परमात्मा) दिशा, काल आदि परिच्छेदकों अर्थात् सीमाओं से परे है, अन्तहीन और चैतन्यस्वरूप है, अनुभूति से ही जो गम्य हो, शान्त एवं तेजोमय हो, ऐसे (परमात्मा) को नमस्कार।

[*श्रीमद्भगवद्गीता* में परमात्मा का अविनाशी, नित्य, अव्यक्त, एवं अचिन्त्य स्वरूप का उल्लेख है। जैसा कि कहा गया है —

अन्तवन्त इमे देहा नित्यस्योक्ताः शरीरिणः।
अनाशिनोऽप्रमेयस्य तस्माद्युध्यस्व भारत ॥ II.18 ॥

अव्यक्तोऽयमचिन्त्योऽयमविकार्योऽयमुच्यते।
तस्मादेवं विदित्वैनं नानुशोचितुमर्हसि ॥ II.25 ॥]

तात्पर्य — संसार में सभी भौतिक वस्तुएं पूर्व, आग्नेय, दक्षिण, नैऋत्य, पश्चिम, वायव्य, उत्तर, ईशान, आकाश (ऊर्ध्व), पाताल (अधः) इन दश दिशायों में से किसी न किसी दिशा से एवं भूत, भविष्य एवं वर्तमान इन तीन कालों में से परिमित एवं सीमित होती हैं। परन्तु अनन्त एवं चैतन्यस्वरूप परमात्मा किसी भी देश एवं काल आदि की सीमा से परिमित या सीमित नहीं है।

सृष्टि की भौतिक वस्तु के अस्तित्व को सिद्ध करने हेतु बाह्य प्रमाणों की अपेक्षा होती है, परन्तु परमब्रह्म के अस्तित्व एवं प्रमेयता की सिद्धि एकमात्र स्वयं परमब्रह्म या परमात्मा की अनुभूति से ही सम्भव है। परमब्रह्म या परमात्मा स्वयम् अनन्त (अन्तहीन) एवं चिन्मात्र मूर्ति अर्थात् केवल नित्य चैतन्यस्वरूप है एवं जिसका साक्षात्कार अन्तरात्मा की अनुभूति से ही सम्भव है ।

Invocation

dikkālādyanavacchinnānantacinmātramūrtaye ।
svānubhūtyekamānāya namaḥ śāntāya tejase ॥ 1 ॥

anvayaḥ — *dikkālādyanavacchinnānantacinmātramūrtaye svānubhūtyekamānāya śāntāya tejase namaḥ* ।

Salutations to the one (God) who is beyond the boundaries or limitations of direction, time, etc. who is infinite and purely consciousness, who is attainable only by self-realization, who is calm and magnificent.

[In the *Śrīmadbhagavadgītā*, God has been mentioned as imperishable, eternal, unmanifested and beyond the subject of mind. As it is told:

antavanta ime dehā nityasyoktāḥ śarīriṇaḥ ।
anāśino'prameyasya tasmādyudhyasva bhārata ॥ II.18 ॥

avyakto'yamacintyo'yamavikāryo'yamucyate ।
tasmādevaṁ viditvainaṁ nānuśocitumarhasi ॥ II.25 ॥]

Purport — All physical substances are limited and conditioned with a certain direction or space, i.e. four cardinal directions such as north, south, east and west; four intermediate directions such as north-east, north-west, south-east and south-west plus above and below. Simultaneously, these are conditioned with three time periods such as past, present and future. But the infinite *Brahman* is not conditioned with any of these variables like space and time. The existence of all material bodies needs to be proved by an external authority, i.e. a *pramāṇa,* but the existence of the infinite *Brahman* can only be experienced by self-realization. That divine spirit is eternal (endless) and only perpetual consciousness and attainable only through the experience of the eternal spirit. Therefore, I salute the calm and magnificent spirit, the infinite *Brahman*.

आसक्ति की निन्दा

यां चिन्तयाम्यनुदिनं[1] मयि सा विरक्ता
साऽप्यन्यमिच्छति नरं स नरोऽन्यसक्तः[2]।
अस्मत्कृतेऽपि परितुष्यति[3] काचिदन्या
धिक्तां च तं च कुसुमेषु[4]मिमां च मां च ॥ 2 ॥

अन्वय — (अहं) याम् अनुदिनं चिन्तयामि सा मयि विरक्ता, सा अपि अन्यं नरम् इच्छति, सः (अपि) जनः अन्यसक्तः। अस्मत्कृते च काचित् अन्या परितुष्यति, (अतः) तां च तं च मदनं च इमां च मां च धिक्।

प्रस्तुत पद्य में भर्तृहरि ने आसक्ति के व्यभिचार वृत्तित्व को अपने जीवन के कुछ अनुभवों को उदाहरण के रूप में प्रस्तुत करते हुए उसकी निन्दा की है । भर्तृहरि कहते हैं — मैं जिस स्त्री से आसक्त हूँ, वह स्त्री मुझसे विरक्त है और किसी अन्य पुरुष पर आसक्त है । वह स्त्री जिस पुरुष पर आसक्त है, वह पुरुष भी किसी अन्य स्त्री पर आसक्त है । मेरे प्रति भी कोई अन्य स्त्री मेरे सभी कार्यों पर सन्तुष्ट एवं प्रसन्न रहती हुई आसक्त है, जिस स्त्री के प्रति मेरा कोई अनुराग नहीं है । अतः उस स्त्री को धिक्कार है जिसके प्रति मैं आसक्त हूँ, उस पुरुष को भी धिक्कार है जिसके प्रति वह स्त्री आसक्त है, मेरे प्रति जो स्त्री आसक्त है उसे भी धिक्कार है, स्वयं मुझे भी धिक्कार है एवं इसी आसक्ति के मूल कारण काम को भी धिक्कार है।

[*श्रीमद्भगवद्गीता* में काम की गर्हणा की गई है। कामरूपी आवरण से ही शाश्वत ज्ञान आच्छन्न रहता है जिससे व्यक्ति क्षणिक एवं तात्कालिक सुख के पीछे-पीछे भागता है। जैसा कि —

आवृतं ज्ञानमेतेन ज्ञानिनो नित्यवैरिणा।
कामरूपेण कौन्तेय दुष्पूरेणानलेन च ॥ III.39 ॥

अतः भगवान् श्रीकृष्ण काम-रूपी शत्रु का दमन करने के लिए कहते हैं —

जहि शत्रुं महाबाहो कामरूपं दुरासदम् ॥ III.43 ॥]

तात्पर्य — मनुष्य को किसी व्यक्ति या वस्तु पर आसक्ति नहीं रखनी चाहिए। क्योंकि आसक्ति कभी ना कभी धोखा एवं दुःख देती है।

---

1 सततं — *JKM.1911.*

2 जनं स जनोऽन्यसक्तः — *JKM.1911.*

3 परिशुष्यति — *JKM.1911.*

4 मदनं — *JKM.1911.*

Disapproval of Addiction

yāṁ cintayāmyanudinaṁ mayi sā viraktā
sā 'pyanyamicchati naraṁ sa naro 'nyasaktaḥ ।
asmatkṛtepi parituṣyati kācidanyā
dhiktāṁ ca taṁ ca kusumeṣumimāṁ ca māṃ ca ॥ 2 ॥

anvayaḥ — (*ahaṁ*) *yām anudinaṁ cintayāmi sā mayi viraktā, sā api anyaṁ naram icchati, saḥ* (*api*) *janaḥ anyasaktaḥ* । *asmatkṛte ca kācit anyā parituṣyati,* (*ataḥ*), *tāṁ ca taṁ ca madanaṁ ca imāṁ ca māṁ ca dhik* ।

In this verse, King Bhartṛhari condemns the betraying nature of affection and attachment, with some of bitter experiences of his life as examples. He states: The woman, I mull over whom, has no affection for me; she, however, adores another who is attached to someone else; while a certain woman is delighted with all I do and loves me even when I do not reciprocate her emotions towards me. Therefore, shame on the woman to whom I am attached, shame on the man to whom that woman is attached, shame on the woman who is attracted to me, shame on myself and also on Madana (the passion), root cause of this attachment, who longs for love and attachment in spite of its betraying characteristics of attachment and affection.

[*Kāma* (lust) has been condemned in the *Śrīmadbhagavadgītā*. As the Eternal knowledge remains covered only by the cover of lust due to which an individual runs after momentary and immediate happiness. Thus told:

āvṛtaṁ jñānametena jñānino nityavairiṇā ।
kāmarūpeṇa kaunteya duṣpūreṇānalena ca ॥ III.39 ॥

Therefore, Lord Kṛṣṇa asks to terminate the enemy of lust:

jahi śatruṁ mahābāho kāmarūpaṁ durāsadam ॥ III.43 ॥]

Purport — One should not get addicted to an object or an individual out of lust or desire. Because, addiction to lust or desire betrays us sooner or later.

समाज में सुभाषितों की अग्राह्यता

बोद्धारो मत्सरग्रस्ता विभवः[5] स्मयदूषिताः ।
अबोधोपहताश्चान्ये जीर्णमङ्गे सुभाषितम् ॥ 3 ॥

अन्वय — बोद्धारः मत्सरग्रस्ताः, विभवः स्मयदूषिताः, अन्ये च अबोधोपहताः। (एवं प्रकारेण) सुभाषितम् अङ्गे जीर्णम् ॥

सुभाषित अर्थात् सुन्दर भाषा में कहा गया है ऐसा कथन जिससे श्रेयः एवं प्रेयः उभय की प्राप्ति होती है। सुभाषितों में सुखी और आदर्श जीवन की अनमोल सीख छुपी हुई रहती है। परन्तु उन्हें ग्रहण करके अपने जीवन के आचरणों में प्रयोग करने वाले ही दुर्लभ हैं। जो इन सुभाषित वचनों के मूल्य समझने वाले विद्वान् हैं वे ईर्ष्या-द्वेष से ग्रस्त होते हैं। जो शासक, स्वामी या प्रभुत्व के अधिकारी होते हैं वे अहंकार से युक्त होते हैं। और दूसरे लोग अज्ञानयुक्त हैं, वे इन सुभाषितों के मूल्य समझने में असमर्थ होते हैं। अतः कवियों के सुन्दर वचन उनके शरीर में ही नष्ट हो जाते हैं अर्थात् उनका उपयोग नहीं हो पाता, और कवियों या उपदेष्टाओं के बीच में ही रह जाते हैं।

[पूर्वाग्रह से ग्रसित व्यक्ति सुभाषितों को उसी प्रकार नहीं समझ पाता जिस प्रकार चन्द्र की शीतल किरण कमलों को प्रकाशित नहीं कर पाती। जैसे कि कहा गया है —

अथवाभिनिविष्टबुद्धिषु व्रजति व्यर्थकतां सुभाषितम्।
रविरागिषु शीतरोचिषः करजालं कमलाकरेष्विव ॥ — *शिशुपालवधम्* 16.43]

तात्पर्य — समाज में प्रायः ऐसा होता है कि महान् और नवीन विचार कभी बोले नहीं जाते अपितु व्यक्ति के भीतर ही पच जाते हैं। अतः अच्छे विचारों को सदैव श्रद्धा से ग्रहण करना चाहिए।

Rejection of Good-Sayings in the Society

boddhāro matsaragrastā vibhavaḥ smayadūṣitāḥ ।
abodhopahatāścānye jīrṇamaṅge subhāṣitam ॥ 3 ॥

anvayaḥ — *boddhāraḥ matsaragrastāḥ, vibhavaḥ smayadūṣitāḥ, anye ca abodhopahatāḥ* । *(evaṁ prakāreṇa) subhāṣitam aṅge jīrṇam* ॥

Subhāṣitas (proverbs) mean good-sayings that lead to both welfare and pleasure. Proverbs contain precious lessons for a happy and ideal life. But rarely these are used in practices. The learned ones, who can understand the value of these

[5] प्रभवः — *JKM*.1911.

proverbs, are consumed by jealousy and hatred and hence do not appreciate these. Those who are rulers, masters or possessors of dominion are full of ego and self-conceit. The rest of the people are senselessly immersed in their own ignorance and, hence, unable to understand the value of these precious proverbs. Thus, good counsel or wisdom is digested within oneself and remains unshared and unused.

[A person subjected to prejudice is not able to understand the well-spoken words in the same way as the cool rays of the moon are not able to illuminate the lotuses. It is stated:

> *athavābhiniviṣṭabuddhiṣu vrajati vyarthakatāṁ subhāṣitam* ।
> *ravirāgiṣu śītarociṣaḥ karajālaṁ kamalākareṣviva* ॥
> — *Śiśupālavadham* 16.43]

Purport — In the society it often happens that the great and innovative ideas are never uttered but digested within the individual. Therefore, good thoughts should always be assumed with grand respect and devotion.

तृष्णा की अनुपशमनीयता

> भ्रान्त्वा[6] देशमनेकदुर्गविषमं प्राप्तं न किञ्चित्फलं
> त्यक्त्वा जातिकुलाभिमानमुचितं सेवा कृता निष्फला ।
> भुक्तं मानविवर्जितं परगृहे साशङ्कमाः[7] काकवत्
> तृष्णे जृम्भसि पापकर्मपिशुने नाद्यापि विश्राम्यसि[8] ॥ 4 ॥

अन्वय — अनेकदुर्गविषमं देशं भ्रान्त्वा किञ्चित् (अपि) फलं न प्राप्तं, उचितं जातिकुलाभिमानं त्यक्त्वा कृता सेवा निष्फला (जाता अस्ति)। परगृहे मानविवर्जितं (यथा स्यात्तथा) काकवत् साशङ्कं भुक्तम्, आः पापकर्मपिशुने तृष्णे! जृम्भसि! अद्यापि न विश्राम्यसि!

मैंने अनेक पर्वत, कण्टकित वृक्ष आदि से दुर्गम देशों में भ्रमण किया, परन्तु उससे कोई फल न मिला। अपनी जाति और कुल के अभिमान को त्यागकर जिनकी सेवा नहीं करनी

---

6 भ्रान्तं — *JKM.1911, GAV.1954.*

7 परगृहेष्वाशङ्कया — *JKM.1911, GAV.1954.*

8 सन्तुष्यसि — *JKM.1911, GAV.1954.*

थी, उसे भी किया पर वह भी निष्फल हुई। अपने मान एवं अपमान का विचार न करते हुए दूसरों के घर कौवे की तरह शंकाकुल होकर भोजन भी किया। परन्तु हे पापकर्म में प्रवृत्त तृष्णे! इतने पर भी तू सन्तुष्ट नहीं हुई, जो शान्त होने के बजाय नित्य-प्रतिदिन बढ़ ही रही है।

[तृष्णा ही व्यक्ति को अकर्त्तव्य कर्मों में प्रेरित करती है। अतः कहा गया है — "अकर्तव्येष्वसाध्वीव तृष्णा प्रेरयते जनम्"।]

तात्पर्य — अन्तहीन समुद्र की लहरों की तरह तृष्णा या लालच पर सवार मनुष्य जीवन सागर में भटकता रहता है, जो उसके विवेक को नष्ट कर देता है। अनियन्त्रित तृष्णा मनुष्य को अच्छा नहीं बनने देती, क्योंकि सभी बुराइयों की जड़ इच्छा ही है।

Absurdity of Desire

bhrāntvā deśamanekadurgaviṣamaṁ prāptaṁ na kiñcitphalaṁ
tyaktvā jātikulābhimānamucitaṁ sevā kṛtā niṣphalā ।
bhuktaṁ mānavivarjitaṁ paragṛhe sāśaṅkamāḥ kākavat
tṛṣṇe jṛmbhasi pāpakarmapiśune nādyāpi viśrāmyasi ॥ 4 ॥

anvayaḥ — *anekadurgaviṣamaṁ deśaṁ bhrāntvā kiñcit (api) phalaṁ na prāptaṁ, ucitaṁ jātikulābhimānaṁ tyaktvā kṛtā sevā niṣphalā (jātā asti)*। *paragṛhe mānavivarjitaṁ (yathā syāttathā) kākavat sāśaṅkaṁ bhuktam, āḥ pāpakarmapiśune tṛṣṇe! jṛmbhasi! adyāpi na viśrāmyasi!*

I obtained no wealth even after travelling many inaccessible and perilous places. The services, rendered by me to unworthy persons, ignoring even the dignity of my ancestry, went in vain. I, devoid of my self-respect, cynically fed myself, like a crow in others' houses. But even then, Oh desire! you being engaged in sinful deeds were not stopped, which, instead of resting, are spreading and bursting upon day by day.

[It is the desire that motivates a person to do wrongful acts. Thus, it is said:

akartavyeṣvasādhvīva tṛṣṇā prerayate janam ।]

Purport — Like the waves of the endless ocean, a man wanders in the ocean of life riding on desire or greed, which destroys his conscience. Uncontrolled desire does not allow a man to be honest, because, the root of all evil is desire.

तृष्णा : असन्तोष का मूल कारण

उत्खातं निधिशङ्कया क्षितितलं ध्माता गिरेर्धातवो
निस्तीर्णः सरितां पतिर्नृपतयो यत्नेन संतोषिताः ।
मन्त्राराधनतत्परेण मनसा नीताः श्मशाने निशाः
सम्प्राप्तश्च वराटकोऽपि न मया तृष्णे सकामा भव[9] ॥ 5 ॥

अन्वय — (मया) निधिशङ्कया क्षितितलम् उत्खातं, गिरेः धातवो ध्माताः, सरितां पतिः निस्तीर्णः, नृपतयो यत्नेन संतोषिताः। मन्त्राराधनतत्परेण मनसा श्मशाने निशाः नीताः, (परन्तु) वराटकोऽपि मया न सम्प्राप्तः। (अतः) हे तृष्णे! (त्वं) सकामा भव ।

मैंने खज़ाने की आशा से धरती की गहराई तक खोद दी; अनेक प्रकार की पर्वतीय धातुओं के लिए चट्टानों को पिघला दिया, रत्नों की खोज में समुद्रों को पार कर लिया; राजाओं को यत्नपूर्वक सन्तुष्ट करने का प्रयास किया; रात-रात भर श्मशान में एकाग्रचित्त से बैठा हुआ जप करता रहा; फिर भी एक कानी कौड़ी हाथ न लगी। अतः, हे तृष्णे! हे इच्छा! इसलिए सन्तुष्ट रहो।

[प्राणी तृष्णा के कारण किस तरह भटकता रहता है उसका एक सुन्दर उदाहरण निम्न श्लोक में बताया गया है। जैसा कि —

प्रत्यग्रोऽत्र यथासुखं मधुरसः पातव्य इत्युत्सुकस्
तृष्णाविभ्रमविप्रलब्धहृदयस्तत्त्वावबोधं विना।
निर्विण्णोऽप्यफलश्रमो न विरमत्यालेख्यपद्माकरे
दुर्बुद्धिर्व्यसनी तथापि मधुपस्तृष्णाशयोद्भ्राम्यति — वल्लभदेव की *सुभाषितावलि* ॥

एक भ्रमर चित्र में चित्रांकित एक पद्म-सरोवर को चित्र नहीं समझता एवं उससे मधुरस पाने की तृष्णा के विभ्रम के कारण प्रतारित होता है। चित्रांकित पद्म-सरोवर से मधुपान से वंचित होता हुआ भी वह भमर तृष्णा के वशवर्ती होकर अपने निष्फल प्रयासों से विरत नहीं होता है। इससे यह प्रमाणित होता है कि तृष्णा किस प्रकार प्राणी को भ्रम में उलझाकर वंचित करता रहता है।]

तात्पर्य — मनुष्य की तृष्णा कभी भी शान्त नहीं होती। तृष्णा के वशवर्ती मनुष्य हमेशा अशान्त ही रहता है।

Desire: The Root Cause of Dissatisfaction

utkhātaṁ nidhiśaṅkayā kṣititalaṁ dhmātā girerdhātavo
nistīrṇaḥ saritāṁ patirnṛpatayo yatnena saṅtoṣitāḥ ।

[9] प्राप्तः काणवराटकोऽपि न मया तृष्णोऽधुना मुञ्च माम् — *JKM.1911.*

mantrārādhanatatpareṇa manasā nītāḥ śmaśāne niśāḥ
samprāptaśca varāṭako 'pi na mayā tṛṣṇe sakāmā bhava ॥ 5 ॥

anvayaḥ — *(mayā) nidhiśaṅkayā kṣititalam utkhātaṁ, gireḥ dhātavo dhmātāḥ, saritāṁ patiḥ nistīrṇaḥ, nṛpatayo yatnena saṅtoṣitāḥ* । *mantrārādhanatatpareṇa manasā śmaśāne niśāḥ nītāḥ, (parantu) varāṭako 'pi mayā na samprāptaḥ* । *(ataḥ) he tṛṣṇe! (tvaṁ) sakāmā bhava* ।

I dug to the depths of the earth in the hope of treasure; smelted down the rocks for precious metals, crossed the seas in search of gems; tried to satisfy the kings diligently; I spent on nights while chanting incantations with a totally absorbed mind in the crematorium; yet I did not get a penny. Oh desire! therefore, remain contented.

[A beautiful example of how an individual keeps wandering due to thirst is given in the following verse:

pratyagro 'tra yathāsukhaṁ madhurasaḥ pātavya ityutsukas
tṛṣṇāvibhramavipralabdhahṛdayastattvāvabodhaṁ vinā ।
nirviṇṇo 'pyaphalaśramo na viramatyālekhyapadmākare
durbuddhirvyasanī tathāpi madhupastṛṣṇāśayodbhrāmyati
— *Subhāṣitāvali* of Vallabhdeva ॥

A bee cannot identify a lake of lotus drawn in a picture and it gets deceived due to the illusion of the desire to get honey from it. Despite being deprived of drinking the honey from the lake of lotus drawn in the picture, the bee does not desist from his fruitless efforts due to his craving. This proves how craving keeps deceiving the creature by entangling it in illusion.]

Purport — The desire of an individual never comes to an end. An individual who is controlled by his desire always remains disgruntled.

तृष्णा की निरर्थकता

खलोल्लापाः[10] सोढाः कथमपि तदाराधनपरैः
निगृह्यान्तर्वाष्पं हसितमपि शून्येन मनसा ।

[10] खल्लोल्लापाः — *Ms eG-1*, खलालापाः — *GAV.1954.*

कृतो वित्तस्तम्भप्रणिहितधियामञ्जलिरपि[11]
त्वमाशे मोघाशे [12]किमपरमतो नर्तयसि माम् ॥ 6 ॥

अन्वय — (अस्माभिः) खलोल्लापाः तदाराधनपरैः कथमपि सोढाः, शून्येन मनसा अन्तर्वाष्पं निगृह्य हसितम् अपि। वित्तस्तम्भप्रणिहितधियाम् (वित्तेन यः स्तम्भो जडीभावस्तं प्रणिहिता केन्द्रिता प्राप्ता वा धीर्येषां तेषां पुरतः) अञ्जलिरपि कृतः। (एवं प्रकारेण) हे मोघाशे आशे! त्वम् अतः परं मां किं नर्तयसि?

हमने दुष्टों की सेवा करते हुए उनकी धोखेबाज़ एवं तिरस्कारपूर्ण बातों को किसी भी तरह सहा; सूने मन से अपने भीतर की भाप को रोककर किसी भी तरह मुस्कराए, धन के कारण जड़बुद्धि वालों के सामने हाथ भी जोड़े; हे झूठी आशा! तुम मुझे और कौन से व्यर्थ कर्मों में नचाएगी?

[आशा या तृष्णा ही मनुष्य को याचना के लिए प्रेरित करती है। किसी वैरागी व्यक्ति की उक्ति है कि आशा या तृष्णा से प्रेरित होकर दीन-याचना की अपेक्षा फटे-पुराने कपड़े पहनते, वन में वास करते अयाचित लब्ध जल मात्र से प्राण धारण करना बेहतर है। जैसे कि —

कामं शीर्णपलाशसंहतिकृतां कन्थां वसानो वने
कुर्यामम्बुभिरप्ययाचितसुखैः प्राणावबन्धस्थितिम्।
साङ्ग्लानि सवेपितं सचकितं सान्तर्निदाघज्वरं
वक्तुं न त्वहमुत्सहेय कृपणं देहीत्यवद्यं वचः ॥
— विद्याकरकृत *सुभाषितरत्नकोश*, 48.23]

तात्पर्य — तृष्णा के कारण मनुष्य अनुचित एवं अयोग्य कार्य करने के लिए मजबूर होता है। अतः तृष्णा सर्वथा वर्जनीय है।

Futility of Desire

khalollāpāḥ soḍhāḥ kathamapi tadārādhanaparaiḥ
nigṛhyāntarvāṣpaṁ hasitamapi śūnyena manasā ।
kṛto vittastambhapraṇihitadhiyāmañjalirapi
tvamāśe moghāśe kimaparamato nartayasi mām ॥ 6 ॥

anvayaḥ — *(asmābhiḥ) khalollāpāḥ tadārādhanaparaiḥ kathamapi soḍhāḥ, śūnyena manasā antarvāṣpaṁ nigṛhya hasitam api*। *vittastambhapraṇihitadhiyām (vittena yaḥ stambho jaḍībhāvastaṁ praṇihitā kendritā prāptā vā dhīryeṣāṁ teṣāṁ purataḥ) añjalirapi kṛtaḥ*। *(evaṁ prakāreṇa) he moghāśe āśe! tvam ataḥ paraṁ māṁ kiṁ nartayasi?*

---

11 कृतो चित्तस्तम्भप्रतिहतधियामञ्जलिरपि — *JKM.1911.*

12 किमुपर — *JKM.1911.*

We somehow put up with the deceitful and contemptuous words while serving the wicked; smiled with vacant mind somehow holding back our tears; bow down before the persons, numbed with wealth; oh insatiable desire! what other futile deeds would you have me dance in?

[It is the hope or desire what motivates a person to entreat. It is said by a recluse that it is better to live in a forest, wearing tattered old clothes and with water only that could be available without begging than the entreat inspired by hope or desire. Thus told:

kāmaṁ śīrṇapalāśasaṁhatikṛtāṁ kanthāṁ vasāno vane
kuryāmambubhirapyayācitasukhaiḥ prāṇāvabandhasthitim ।
sāṅgaglāni savepitaṁ sacakitaṁ sāntarnidāghajvaraṁ
vaktuṁ na tvahamutsaheya kṛpaṇaṁ dehītyavadyaṁ vacaḥ ॥
— *Subhāṣitaratnakośaḥ* of Vidyākara, 48.23]

Purport — Due to desire, man is forced to do unacceptable and undeserving jobs. That is why desire is totally avoidable.

सम्पूर्ण संसार मोह के नशे में

आदित्यस्य गतागतैरहरहस्सङ्क्षीयते जीवितं
व्यापारैर्बहुकार्यभारगुरुभिः कालो न विज्ञायते।
दृष्ट्वा जन्मजराविपत्तिमरणं त्रासश्च नोत्पद्यते
पीत्वा मोहमयीं प्रमादमदिरामुन्मत्तभूतं जगत्॥ 7 ॥

अन्वय — आदित्यस्य गतागतैः अहरहः जीवितं सङ्क्षीयते, बहुकार्यभारगुरुभिः व्यापारैः कालो न विज्ञायते। जन्मजराविपत्तिमरणं दृष्ट्वा त्रासश्च न उत्पद्यते, मोहमयीं प्रमादमदिरां पीत्वा जगत् उन्मत्तभूतं (जायते)।

सूर्य के उदय और अस्त के साथ प्राणी का जीवन दिन-प्रतिदिन घटता जाता है। तरह-तरह के कारोबारों में व्यग्र रहने के कारण काल कैसे बीत जाता है, उसे पता ही नहीं चलता। जन्म, बुढ़ापा, विपत्ति एवं मरण को देखकर भी उसे भय नहीं होता। इसी प्रकार मोहमय प्रमादरूपी मदिरा के नशे में सम्पूर्ण संसार उन्मत्त हो रहा है।

तात्पर्य — मोहरूपी मदिरा के आवेश में प्राणी सत्य को भी भुलाकर उन्मत्त सा हो जाता है।

World Is under the Wine of Infatuation

ādityasya gatāgatairaharahassaṅkṣīyate jīvitaṁ
vyāpārairbahukāryabhāragurubhiḥ kālo na vijñāyate ।

dṛṣṭvā janmajarāvipattimaraṇaṁ trāsaśca notpadyate
pītvā mohamayīṁ pramādamadirāmunmattabhūtaṁ jagat ॥ 7 ॥

anvayaḥ — *ādityasya gatāgataiḥ aharahaḥ jīvitaṁ saṅkṣīyate, bahukārya-bhāragurubhiḥ vyāpāraiḥ kālo na vijñāyate*। *janmajarāvipattimaraṇaṁ dṛṣṭvā trāsaśca na utpadyate, mohamayīṁ pramādamadirāṁ pītvā jagat unmattabhūtaṁ (jāyate)*।

With the rising and setting of the sun, the life of a living being ebbs away day by day. Time passes away unknowingly under the heavy burden of various activities. He is not afraid even after watching birth, ageing, suffering and death. For the world has become insane by drinking the intoxicating wine of infatuation.

Purport — An individual, drunk with the wine of infatuation, forgets the truth and becomes maniac.

मनस्वी पुरुष की याचना से विमुखता

दीनां दीनमुखैः सहैव शिशुकैराकृष्टजीर्णाम्बरां
क्रोशद्भिर्विधुरैः क्षुधातिविधुरां पश्येन्न चेद्गेहिनीम्।[13]
याच्ञाभङ्गभयेन गद्गदगलत्त्रुट्यद्विलीनाक्षरं
को देहीति वदेत्स्वदग्धजठरस्यार्थे मनस्वी जनः ॥ 8 ॥

अन्वय — दीनमुखैः क्षुधा क्रोशद्भिः विधुरैः शिशुकैः सहैव आकृष्टजीर्णाम्बराम् अतिविधुरां दीनां गेहिनीं न पश्येत् चेत्, याच्ञाभङ्गभयेन गद्गदगलत्त्रुट्यद्विलीनाक्षरं स्वदग्धजठरस्यार्थे कः मनस्वी जनः देहीति वदेत्?

दीन-हीन मुख वाले भूख से बिलखते व्यथित बच्चों के साथ, अपने फटे-पुराने वस्त्रों से शरीर को किसी भी तरह ढकी हुई गृहिणी को जब तक नहीं देखता, तब तक वह कौन स्वाभिमानी मनस्वी व्यक्ति रूंधे हुए गले से अपनी धधकती हुई पेट की आग को शान्त करने के लिए याचना करेगा?

[गृहस्थाश्रम बन्धन का कारण है; जिसमें ज़रा भी सुख नहीं है। स्त्री एवं सन्तति के लिए पुरुष को याचना के लिए मजबूर होना पड़ता है। अतः व्यक्ति को अपने स्वाभिमान को बनाए रखने के लिए गृहस्थाश्रम के बन्धन से दूर रहना चाहिए।]

तात्पर्य — मनस्वी व्यक्ति सदैव याचना से विमुख रहने के लिए गार्हस्थ्य से दूर रहते हैं।

---

13 दीना दीनमुखैः सहैव शिशुकैराकृष्टजीर्णाम्बरा क्रोशद्भिः क्षुधितैर्निरन्नैर्विधुरा दृश्येत चेद्गेहिनी। — *JKM.1911*

Alienation from Entreaty of the Individuals with Magnanimity

dīnāṁ dīnamukhaiḥ sahaiva śiśukairākṛṣṭajīrṇāmbarāṁ
krośadbhirvidhuraiḥ kṣudhātividhurāṁ paśyenna cedgehinīm ।
yācñābhaṅgabhayena gadgadagalattruṭyadvilīnākṣaraṁ
ko dehīti vadetsvadagdhajaṭharasyārthe manasvī janaḥ ॥ 8 ॥

anvayaḥ — *dīnamukhaiḥ kṣudhā krośadbhiḥ vidhuraiḥ śiśukaiḥ sahaiva ākṛṣṭajīrṇāmbarām atividhurāṁ dīnāṁ gehinīṁ na paśyet cet, yācñābhaṅga-bhayena gadgadagalattruṭyadvilīnākṣaraṁ svadagdhajaṭharasyārthe kaḥ manasvī janaḥ dehīti vadet?*

Until a resolute man of self-respect sees the poor-faced housewife, whose body somehow covered with tattered clothes, with her children crying out of hunger, will plead with a choked and faltering voice, to calm his hunger?

[*Gṛhasthāśrama* (estate of a householder) is the cause of bondage. There is no happiness at all in this. A man is forced to beg for his wife and children. Therefore, to maintain one's self-respect, a person should stay away from the bondage of household life.]

Purport — Individuals with magnanimity always stay away from the estate of a householder in order to refrain from entreaty.

दासत्व से आजीविका की तुच्छता

स्वादिष्टं मधुनो घृताच्च रसवद्यत्प्रस्रवत्यक्षरं
दैवी वागमृतात्मनो रसवता तेनैव तृप्ता वयम्।
कुक्षौ यावदमी भवन्ति धृतये भिक्षाहृताः सक्तव-
स्तावद्दास्यकृतार्जनैर्न हि धनैर्वृत्तिं समीहामहे ॥ 9 ॥

अन्वय — मधुनः स्वादिष्टं घृताच्च रसवद् अमृतात्मनो यद् अक्षरं दैवी वाक् प्रस्रवति तेनैव रसवता (अक्षरेण) वयं तृप्ताः। हि धृतये कुक्षौ यावत् अमी भिक्षाहृताः सक्तवो भवन्ति तावद् दास्यकृतार्जनैः धनैः वृत्तिं न समीहामहे।

अमृत आत्मा से जो अक्षर-रूप दैवी वाणी बहती है, मधु से भी स्वादिष्ट एवं घृत से भी रसपूर्ण उस अक्षर से ही हम तृप्त हैं। क्योंकि अपने धारण के लिए अपने उदर में जब तक

भिक्षा के रूप में गृहीत सत्तुएं होती हैं तब तक हम दासत्व वृत्ति से उपार्जित धनों से अपनी आजीविका की इच्छा नहीं रखते।

तात्पर्य — दासत्व वृत्ति से आजीविका निर्वाह करने की अपेक्षा भिक्षा-याचना करके उदर पोषण करना बेहतर है।

Insignificance of Livelihood by Servitude

svādiṣṭaṁ madhuno ghṛtācca rasavadyatprasravatyakṣaraṁ
daivī vāgamṛtātmano rasavatā tenaiva tṛptā vayam ।
kukṣau yāvadamī bhavanti dhṛtaye bhikṣāhṛtāḥ saktava-
stāvaddāsyakṛtārjanairna hi dhanairvṛttiṁ samīhāmahe ॥ 9 ॥

anvayaḥ — *madhunaḥ svādiṣṭaṁ ghṛtācca rasavad amṛtātmano yad akṣaraṁ daivī vāk prasravati tenaiva rasavatā (akṣareṇa) vayaṁ tṛptāḥ* । *hi dhṛtaye kukṣau yāvat amī bhikṣāhṛtāḥ saktavo bhavanti tāvad dāsyakṛtārjanaiḥ dhanaiḥ vṛttiṁ na samīhāmahe* ।

We are satisfied only with that *akṣara* (word), which flows from the eternal soul in the form of divine speech, tastier than honey and more luscious than ghee or aloe. Because as long as there is flour or barley in the form of alms in the stomach for our sustenance, we never wish for our livelihood with the money earned from servitude.

Purport — It is better to feed the stomach by begging than to earn livelihood by servitude.

मृत्यु की अवश्यम्भाव्यता

निवृत्ता भोगेच्छा पुरुषबहुमानो विगलितः
समानाः स्वर्याताः सपदि सुहृदो जीवितसमाः।
शनैर्यष्ट्युत्थानं घनतिमिररुद्धे च नयने
अहो भ्रष्टः[14] कायस्तदपि मरणापायचकितः ॥ 10 ॥

अन्वय — भोगेच्छा निवृत्ता, पुरुषबहुमानो विगलितः, जीवितसमाः समानाः सुहृदः सपदि स्वर्याताः। शनैः यष्ट्युत्थानं, नयने च घनतिमिररुद्धे, कायः भ्रष्टः, अहो! तदपि मरणापायचकितः।

---

[14] धृष्टः — *JKM.1911*, मूढः — *GAV.1954.*

सुख की इच्छा समाप्त हो गई, पौरुषत्व का अहंकार नष्ट हो गया, जीवन-तुल्य प्रिय मित्र एवं स्वजन स्वर्ग को चल बसे, अब छड़ी के सहारे धीरे-धीरे खड़ा होना होता है, आँखों में अँधेरी छा गई है, शरीर शिथिल हो चुका है। इतना सब होने पर भी, व्यक्ति अपनी मूर्खता के कारण, मृत्यु की सम्भावना पर आश्चर्य करता है!

तात्पर्य — मृत्यु की अवश्यम्भाव्यता पर अविश्वास नहीं करना चाहिए।

Inevitability of Death

nivṛttā bhogecchā puruṣabahumāno vigalitaḥ
samānāḥ svaryātāḥ sapadi suhṛdo jīvitasamāḥ ।
śanairyaṣṭyutthānaṁ ghanatimiraruddhe ca nayane
aho bhraṣṭaḥ kāyastadapi maraṇāpāyacakitaḥ ॥ 10 ॥

anvayaḥ — *bhogecchā nivṛttā, puruṣabahumāno vigalitaḥ, jīvitasamāḥ samānāḥ suhṛdaḥ sapadi svaryātāḥ* । *śanaiḥ yaṣṭyutthānaṁ, nayane ca ghanatimiraruddhe, kāyaḥ bhraṣṭaḥ, aho! tadapi maraṇāpāyacakitaḥ* ।

The desire for pleasures has ended, the pride of masculinity has been disappeared, life-like dear friends and relatives have gone to heaven, now one has to stand slowly with the help of a staff, darkness has engulfed the eyes, the body has become feeble. In spite of all this, one still wonders at the possibility of death, due to one's own stupidity!

Purport — One should not distrust over inevitability of death.

पराश्रित वृत्ति की निन्दा

हिंसाशून्यमयत्नलभ्यमशनं धात्रा मरुत्कल्पितं
व्यालानां पशवस्तृणाङ्कुरभुजः सृष्टा[15] [16]महीशायिनः ।
संसारार्णवलङ्घनक्षमधियां वृत्तिः कृता सा नृणां
या[17]मन्वेषयतां प्रयान्ति सहसा[18] सर्वे समाप्तिं गुणाः ॥ 11 ॥

---

15 तुष्टाः — *GAV.1954.*

16 स्थली — *JKM.1911, GAV.1954.*

17 ताम् — *GAV.1954.*

18 सततं — *JKM.1911, GAV.1954.*

अन्वय — व्यालानां हिंसाशून्यम् अयत्नलभ्यम् अशनं मरुत् धात्रा कल्पितं, महीशायिनः पशवः तृणाङ्कुरभुजः सृष्टाः। संसारार्णवलङ्घनक्षमधियां नृणां सा वृत्तिः कृता, याम् अन्वेषयतां (नृणां) सहसा सर्वे गुणाः समाप्तिं प्रयान्ति।

सृष्टिकर्ता ब्रह्मा ने हिंसारहित और बिना प्रयास से मिलने वाली वायु को सर्पों का भोजन बनाया, उसी तरह पशुओं को सहजसाध्य तृणों के अंकुरों को भोजन के रूप में एवं भूमि को शय्या के रूप में बनाकर आत्मनिर्भर बनाया। परन्तु संसाररूपी समुद्र को पार करने में समर्थ मनुष्यों की वह पराश्रित वृत्ति बनाई, जिसकी खोज में उनके (अपनी बुद्धि के बल से) परमार्थ पाने में समर्थ समस्त गुण समाप्तप्रायः हो गए। इसी पराश्रितता से दूर रहने के लिए योगी लोग हिंसारहित यदृच्छालभ्य पाथेय से सन्तुष्ट होने की वृत्ति को अपनाते हैं।

तात्पर्य: संसार में मनुष्य ही एकमात्र ऐसा प्राणी है जो अपनी बुद्धि के बल से परमार्थ (मोक्ष) प्राप्त कर सकता है। परन्तु पराश्रित वृत्ति की खोज मनुष्य को परमार्थ की प्राप्ति से दूर रखती है।

Condemnation of Enslaved Livelihood

hiṁsāśūnyamayatnalabhyamaśanaṁ dhātrā marutkalpitaṁ
vyālānāṁ paśavastṛṇāṅkurabhujaḥ sṛṣṭā mahīśāyinaḥ ।
saṁsārārṇavalaṅghanakṣamadhiyāṁ vṛttiḥ kṛtā sā nṛṇāṁ
yāmanveṣayatāṁ prayānti sahasā sarve samāptiṁ guṇāḥ ॥ 11 ॥

anvayaḥ — *vyālānāṁ hiṁsāśūnyam ayatnalabhyam aśanaṁ marut dhātrā kalpitaṁ, mahīśāyinaḥ paśavaḥ tṛṇāṅkurabhujaḥ sṛṣṭāḥ* । *saṁsārārṇavalaṅghanakṣamadhiyāṁ nṛṇāṁ sā vṛttiḥ kṛtā, yām anveṣayatāṁ (nṛṇāṁ) sahasā sarve guṇāḥ samāptiṁ prayānti* ।

The creator Brahmā has provided air as food for serpents, obtained without violence and without effort. In the same way, he has made the animals self-sufficient by making the shoots of easily available grasses as food and the land as a bed. In contrary, he has created such dependent means of earning livelihood for the humans, capable of crossing the worldly ocean, in the search of which all their qualities, i.e. essential for attaining the ultimate goal (with the power of their intellect) almost exhausted. In order to stay away from this dependency, *yogī*s adopt a way of satisfied with effortlessly available non-violent livelihood.

Purport — Man is the only living being in the world who can attain salvation by the power of his intellect. But the pursuit of dependent means of earning his livelihood keeps the human being away from the attainment of the Supreme.

जीवन की सार्थकता का रहस्य

न ध्यातं पदमीश्वरस्य विधिवत्संसारविच्छित्तये
स्वर्गद्वारकवाट[19]पाटनपटुर्धर्मोऽपि नोपार्जितः ।
नारीपीनपयोधरोरुयुगलं स्वप्नेऽपि नालिङ्गितं
मातुः केवलमेव यौवनवनच्छेदे कुठारा वयम् ॥ 12 ॥

अन्वय — संसारविच्छित्तये ईश्वरस्य पदं विधिवत् न ध्यातं, (संसारविच्छित्तये) स्वर्गद्वारकवाटपाटनपटुः धर्मः अपि न उपार्जितः । (संसारविच्छित्तये) नारीपीनपयोधरोरुयुगलं स्वप्नेऽपि नालिङ्गितम् । केवलं मातुः यौवनवनच्छेदे एव वयं कुठाराः (स्मः) ।

हमने संसार बन्धन को काटने के लिए, यथाविधि, ईश्वर के चरणों का एकाग्र मन से ध्यान नहीं किया, जिससे इस जन्म में मोक्ष-प्राप्ति सम्भव नहीं; हमने स्वर्ग के दरवाज़े खुलवाने वाले धर्म का सञ्चय भी नहीं किया, क्योंकि "ज्योतिष्टोमेन स्वर्गकामो यजेत" इस श्रुतिवचन से ज्योतिष्टोम यज्ञ आदि धार्मिक कार्यों से स्वर्ग-प्राप्ति होती है, इस प्रकार हमने धर्म का अर्जन भी नहीं किया; और हमने स्वप्न में भी स्त्रियों के कठोर स्तन एवं जघनों का आलिंगन नहीं किया, जिससे काम-रूपी पुरुषार्थ भी सिद्ध नहीं हुआ। हम तो अपनी माँ के यौवन-रूपी वन को काटने के लिए कुल्हाड़े ही हुए।

तात्पर्य — मानव जीवन का परम उद्देश्य है धर्म, अर्थ, काम एवं मोक्ष जैसे चार पुरुषार्थों की प्राप्ति। अतः जो मनुष्य अपने जीवन काल में इन पुरुषार्थों में से एक को भी प्राप्त नहीं करता है, तो उसका जन्म ही निष्फल होता है।

Secret of the Significance of Life

na dhyātaṁ padamīśvarasya vidhivatsaṁsāravicchittaye
svargadvārakavāṭapāṭanapaṭurdharmo 'pi nopārjitaḥ ।
nārīpīnapayodharoruyugalaṁ svapne 'pi nāliṅgitaṁ
mātuḥ kevalameva yauvanavanacchede kuṭhārā vayam ॥ 12 ॥

---

19 कपाट — *Ms ORLS-3, JKM.1911.*

anvayaḥ — *saṁsāravicchittaye īśvarasya padaṁ vidhivat na dhyātaṁ, (saṁsāravicchittaye) svargadvārakavāṭapāṭanapaṭuḥ dharmaḥ api na upārjitaḥ* । *(saṁsāravicchittaye) nārīpīnapayodharoruyugalaṁ svapne 'pi nāliṅgitam* । *kevalaṁ mātuḥ yauvanavanacchede eva vayaṁ kuṭhārāḥ (smaḥ)* ।

In order to cut off the bondage of the world, we have neither meditated on the feet of God with concentration, due to which salvation is not attainable in this birth; nor have we even accumulated *dharma* that opens the doors of heaven, because it is mentioned in the Veda *jyotiṣṭomena svargakāmo yajeta* (one who desires *svarga* should sacrifice with the Jyotiṣṭoma ritual). Thus we did not even acquire religion. The ritual Jyotiṣṭoma and similar religious works lead to heaven; nor, even in our dreams, have we embraced a woman with full-grown breasts that directed us towards non-achievement of *kāma,* one of the four essences of life. We have, by being born, only served the purpose of life, like an axe, to cut the bloom of our mother's youth.

Purport — The ultimate aim of human life is the attainment of four *puruṣārtha*s (essences of life) like *dharma, artha, kāma* and *mokṣa.* Therefore, the person who does not achieve even one of these *puruṣārtha*s in his lifetime, his birth itself becomes useless.

तृष्णा की अन्तहीनता

भोगा न भुक्ता वयमेव भुक्तास्तपो न तप्तं वयमेव तप्ताः ।
कालो न यातो वयमेव यातास्तृष्णा न जीर्णा वयमेव जीर्णाः ॥ 13 ॥

अन्वय — भोगा न भुक्ताः, वयमेव भुक्ताः, तपः न तप्तं, वयमेव तप्ताः । कालो न यातः, वयमेव याताः । तृष्णा न जीर्णा, वयमेव जीर्णाः ।

सांसारिक सुखों को हमने भोगा नहीं, अपितु हम स्वयं ही वासनाओं के शिकार हो गए हैं। हमारे द्वारा कोई तपस्या नहीं की गई, बल्कि हम खुद ही झुलस गए हैं। समय, जो कि त्रिकाल-विद्यमान और अनन्त होता है, नहीं गया है लेकिन हम खुद ही मृत्यु के करीब आने के कारण अन्त की ओर चले जा रहे हैं। इच्छाएं कम नहीं होती, हालाँकि हम स्वयं बुढ़ापे से ग्रसित हो गए हैं।

तात्पर्य — शरीर भोग, वासना एवं समय से ग्रसित होकर मृत्यु के जठराग्नि में जीर्ण हो जाता है, परन्तु तृष्णा मरती नहीं।

The Endlessness of Craving

bhogā na bhuktā vayameva bhuktā-
stapo na taptaṁ vayameva taptāḥ ।
kālo na yāto vayameva yātā-
stṛṣṇā na jīrṇā vayameva jīrṇāḥ ॥ 13 ॥

anvayaḥ — *bhogā na bhuktāḥ, vayameva bhuktāḥ, tapaḥ na taptaṁ, vayameva taptāḥ* । *kālo na yātaḥ, vayameva yātāḥ* । *tṛṣṇā na jīrṇā, vayameva jīrṇāḥ* ।

Worldly pleasures have not been enjoyed by us, but we ourselves have been devoured by desires. No austerity has been performed by us, but we ourselves got scorched, time (being ever present and infinite) is not gone but we ourselves have gone (because of approaching the death). Desires are not diminished, though we ourselves are struck down by senility.

Purport — The body becomes dilapidated in the fire of death after being affected by enjoyment, lust and time, but the thirst does not die.

अनासक्त कर्मोपासना से ही शाश्वत सिद्धि की प्राप्ति

क्षान्तं न क्षमया गृहोचितसुखं त्यक्तं न सन्तोषतः[20]
सोढा दुःसहशीतवाततपनक्लेशा[21] न तप्तं तपः ।
ध्यातं वित्तमहर्निशं [22]नियमितैः प्राणैर्न शम्भोः पदं
तत्तत्कर्म कृतं यदेव मुनिभिस्तैस्तैः फलैर्वञ्चितम्[23] ॥ 14 ॥

अन्वय — (मया) क्षान्तं, (परं) न क्षमया, गृहोचितसुखं त्यक्तं (परं) न सन्तोषतः, दुःसहशीतवात-तपनक्लेशाः सोढाः, (परं) न तपः तप्तम्। नियमितैः प्राणैः अहर्निशं वित्तं ध्यातं न शम्भोः पदम्। मुनिभिः यदेव कृतं तत्तत्कर्म (मयाऽपि कृतं) परं फलैः वञ्चितम्।

---

20 संतोषितः — *Ms eG-1.*

21 सोढो दुःसहशीतवाततपनक्लेशो। — *JKM.1911, GAV.1954*

22 नियमितप्रणैः — *JKM.1911.*

23 वञ्चिताः — *JKM.1911, GAV.1954.*

हमने दूसरों से प्राप्त दुःख आदि को सहकर क्षमा तो की, परन्तु आन्तरिक क्षमाभाव से नहीं की, अपितु असामर्थ्य या भय के कारण की। स्वादिष्ट भोजन, पत्नी-समागम आदि गृहयोग्य भोग-विलासों को छोड़ा, परन्तु सन्तोष के कारण नहीं छोड़ा, अपितु अनिच्छा या परतन्त्रता के कारण छोड़ा। हमने असह्य सर्दी-गर्मी और हवा के दुःख तो सहे; किन्तु ये सब दुःख हमने तप की गरज से नहीं, वरन् दरिद्रता या अभाव के कारण सहे। हम प्राणों को नियन्त्रित करके एकाग्र होकर दिन-रात ध्यान में लगे तो रहे, परन्तु धन के ध्यान में लगे रहे, न कि प्राणायाम-क्रिया द्वारा शम्भू के चरणों के ध्यान में। इस प्रकार हमने मुनियों की तरह क्षमा, त्याग, तपस्या,ध्यान आदि समस्त कर्मों का आचरण किया, परन्तु आसक्ति से किए हुए कर्मों के कारण उनकी तरह शाश्वत सिद्धि नहीं मिली।

[*श्रीमद्भगवद्गीता* में कहा गया है —

न कर्मणामनारम्भान्नैष्कर्म्यं पुरुषोऽश्नुते।
न च सन्न्यसनादेव सिद्धिं समधिगच्छति ॥ III.4 ॥

कर्मेन्द्रियाणि संयम्य य आस्ते मनसा स्मरन्।
इन्द्रियार्थान्विमूढात्मा मिथ्याचारः स उच्यते ॥ III.6 ॥

यस्त्विन्द्रियाणि मनसा नियम्याऽरभतेऽर्जुन।
कर्मेन्द्रियैः कर्मयोगमसक्तः स विशिष्यते ॥ III.7 ॥

सार यह है कि कर्म के न करने से या कर्म के त्याग मात्र से मनुष्य को योग-सिद्धि नहीं मिलती। अपितु केवल कर्मेन्द्रियों को संयत करके जो व्यक्ति मन से इन्द्रियों के विषयों पर आसक्त रहता है उसे मिथ्याचार कहा जाता है। योग-सिद्धि तो उन्हें प्राप्त होती है जो मन से इन्द्रियों को संयत करके अनासक्ति भाव से कर्म करते हैं।]

तात्पर्य — आसक्तिपूर्वक किया हुआ कर्म व्यक्ति को शाश्वत-सिद्धि की प्राप्ति से दूर रखता है। अतः परम सत्य की प्राप्ति हेतु मनुष्य को अनासक्ति भाव से शास्त्रविहित आचरण करना चाहिए।

Absolute Success Is the Result of Disassociation with Karma

kṣāntaṁ na kṣamayā gṛhocitasukhaṁ tyaktaṁ na saṅtoṣataḥ
soḍhā duḥsahaśītavātatapanakleśā na taptaṁ tapaḥ ।
dhyātaṁ vittamaharniśaṁ niyamitaiḥ prāṇairna śambhoḥ padaṁ
tattatkarma kṛtaṁ yadeva munibhistaistaiḥ phalairvañcitam ॥ 14 ॥

anvayaḥ — *(mayā) kṣāntaṁ (paraṁ) na kṣamayā, gṛhocitasukhaṁ tyaktaṁ (paraṁ) na santoṣataḥ, duḥsahaśītavātatapanakleśāḥ soḍhāḥ, (paraṁ) na tapaḥ taptam* । *niyamitaiḥ prāṇaiḥ aharniśaṁ vittaṁ dhyātaṁ na śambhoḥ padam* । *munibhiḥ yadeva kṛtaṁ tattatkarma (mayā 'pi kṛtaṁ) paraṁ phalaiḥ vañcitam* ।

We exonerated after tolerating the loss and pain, etc. received from others, but not with inner forgiveness, rather due to inability or fear. We gave up the homely pleasures like delicious food, association of wife, etc. but not because of satisfaction, rather because of reluctance or dependence. We have suffered the unbearable cold, heat and wind, but we did not suffer all these sorrows due to penance, rather than because of poverty or paucity. We remained focused and engaged in the meditation of money day and night within tense energy, but not in the meditation of the feet of Śambhū through *prāṇāyāma*. Thus have we performed the actions of the ascetic recluse, i.e. forgiveness, sacrifice, penance, meditation, etc. but devoid of the benefits out of those.

[It is alluded in the *Śrīmadbhagavadgītā*:

> *na karmaṇāmanārambhānnaiṣkarmyaṁ puruṣo 'śnute* ।
> *na ca sannyasanādeva siddhiṁ samadhigacchati* ॥ III.4 ॥
>
> *karmendriyāṇi saṁyamya ya āste manasā smaran* ।
> *indriyārthānvimūḍhātmā mithyācāraḥ sa ucyate* ॥ III.6 ॥
>
> *yastvindriyāṇi manasā niyamyā 'rabhate 'rjuna* ।
> *karmendriyaiḥ karmayogamasaktaḥ sa viśiṣyate* ॥ III.7 ॥

The essence is that a man does not get eternal achievement by not doing work or by simply renunciation of work. Rather, a person, who remains attached to the objects of the senses by restraining only the physical senses, is called a liar. Eternal achievement is attained by those who restrain the senses from the mind and work with non-attachment.]

Purport — Action done with attachment keeps one away from the attainment of eternal perfection. Therefore, in order to attain the Ultimate Truth, an individual should carry out the conducts with non-attachment according to the guidelines of the scriptures.

तृष्णा की नित्य नवीनता

वलिभिर्मुखमाक्रान्तं पलितैरङ्कितं शिरः।
गात्राणि शिथिलायन्ते तृष्णैका तरुणायते॥ 15॥

अन्वय — वलिभिः मुखम् आक्रान्तं, पलितैः शिरः अङ्कितं, गात्राणि शिथिलायन्ते, (परं) तृष्णैका तरुणायते।

चेहरे पर झुर्रियां पड़ गई, शिर के बाल पककर सफ़ेद हो गए, सारे अंग शिथिल हो गए, परन्तु तृष्णा तो तरुण होती जाती है।

तात्पर्य — व्यक्ति अपने शरीर की क्षीणता एवं नश्वरता को देखते हुए भी अपनी तृष्णा को नहीं त्यागता, यही बिडम्बना है।

Agelessness of Desire

valibhirmukhamākrāntaṁ palitairaṅkitaṁ śiraḥ।
gātrāṇi śithilāyante tṛṣṇaikā taruṇāyate॥ 15॥

anvayaḥ — *valibhiḥ mukham ākrāntaṁ, palitaiḥ śiraḥ aṅkitaṁ, gātrāṇi śithilāyante, (paraṁ) tṛṣṇaikā taruṇāyate*।

Face has been covered with wrinkles, the head painted white with gray hair, the limbs turned feeble, yet the rejuvenating desire alone stays youthful.

Purport — The irony is that a person does not give up his passion, even after observing the frailty and impermanence of his body.

भौतिक वस्तु पर अनन्य प्रभुत्व की निन्दा

येनैवाम्बरखण्डेन संवीतो निशि चन्द्रमा:।
तेनैव च दिवा भानुरहो दौर्गत्यमेतयो:॥ 16॥

अन्वय — येनैव अम्बरखण्डेन निशि चन्द्रमा: संवीतः। तेनैव च दिवा भानुः संवीतः। अहो एतयो: दौर्गत्यम्! (अम्बरखण्डेन = आकाशशकलेन वस्त्रखण्डेन वा)।

आकाश के जिस टुकड़े को वस्त्र के रूप में ओढ़कर या पहनकर चन्द्रमा रात बिताता है, उसी आकाशरूपी वस्त्र को पहनकर सूर्य दिन बिताता है। (सम्पूर्ण संसार को प्रकाशित करके अपने प्रभाव से जगत् में प्रतिष्ठित सूर्य एवं चन्द्र के अपने वस्त्र-खण्ड पर भी एकाधिकार न होने से) इन दोनों की कैसी दुर्गति होती है!

तात्पर्य — इस नश्वर संसार में व्यक्ति को किसी वस्तु या पद पर सम्पूर्ण स्वत्व-युक्त एकाधिकार का भ्रम नहीं पालना चाहिए।

Censuring Exclusive Dominion over Material Things

yenaivāmbarakhaṇḍena saṁvīto niśi candramāḥ ।
tenaiva ca divā bhānuraho daurgatyametayoḥ ॥ 16 ॥

anvayaḥ — *yenaiva ambarakhaṇḍena niśi candramāḥ saṁvītaḥ* । *tenaiva ca divā bhānuḥ saṁvītaḥ* । *aho etayoḥ daurgatyam*!

The sun spends the day wearing the piece of sky that the moon spends the night wearing as a garment. (By illuminating the whole world with their influence, the sun and the moon, that are respected in the world, do not have their dominion even over their piece of clothing). What a misery these two are in?

Purport — In this mortal world, a person should not have the illusion of absolute proprietary dominion over any material or position.

विषयों का परित्याग : अनन्त सुख का कारण

अवश्यं यातारश्चिरतरमुषित्वापि विषया
वियोगे को भेदस्त्यजति न जनो यत्स्वयममून्।
व्रजन्तः स्वातन्त्र्यादतुलपरितापाय मनसः
स्वयं त्यक्ता ह्येते शमसुखमनन्तं विदधते[24] ॥ 17 ॥

अन्वय — चिरतरम् उषित्वापि विषया अवश्यं यातारः, वियोगे को भेदो यद् जनः स्वयम् अमून् न त्यजति। (इमे विषयाः) स्वातन्त्र्याद् व्रजन्तः मनसः अतुलपरितापाय (भवन्ति), हि एते (विषयाः) स्वयं त्यक्ता अनन्तं शमसुखं विदधते।

इन्द्रियों के शब्द, रूप, रस, गन्ध एवं स्पर्श आदि विषयों को हम चाहे कितने दिन तक क्यों न भोगें, एक दिन वे निश्चय ही हमसे अलग हो जाएंगे; तब मनुष्य उन्हें स्वयं अपनी इच्छा से ही क्यों न छोड़ दे? इस वियोग में क्या अन्तर है? यदि मनुष्य विषयों को नहीं छोड़ेगा तो, वे विषय ही मनुष्य को छोड़ देंगे। और जब वे स्वयं मनुष्य को छोड़ेंगे, तब उससे मनुष्य को बड़ा दुःख और मनःक्लेश होगा। अगर मनुष्य उन्हें स्वयं छोड़ देगा, तो उसे अनन्त सुख और शान्ति प्राप्त होगी।

---

24 विदधति — *JKM.1911, GAV.1954.*

[श्रोत्र, त्वक्, जिह्वा, घ्राण एवं चक्षुः इन पाँच इन्द्रियों के जो शब्द, स्पर्श, रस, गन्ध एवं रूप ये विषय अस्थिर एवं गमनशील हैं, जिनके चले जाने पर मनुष्य को दुःख होता है। अतः इन विषयों को त्यागकर मनुष्य क्यों न शमसुख को प्राप्त करे? क्योंकि विषयों के उपभोग की तृष्णा के त्याग के समान कोई सुख नहीं होता। जैसा कि *महाभारत* में कहा गया है —

यच्च कामसुखं लोके यच्च दिव्यं महत्सुखम्।
तृष्णाक्षयसुखस्यैते नार्हतः षोडशीं कलाम् ॥] — शान्तिपर्व 176.51

तात्पर्य — अनन्त एवं पारलौकिक सुख इन्द्रियों के विषयों के परित्याग से ही सम्भव है। अतः मनुष्य को विषयों की आसक्ति से विरत रहना चाहिए।

Extrication to Sensual Objects: The Cause of Eternal Happiness

avaśyaṁ yātāraściratarамuṣitvāpi viṣayā
viyoge ko bhedastyajati na jano yatsvayamamūn ।
vrajantaḥ svātantryādatulaparitāpāya manasaḥ
svayaṁ tyaktā hyete śamasukhamanantaṁ vidadhate ॥ 17 ॥

anvayaḥ — *cirataram uṣitvāpi viṣayā avaśyaṁ yātāraḥ, viyoge ko bhedo yad janaḥ svayam amūn na tyajati* । *(ime viṣayāḥ) svātantryād vrajantaḥ manasaḥ atulaparitāpāya (bhavanti), hi ete (viṣayāḥ) svayaṁ tyaktā anantaṁ śamasukhaṁ vidadhate* ।

No matter how many days we enjoy the objects of the senses like sound, form, taste, smell and touch, they will definitely leave us sometime; then why should not man leave them of his own free will? Then, what difference does it make if the people discard them by their own choice? The mind is sorely attached to those objects of the senses which derive material pleasures, and gets afflicted if they leave us of their own accord. If men voluntarily renounce those, they conduce to the eternal bliss of self-possession.

[Sound, touch, taste, smell and form are the objects of our five senses, i.e. ears, skin, tongue, nose and eyes, which are volatile and mutable. We get afflicted when they leave us. Therefore, leaving these subjects, why should not we attain the eternal bliss of self-possession, by renouncing those? Because there is no happiness like renunciation of the passion for the enjoyment of those objects of our senses. It is stated in the *Mahābhārata*:

> *yacca kāmasukhaṁ loke yacca divyaṁ mahatsukham* ।
> *tṛṣṇākṣayasukhasyaite nārhataḥ ṣoḍaśīṁ kalām* ॥
> — Śantiparva 176.51

Meaning: "Whatever is the happiness of desire in this world and whatever is the ultimate divine pleasure. Those are not equal to the sixteenth part of happiness of renunciation of the passion".]

Purport — Eternal and transcendent happiness is possible only by abandoning the objects of the senses. Therefore, man should abstain from attachment to objects of the senses.

काम-वासना की सर्वव्यापकता

कृशः काणः खञ्जः श्रवणरहितः पुच्छविकलो
व्रणी पूयक्लिन्नः कृमिकुलशतैरावृततनुः ।
क्षुधाक्षामो जीर्णः [25]पिठिरककपालार्पितगलः
शुनीमन्वेति श्वा हतमपि निहन्त्येव[26] मदनः ॥ 18 ॥

अन्वय — कृशः काणः खञ्जः श्रवणरहितः पुच्छविकलो व्रणी पूयक्लिन्नः कृमिकुलशतैः आवृततनुः क्षुधाक्षामो जीर्णः पिठिरककपालार्पितगलः श्वा शुनीम् अन्वेति। (हन्त!) मदनः हतमपि निहन्ति एव।

एक कुत्ता, क्षीण और काना, लंगड़ा और बहरा, पूँछरहित और जख्मी, जिसके जख्मों में राध बह रही है, जिसके शरीर में कीड़े बिलबिला रहे हैं, जो भूखा और बूढ़ा है, टूटे हुए कटोरे में जिसकी गर्दन फँसी हुई है, ऐसी अवस्था में भी कामातुर होकर एक कुतिया के पीछे भाग रहा है। हाय! कामदेव जब मरे हुए प्राणी पर भी हमला करता है, तब स्वादिष्ट भोजी, सुखी एवं स्वस्थ मनुष्य को कैसे छोड़ेगा?

[काम एक ऐसी तीव्र दाहक अग्नि है जो कि सभी प्राणियों को जला देती है। काम के वश में आकर प्राणी अपना ज्ञान खो देता है जिससे उसे शान्ति नहीं मिलती। परन्तु मनुष्य ही एकमात्र ऐसा प्राणी है जो अपनी बुद्धि के बल से इसी काम को नियन्त्रित करके परम शान्ति प्राप्त कर सकता है। क्योंकि *श्रीमद्भगवद्गीता* III.38-40 में कहा गया है —

> धूमेनाव्रियते वह्निर्यथादर्शो मलेन च।
> यथोल्बेनावृतो गर्भस्तथा तेनेदमावृतम्॥

---

[25] पिठरक — *JKM.1911.*

[26] च हन्त्येव — *JKM.1911.*

आवृतं ज्ञानमेतेन ज्ञानिनो नित्यवैरिणा।
कामरूपेण कौन्तेय दुष्पूरेणानलेन च॥

इन्द्रियाणि मनो बुद्धिरस्याधिष्ठानमुच्यते।
एतैर्विमोहयत्येष ज्ञानमावृत्य देहिनम्॥

अर्थात् जिस प्रकार धुएं से अग्नि और मैल से दर्पण ढका जाता है तथा जिस प्रकार जेर से गर्भ ढका रहता है, वैसे ही उस काम के द्वारा यह ज्ञान ढका रहता है। कभी न शान्त होने वाले, नित्य वैरी इस कमाग्नि से ज्ञानियों का ज्ञान ढका हुआ है। इन्द्रिय, मन और बुद्धि — ये सब इसके वासस्थान कहे जाते हैं। यह काम मन, बुद्धि और इन्द्रियों के द्वारा ही ज्ञान को आच्छादित करके जीवात्मा को मोहित करता है।]

तात्पर्य — काम-वासना अमृतमय जीवन को मृत्यु में बदल देती है। अतः जीवन को शाश्वत आनन्दोन्मुखी बनाने हेतु सर्वादौ काम-वासना का त्याग करना चाहिए।

Ubiquity of Lust

kṛśaḥ kāṇaḥ khañjaḥ śravaṇarahitaḥ pucchavikalo
vraṇī pūyaklinnaḥ kṛmikulaśatairāvṛtatanuḥ।
kṣudhākṣāmo jīrṇaḥ piṭhirakakapālārpitagalaḥ
śunīmanveti śvā hatamapi nihantyeva madanaḥ ॥ 18 ॥

anvayaḥ — *kṛśaḥ kāṇaḥ khañjaḥ śravaṇarahitaḥ pucchavikalo vraṇī pūyaklinnaḥ kṛmikulaśataiḥ āvṛtatanuḥ kṣudhākṣāmo jīrṇaḥ piṭhirakakapālārpitagalaḥ śvā śunīm anveti*। *(hanta!) madanaḥ hatamapi nihanti eva*।

A dog, emaciated and with a perforated eye, lame and deaf, tailless and wounded, bleeding from its wounds, worms writhing in its body, hungry and old, with its neck stuck in a broken bowl, he, having been lustful even in such a state of infirmity, runs after a bitch. Oh! when cupid leaves not even a tormented creature, then how will he leave a healthy and happy man, capable of arranging delicious food for him?

[Lust is such an intense burning fire that it burns all organisms. By coming under the control of lust, the creature loses its knowledge, due to which it does not get peace. But, man is the only creature who can achieve ultimate peace by controlling the lust with the power of his intellect. Because it is said in *Śrīmadbhagavadgītā* III.38-40:

dhūmenāvriyate vahniryathādarśo malena ca ।
yatholbenāvṛto garbhastathā tenedamāvṛtam ॥

āvṛtaṁ jñānametena jñānino nityavairiṇā ।
kāmarūpeṇa kaunteya duṣpūreṇānalena ca ॥

indriyāṇi mano buddhirasyādhiṣṭhānamucyate ।
etairvimohayatyeṣa jñānamāvṛtya dehinam ॥

Meaning: Just as the fire is covered by smoke, just as mirror is covered by dust and just as the embryo is covered by amnion, similarly knowledge is covered and surrounded by one's desires and lust. The knowledge of the wise is covered by this fire of lust that never calms down and acts as an enemy. The senses, mind and one's intellect are the home of the desire or lust. This covers the knowledge and deluges the spirit.]

Purport — It is the lust that turns the nectarlike life into death. Therefore, to make the life prone towards eternal happiness, one should give up all sexual desires.

विषयों की अपरित्याज्यता

भिक्षाशनं तदपि नीरसमेकवारं
शय्या च भूः परिजनो निजदेहमात्रम्।
वस्त्रं [27]च जीर्णशतखण्डमयी च कन्था
हा हा तथापि विषया न परित्यजन्ति[28] ॥ 19 ॥

अन्वय — एकवारं भिक्षाशनं तदपि नीरसं, शय्या च भूः, परिजनो निजदेहमात्रम्। जीर्णं च वस्त्रं, शतखण्डमयी च कन्था। हा! हा! तथापि विषया (मनुष्यं) न परित्यजन्ति।

आश्चर्य है कि ऐसे दीन-हीन प्राणी को भी विषय नहीं छोड़ते, जो भीख माँगकर दिन में एक समय ही नीरस अन्न खाता है, धरती पर सोता है, जिसका शरीर ही उसका कुटुम्बी है, जिसके पहने हुए वस्त्र अत्यन्त जीर्ण हो गए हैं, जो सौ चीथड़ों की गुदड़ी ओढ़ता है।

[इस सन्दर्भ में *श्रीमद्भगवद्गीता* का उपदेश ग्राह्य है —

श्रोत्रं चक्षुः स्पर्शनं च रसनं घ्राणमेव च।
अधिष्ठाय मनश्चायं विषयानुपसेवते ॥ XV.9 ॥

---

27 सुजीर्ण — *JKM.1911*, विशीर्ण — *GAV.1954.*

28 विषयान्न जहाति चेतः — *JKM.1911.*

ध्यायतो विषयान्पुंसः सङ्गस्तेषूपजायते।
सङ्गात्सञ्जायते कामः कामात्क्रोधोऽभिजायते ॥ II.62 ॥

क्रोधाद्भवति संमोहः संमोहात्स्मृतिविभ्रमः।
स्मृतिभ्रंशाद्बुद्धिनाशो बुद्धिनाशात्प्रणश्यति ॥ II.63 ॥

आपूर्यमाणमचलप्रतिष्ठं समुद्रमापः प्रविशन्ति यद्वत्।
तद्वत्कामा यं प्रविशन्ति सर्वे स शान्तिमाप्नोति न कामकामी ॥ II.70 ॥

अर्थात् श्रोत्र, चक्षु, त्वचा, जिह्वा, घ्राण और मन इन इन्द्रियों के विषय हैं शब्द, रूप, स्पर्श, रस एवं गन्ध आदि। मनुष्य इन विषयों का सेवन करता है। विषयों का चिन्तन करने वाले पुरुष की उन विषयों में आसक्ति हो जाती है, आसक्ति से उन विषयों की कामना उत्पन्न होती है और कामना में विघ्न पड़ने से क्रोध उत्पन्न होता है। क्रोध से सम्मोह उत्पन्न हो जाता है, सम्मोह से स्मृति में भ्रम हो जाता है, स्मृति के भ्रष्ट हो जाने से बुद्धि अर्थात् ज्ञान-शक्ति का नाश हो जाता है और बुद्धि के नाश हो जाने से पुरुष विनाश को प्राप्त करता है।

अतः, जैसे नाना नदियों के जल सभी ओर से परिपूर्ण, अचल प्रतिष्ठा वाले समुद्र में उसको विचलित न करते हुए ही समा जाते हैं, वैसे ही सभी विषय-भोग जिस स्थितप्रज्ञ पुरुष में किसी प्रकार का विकार उत्पन्न किए बिना ही समा जाते हैं, वही पुरुष परम शान्ति को प्राप्त करता है, न कि विषयों में आसक्त पुरुष।]

तात्पर्य — इन्द्रियों की विषयासक्ति इतनी व्यापक है कि दीन-हीन प्राणी को भी अपने वश में करके उसका विनाश कर देती हैं। अतः विवेकी पुरुष ही इन विषयों पर आसक्त न होकर शाश्वत शान्ति प्राप्त कर सकता है।

Irreconcilability of Sensual Desires

bhikṣāśanaṁ tadapi nīrasamekavāraṁ
śayyā ca bhūḥ parijano nijadehamātram ।
vastraṁ ca jīrṇaśatakhaṇḍamayī ca kanthā
hā hā tathāpi viṣayā na parityajanti ॥ 19 ॥

anvayaḥ — *ekavāraṁ bhikṣāśanaṁ tadapi nīrasaṁ, śayyā ca bhūḥ, parijano nijadehamātram* । *jīrṇaṁ ca vastraṁ, śatakhaṇḍamayī ca kanthā* । *hā! hā! tathāpi viṣayā (manuṣyaṁ) na parityajanti* ।

Sensual desires do not leave even such a person who feeds on tasteless food once a day, after begging of alms, who has no other bed than the bare earth, no other member in his family than his body itself, whose dress has become dilapidated and who uses a bundle of rags as a blanket.

[Here the advice of the *Śrīmadbhagavadgītā* may be followed:

śrotraṁ cakṣuḥ sparśanaṁ ca rasanaṁ ghrāṇameva ca ।
adhiṣṭhāya manaścāyaṁ viṣayānupasevate ॥ XV.9 ॥

dhyāyato viṣayānpuṁsaḥ saṅgasteṣūpajāyate ।
saṅgātsañjāyate kāmaḥ kāmātkrodho 'bhijāyate ॥ II.62 ॥

krodhādbhavati sammohaḥ sammohātsmṛtivibhramaḥ ।
smṛtibhraṁśādbuddhināśo buddhināśātpraṇaśyati ॥ II.63 ॥

āpūryamāṇamacalapratiṣṭhaṁ
samudramāpaḥ praviśanti yadvat ।
tadvatkāmā yaṁ praviśanti sarve
sa śāntimāpnoti na kāmakāmī ॥ II.70 ॥

Meaning: The objects of the senses are sound, form, touch, taste, smell, etc. A being is able to experience these objects in this world through his senses. A man who contemplates on these objects becomes attached to these, attachment arouses desires and when one does not get what one desires, irritation is aroused, and from irritation stem anger and frustration. From anger stems delusion (false beliefs or assumptions); delusion causes loss of one's confused mind; the confused mind makes a person lose his/her ability to reason and lose their power to solve his/her problems. When one loses his/her power to reason, the person will suffer ultimate death and destruction.

Therefore, as the river enters the ocean without affecting the ocean or disturbing it, so the desires enter the person who has obtained Supreme Peace, but not the person who is already filled with desires and wants more and more.]

Purport — The sensual attachment of the senses is so widespread that it destroys even an anemic creature by taking it under its control. Therefore, without being attached to the senses, a wise man can attain eternal peace.

कामिनी-कामुकता की वीभत्सता

स्तनौ मांसग्रन्थी कनककलशावित्युपमितौ
मुखं श्लेष्मागारं तदपि च शशाङ्केन तुलितम् ।

स्रवन्मूत्रक्लिन्नं करिवरकरस्पर्धि जघनं
[29]मुहुर्निन्द्यं रूपं कविवर[30] विशेषैर्गुरुकृतम् ॥ 20 ॥

अन्वय — स्तनौ मांसग्रन्थी (तथापि कविवरविशेषैः) कनककलशौ इति उपमितौ। मुखं श्लेष्मागारं तदपि च (तथापि कविवरविशेषैः) शशाङ्केन तुलितम्। जघनं स्रवन्मूत्रक्लिन्नं (तथापि कविवरविशेषैः) करिवरकरस्पर्धि (वर्णितम्)। (एवं) मुहुः निन्द्यम् (अपि) रूपं कविवरविशेषैः गुरुकृतम्।

कवियों ने स्त्रियों के जिन स्तनों को सोने के कलशों की उपमा दी है वे मांस के ग्रन्थि मात्र हैं। स्त्रियों का मुँह, जो कि कफ़ का घर है, परन्तु कविवर उसे चन्द्रमा के समान बताते हैं और बहते हुए पेशाब से जो गीली रहती हैं वैसी उनकी जाँघो को, श्रेष्ठ हाथी की सूँड से स्पर्द्धा करने का वर्णन किया है। इस प्रकार स्त्रियों के घृणा योग्य रूप को भी कवियों ने उपमा और अतिशयोक्ति आदि अलंकारों से अलंकृत करके बढ़ा-चढ़ाकर उसकी तारीफ की है।

[काव्यों में स्त्रियों की शरीर-रचना का वर्णन करने का चलन है, जहाँ स्तन, जघन, नितम्ब, आदि कामिनी अवयवों के वर्णन में प्रायः दुनिया की श्रेष्ठ एवं सुन्दरतम वस्तुओं की तुलना में परन्तु प्रचुर मात्रा में आख्यानों के साथ शृंगार रस को छिड़का जाता है। कवि भर्तृहरि ने शृङ्गारशतक में स्त्रियों के शरीर की सुन्दरता वर्णन करते हुए उसकी नश्वरता का भी उल्लेख किया है। इस कविता में कवि भर्तृहरि ने महिलाओं के प्रति आकर्षण को कम करने के उद्देश्य से घृणा की भावना को बढ़ाने में मदद की है, जो कि भारतीय सौन्दर्यशास्त्रियों का कहना है कि यह शान्ति की भावना की ओर ले जाती है।]

तात्पर्य — विषयासक्ति में कामिनियों के प्रति आकर्षण की प्रधान भूमिका है, जिसे कवियों ने अत्यधिक रूप में तूल दी है। अतः मनुष्य को स्त्रियों के शरीर की वास्तविक बीभत्स संरचना को नहीं भूलना चाहिए, जिसे न समझकर पुरुष ने स्त्रियों के शरीर को आकर्षण के रूप में मानने का भ्रम पाल रखा है।

Repulsiveness of Lasciviousness to Feminine

stanau māṁsagranthī kanakakalaśāvityupamitau
mukhaṁ śleṣmāgāraṁ tadapi ca śaśāṅkena tulitam ।
sravanmūtraklinnaṁ karivarakaraspardhi jaghanaṁ
muhurnindyaṁ rūpaṁ kavivaraviśeṣairgurukṛtam ॥ 20 ॥

anvayaḥ — *stanau māṁsagranthī* (*tathāpi kavivaraviśeṣaiḥ*) *kanakakalaśau iti upamitau* । *mukhaṁ śleṣmāgāraṁ tadapi ca* (*tathāpi kavivaraviśeṣaiḥ*)

[29] अहो — *JKM.1911.*

[30] कविजन — *JKM.1911, GAV.1954.*

śaśāṅkena tulitam । *jaghanaṁ sravanmūtraklinnaṁ* (*tathāpi kavivaraviśeṣaiḥ*) *karivarakaraspardhi* (*varṇitam*) । (*evaṁ*) *muhuḥ nindyam* (*api*) *rūpaṁ kavivaraviśeṣaiḥ gurukṛtam* ।

The breasts of women, which have been compared by poets to urns of gold, are just lumps of flesh. The mouth of a woman, which is the base of phlegm, but poets describe it as the moon. And their loins, which are wet with flowing urine, have been described as contesting with the trunk of a paramount elephant. In this way, the poets have praised the disgusting form of women by embellishing them with similes, exaggerations, etc.

[In the poetries there is a trend for describing female anatomy, where verses on *śṛṅgāra* are invariably sprinkled with generous amounts of narrations on *stana* (breasts), *jaghana* (loins), *nitamba* (buttocks), etc. comparing with magnificent objects of the world. Poet Bhartṛhari in his *Śṛṅgāraśataka,* while describing the beauty of women, has mentioned its transitoriness also. In this poem the poet Bhartṛhari has helped to heighten the sentiment of disgust, aiming to reduce the allure towards women, which, Indian aestheticians aver, leads to the sentiment of serenity.]

Purport — There is a major role of attraction towards women in sensual attachment, which has been greatly exaggerated by the poets. So, man should not forget the real repugnant structure of women's body. Not understanding this, man is in illusion of considering the women's body as a cause of attraction.

मोह ही विवेकशून्यता का कारण

अजानन्माहात्म्यं पतति[31] शलभस्तीव्रदहने[32]
स मीनोऽविज्ञाना[33]द्बडिशयुतमश्नाति[34] पिशितम् ।

---

[31] पततु — *JKM.1911, GAV.1954.*

[32] दीपदहने — *JKM.1911.*

[33] अप्यज्ञानात् — *JKM.1911.*

[34] अश्नातु — *JKM.1911, GAV.1954.*

विजानन्तोऽप्येवं[35] वयमिह विपज्जालजटिलान्न
मुञ्चामः कामानहह गहनो मोहमहिमा ॥ 21 ॥

अन्वय — शलभः माहात्म्यम् अजानन् तीव्रदहने पतति, स मीनः अविज्ञानाद् वडिशयुतं पिशितम् अश्नाति। (परन्तु) वयं विजानन्तः अपि विपज्जालजटिलात् कामात् न मुञ्चामः। अहह गहनः (अयं) मोहमहिमा।

अज्ञानवश, पतंगा अग्नि की लौ पर गिरकर भस्म हो जाता है; इसी तरह मछली भी अज्ञानता के कारण काँटे से सने हुए मांस को खाकर अपने प्राण खो देती है; परन्तु हम मनुष्य लोग तो अच्छी तरह जानबूझकर भी विपत्तियों से जटिल काम आदि विषयों की अभिलाषा नहीं त्यागते। इससे प्रतीत होता है कि मनुष्य के मोह की महिमा कितनी गहन या विस्मयकर है।

[प्रस्तुत सन्दर्भ में *श्रीमद्भगवद्गीता* II.67 का उपदेश स्मर्तव्य है —

इन्द्रियाणां हि चरतां यन्मनोऽनुविधीयते ॥
तदस्य हरति प्रज्ञां वायुर्नावमिवाम्भसि ॥

जिस प्रकार प्रचण्ड वायु अपने तीव्र वेग से जल पर तैरती हुई नाव को दूर तक बहाकर ले जाती है उसी प्रकार से अनियन्त्रित इन्द्रियों में से कोई एक जिसमें मन अधिक लिप्त रहता है, बुद्धि का विनाश कर देती है।

अन्यत्र भी उदाहरण प्रस्तुत है –

कुरङ्गमातङ्गपतङ्गभृङ्गा मीना हताः पञ्चभिरेव पञ्च।
एकः प्रमादी स कथं न हन्यते यः सेवते पञ्चभिरेव पञ्च ॥ — *गरुडपुराणम्*, 2.12.18

हरिण संगीत श्रवण की लालसा से शिकारी के जाल में फँस जाता है और मृत्यु को प्राप्त करता है, हाथी हथिनी का स्पर्श प्राप्त करने की लालच से फँसता है। पतंगा अर्थात् कीट अग्नि के तेज-रूप के आकर्षण से उसमें गिरकर मर जाता है, मछली जिह्वा द्वारा रस के स्वाद की लालसा से काँटे से सने हुए मांस को खाकर मरती है, भ्रमर पुष्प की गन्ध के प्रति आसक्त होकर मधु में फँस जाता है और मरता है। इस प्रकार ये जीव तो एक-एक इन्द्रिय पर अत्यन्त आसक्त होकर विनाश को प्राप्त करते हैं। परन्तु मनुष्य का मन जब श्रोत्र, त्वचा, चक्षु, जिह्वा एवं घ्राण इन सभी पाँच इन्द्रियों के विषय शब्द, स्पर्श, रूप, रस एवं गन्ध पर आसक्त रहता है, तब कैसे विनाश को प्राप्त नहीं करेगा?]

तात्पर्य — इन्द्रियों के विषयों के उपभोग से प्राणियों की दुर्दशा होती है, इससे मनुष्य अच्छी तरह से अवगत होकर भी अपने मोह के कारण विषयों पर आसक्ति नहीं छोड़ता।

---

[35] अप्येते — *JKM.1911, GAV.1954.*

Delusion Causes Imprudence

ajānanmāhātmyaṁ patati śalabhastīvradahane
sa mīno 'vijñānādvaḍiśayutamaśnāti piśitam ।
vijānanto 'pyevaṁ vayamiha vipajjālajaṭilānna
muñcāmaḥ kāmānahaha gahano mohamahimā ॥ 21 ॥

anvayaḥ — *śalabhaḥ māhātmyam ajānan tīvradahane patati, sa mīnaḥ avijñānād vaḍiśayutaṁ piśitam aśnāti* । *(parantu) vayaṁ vijānantaḥ api vipajjālajaṭilāt kāmāt na muñcāmaḥ* । *ahaha gahanaḥ (ayaṁ) mohamahimā* ।

Out of ignorance, the moth falls into the flames of the fire and dies; similarly, a fish, due to ignorance, also loses its life by eating meat studded with thorns; we, despite knowing the consequences, do not renounce sensual pleasures, complicated by calamities. This implies that it is astonishing how deeply rooted is the glory of attachment.

[In the present context the reference of *Śrīmadbhagavadgītā* II.67 may be cited here:

indriyāṇāṁ hi caratāṁ yanmano 'nuvidhīyate ।
tadasya harati prajñāṁ vāyurnāvamivāmbhasi ॥

Just as a fierce wind with its strong velocity carries away a boat floating on water, in the same way any one of the uncontrolled senses in which the mind is more involved, destroys the intellect.

Example is also available elsewhere:

kuraṅgamātaṅgapataṅgabhṛṅgā
mīnā hatāḥ pañcabhireva pañca ।
ekaḥ pramādī sa kathaṁ na hanyate
yaḥ sevate pañcabhireva pañca ॥ — *Garuḍapurāṇam* 2.12.18

Deer gets entangled in hunter's net by longing to hear music and gets death, elephant gets trapped by longing to get touch of female elephant. The kite, that is, the insect, falls into it and dies due to the attraction of the fiery form of the fire, the fish dies after eating the thorn-studded flesh through the tongue, longing for the taste of the juice, the honey bee, being attached to the smell of the flower, gets entangled in the honey and dies. In this way, these living beings get destroyed by their acute attachment to each and every sense. But when a man's mind adheres to the objects of all these five senses, hearing, skin, eyes, tongue and smell, how can he not get extinguished?]

Purport — Consuming the objects of the senses leads to the plight of the living beings, despite being well aware of this, man does not give up attachment to the objects because of his enchantment.

सन्तोष से स्वाभिमान-रक्षा

फलमलमशनाय स्वादु पानाय तोयं
शयनमवनिपृष्ठे[36] वाससी वल्कले[37] च[38] ।
[39]धनलवमधुपानभ्रान्तसर्वेन्द्रियाणा-
[40]मभिनयमनुमन्तुं नोत्सहे दुर्जनानाम् ॥ 22 ॥

अन्वय — अशनाय फलम् अलम्, पानाय स्वादु तोयम् (अलम्), शयनम् अवनिपृष्ठे (अलम्), वाससी च वल्कले (अलम्)। धनलवमधुपानभ्रान्तसर्वेन्द्रियाणाम् दुर्जनानाम् अभिनयम् अनुमन्तुं नोत्सहे।

खाने के लिए अनायास उपलब्ध फल ही पर्याप्त है, पीने के लिए सर्व-सुलभ मीठा जल है, सोने के लिए धरती है ही, और पहनने के लिए वृक्षों की छाल; फिर हम थोड़े धनरूपी मदिरा के पान से उन्मत्त इन्द्रिय वाले दुष्टों की बातें क्यों सहें?

[*महाभारत* में भी व्यासदेव ने कहा है –

यच्च कामसुखं लोके यच्च दिव्यं महत्सुखम्।
तृष्णाक्षयसुखस्यैते नार्हतः षोडशीं कलाम् ॥ — शान्तिपर्व 176.51

अर्थात् संसार में इच्छाओं की पूर्ति से जो सुख मिलता है, या स्वर्ग में जो दिव्य सुख मिलता है, वह वास्तविक सुख के सोलहवें अंश के बराबर भी नहीं होता, जो इच्छाओं को सीमित करके प्राप्त होता है। अतः तृष्णा का परित्याग करना चाहिए। क्योंकि कहा गया है कि तृष्णा असाध्वी वेश्या की तरह अकर्त्तव्य कार्यों में प्रेरित करती है। जैसे कि — अकर्तव्येष्वसाध्वीव तृष्णा प्रेरयते जनम् ।

जैसे समुद्र में अगाध जल होते हुए भी वह पिपासा को शान्त नहीं कर सकता वैसे ही धनवान् की अपार सम्पत्ति तृष्णा को कम नहीं कर सकती। अतः अल्पमात्र जल या धन ही पर्याप्त है जो पराश्रित न हो और तृष्णा या पिपासा को नष्ट करने में समर्थ हो। जैसे कि —

---

36 अवनिपृष्ठं — *JKM.1911.*

37 वल्कले वाससी — *JKM.1911.*

38 क्षितिरपि शयनार्थं वाससे वल्कलं च — *GAV.1954.*

39 नवधनमधुपान — *JKM.1911, GAV.1954.*

40 अविनयम् — *Ms eG-2, JKM.1911, GAV.1954.*

अगाधेनापि किं तेन तोयेन लवणाम्बुधेः ।
जनुमात्रं वरं वारि तृष्णाच्छेदकरं नृणाम् ॥ — *महासुभाषितसंग्रह*]

***तात्पर्य* —** तृष्णा के कारण समाज में मनुष्य का स्वाभिमान भंग होता है। अतः तृष्णा को त्यागकर सन्तोष को अपनाना चाहिए।

Complacent Safeguards Self-Respect

phalamalamaśanāya svādu pānāya toyaṁ
śayanamavanipṛṣṭhe vāsasī valkale ca ।
dhanalavamadhupānabhrāntasarvendriyāṇā-
mabhinayamanumantuṁ notsahe durjanānām ॥ 22 ॥

***anvayaḥ* —** *aśanāya phalam alam, pānāya svādu toyam (alam), śayanam avanipṛṣṭhe (alam), vāsasī ca valkale (alam)* । *dhanalavamadhupānabhrāntasarvendriyāṇām durjanānām abhinayam anumantuṁ notsahe* ।

Enough are fruits, available easily for food, sweet water is also effortlessly available to drink, there is earth for a bed and bark of trees for dress; then why should we tolerate the words of the rascals whose senses are deluded by drinking the wine of wealth?

[Vyāsadeva advises in the *Mahābhārata*:

yacca kāmasukhaṁ loke yacca divyaṁ mahatsukham ।
tṛṣṇākṣayasukhasyaite nārhataḥ ṣoḍaśīṁ kalām ॥
— Śānti-Parva 176.51

Meaning: "The happiness got by satisfying your desires, or the happiness got in heaven, does not even match up to a sixteenth portion of the real happiness that is attained through limiting your desires." That is why greed should be discarded. Because, it has been said that greed deludes in unrighteous actions like a promiscuous prostitute. Thus told: *akartavyeṣvasādhvīva tṛṣṇā prerayate janam* ।

Although there is deep water in the ocean, still it cannot quench the thirst; similarly, the abundant wealth of the rich cannot reduce the greed. Therefore, only a little water or money, got without solicitation is enough and is able to root out thirst or greed. As it is cited elsewhere:

agādhenāpi kiṁ tena toyena lavaṇāmbudheḥ ।
janumātraṁ varaṁ vāri tṛṣṇācchedakaraṁ nṛṇām ॥
— *Mahāsubhāṣitasaṁgraha*]

Purport — Self-respect of man is hampered in the society due to greed. Therefore, we should adopt contentment by abandoning greed.

अहंकार की निन्दा

विपुलहृदयैरन्यैः[41] कैश्चिज्जगज्जनितं पुरा
विधृतमपरैर्दत्तं चान्यैर्विजित्य तृणं यथा।
इह हि भुवनान्यन्ये धीराश्चतुर्दश भुञ्जते
कतिपयपुरस्वाम्ये पुंसां क एष मदज्वरः ॥ 23 ॥

अन्वय — पुरा कैश्चिद् विपुलहृदयैः जगद् जनितं, अन्यैः विधृतं, अपरैः (जगद्) विजित्य दत्तम्। इह हि अन्ये धीराः चतुर्दश भुवनानि भुञ्जते। पुंसां कतिपयपुरस्वाम्ये एष मदज्वरः कः?

प्राचीनकाल में कुछ तो ऐसे बड़े दिल वाले लोग हुए, जिन्होंने इस इस जगत् की रचना की अर्थात् नए-नए राज्यों का निर्माण किया; कुछ ऐसे हुए जिन्होंने इस जगत् को अपनी भुजाओं की शक्ति से धारण या रक्षण किया; कुछ ऐसे हुए जिन्होंने समग्र पृथ्वी जीती और फिर तुच्छ समझकर दूसरों को दान कर दी; और कुछ ऐसे भी हैं जो चौदह भुवन का पालन करते हैं। परन्तु कुछ नगरों पर राज करने वाले पुरुषों का यह उग्र अहंकार किसलिए है?

[मूढ़ व्यक्ति कर्त्तव्य कर्मों में स्वयं के कर्तृत्व का अहंकार पालता है। जैसा कि *श्रीमद्भगवद्गीता* III.27 में उल्लेख है —

प्रकृतेः क्रियमाणानि गुणैः कर्माणि सर्वशः।
अहङ्कारविमूढात्मा कर्ताहमिति मन्यते॥

जीवात्मा देह के मिथ्या ज्ञान के कारण स्वयं को अपने सभी कर्मों का कर्ता समझती है। यद्यपि विश्व के सभी कार्य प्रकृति के तीन गुणों के अन्तर्गत सम्पन्न होते हैं, परन्तु जिसका अन्तःकरण अहंकार से मोहित हो रहा है, ऐसा अज्ञानी "मैं कर्ता हूँ" ऐसा मानता है।]

तात्पर्य — मनुष्य अपनी सत्त्व, रजः एवं तमः आदि प्रकृति एवं स्वभाव के कारण ही समस्त कर्त्तव्यों का निर्वहण करता है, अतः किए जाने वाले कर्म पर अहंकार नहीं करना चाहिए। क्योंकि संसार में समस्त कर्म प्रकृति या ईश्वर के द्वारा ही संचालित हैं।

---

[41] धन्यैः — *JKM.1911*, ईशितैः — *GAV.1954.*

Condemnation of Arrogance

vipulahṛdayairanyaiḥ kaiścijjagajjanitaṁ purā
vidhṛtamaparairdattaṁ cānyairvijitya tṛṇaṁ yathā ।
iha hi bhuvanānyanye dhīrāścaturdaśa bhuñjate
katipayapurasvāmye puṁsāṁ ka eṣa madajvaraḥ ॥ 23 ॥

anvayaḥ — *purā kaiścid vipulahṛdayaiḥ jagad janitaṁ, anyaiḥ vidhṛtaṁ, aparaiḥ (jagad) vijitya dattam* । *iha hi anye dhīrāḥ caturdaśa bhuvanāni bhuñjate* । *puṁsāṁ katipayapurasvāmye eṣa madajvaraḥ kaḥ?*

In days of yore, many of these kingdoms were created by the kings with generous hearts; ruled by others, conquered and then squandered like straws by still others. Some heroes even now enjoy everything in the universe. Why then this inordinate arrogance of ruling over a few towns?

[An ignorant person develops the ego of his own doership over those actions. As mentioned in *Śrīmadbhagavadgītā* III.27:

prakṛteḥ kriyamāṇāni guṇaiḥ karmāṇi sarvaśaḥ ।
ahaṅkāravimūḍhātmā kartāhamiti manyate ॥

All actions, that are performed by beings, are done so by three modes of *prakṛti* (three aspects of nature). However, ignorant people claim themselves as the performer of their actions.]

Purport — Man performs all his duties due to the modes of his very nature *sattva, rajaḥ* and *tamaḥ*. So, man should not arrogate over the work. Because all the work in the world is governed by Nature or God only.

वैदुष्य का स्वाभिमान

त्वं राजा वयमप्युपासितगुरुप्रज्ञाभिमानोन्नताः
ख्यातस्त्वं विभवैर्यशांसि कवयो दिक्षु प्रतन्वन्ति[42] नः ।
इत्थं [43]मानधनातिदूरमुभयोरप्यावयोरन्तरं
यद्यस्मासु पराङ्मुखोऽसि वयमप्येकान्ततो निःस्पृहाः ॥ 24 ॥

---

[42] वितन्वन्ति — *Ms ORLS-3.*

[43] मानदनातिदूर — *Ms ORLS-3.*

अन्वय — त्वं राजा, वयम् अपि उपासितगुरुप्रज्ञाभिमानोन्नताः। त्वं विभवैः ख्यातः, कवयो नः यशांसि दिक्षु प्रतन्वन्ति । इत्थम् उभयोः अपि आवयोः मानधनातिदूरम् अन्तरम्। यदि अस्मासु पराङ्मुखः असि (तर्हि) वयम् अपि एकान्ततः निःस्पृहाः।

एक विद्वान् किसी एक राजा को सम्बोधित करके बोल रहा है कि — तू राजा है, तो हम भी गुरु की सेवा से सीखी हुई विद्या के अभिमान से ऊँचे हैं। तू अपने धन और वैभव के लिए प्रसिद्ध है, तो कवियों ने हमारी विद्या की कीर्ति भी चारों और फैला रखी है। इस प्रकार हम दोनों में स्वाभिमान एवं धन से महान् अन्तर है। यदि तुम हमसे विमुख हो, तो हम भी आपके प्रति अनुरागहीन हैं।

[कहा भी गया है —

विद्वत्त्वं च नृपत्वं च नैव तुल्यं कदाचन।
स्वदेशे पूज्यते राजा विद्वान् सर्वत्र पूज्यते॥ — *पञ्चतन्त्र* 2.59

विद्वत्त्व के साथ नृपत्व की तुलना कभी नहीं करनी चाहिए। क्योंकि राजा अपने ही देश में पूजा जाता है, जबकि विद्वान् सम्पूर्ण विश्व में पूजा का पात्र बनता है।

भर्तृहरि स्वयं अपने *नीतिशतक* 16 में कहते हैं —

हर्तुर्याति न गोचरं किमपि शं पुष्णाति यत्सर्वदा
ह्यर्थिभ्यः प्रतिपाद्यमानमनिशं प्राप्नोति वृद्धिं पराम्।
कल्पान्तेष्वपि न प्रयाति निधनं विद्याख्यमन्तर्धनं
येषां तान्प्रति मानमुज्झत नृपाः कस्तैः सह स्पर्धते॥

अर्थात् विद्या एक ऐसा गुप्त धन है, जिसे चोर देख नहीं सकते, जो सदा कल्याण एवं प्रसन्नता की वृद्धि करता रहता है, याचक को निरन्तर दिए जाते हुए भी प्रतिदिन अधिक से अधिक बढ़ता रहता है, और कल्प के अन्त या प्रलयकाल में भी समाप्त नहीं होता। हे राजाओं! जिनके पास ऐसा अद्भुत धन है, उनके प्रति अभिमान का त्याग करें। कौन उन विद्वानों के साथ प्रतिस्पर्धा कर सकता? अर्थात् कोई भी ज्ञानधनी विद्वानों के साथ बराबरी नहीं कर सकता।]

तात्पर्य — एक राजा की अपेक्षा एक मनीषी विद्वान् अधिक आदरणीय है। क्योंकि, राजा अधिक से अधिक अपने ही राज्य का उपकार कर सकता है, परन्तु विद्वान् अपने अध्यवसाय से अर्जित ज्ञान से सम्पूर्ण संसार का कल्याण करता है।

Dignity of Scholarship

tvaṁ rājā vayamapyupāsitaguruprajñābhimānonnatāḥ
khyātastvaṁ vibhavairyaśāṁsi kavayo dikṣu pratanvanti naḥ ।
itthaṁ mānadhanātidūramubhayorapyāvayorantaraṁ
yadyasmāsu parāṅmukho 'si vayamapyekāntato niḥspṛhāḥ ॥ 24 ॥

anvayaḥ — *tvaṁ rājā, vayam api upāsitaguruprajñābhimānonnatāḥ* । *tvaṁ vibhavaiḥ khyātaḥ, kavayo naḥ yaśāṁsi dikṣu pratanvanti* । *ittham ubhayoḥ api āvayoḥ mānadhanātidūram antaram* । *yadi asmāsu parāṅmukhaḥ asi* (*tarhi*) *vayam api ekāntataḥ niḥspṛhāḥ* ।

A diligent erudite scholar, addressing a king, says: You are a king; we also, through service to our teacher, have been uplifted in wisdom. You are famous for your wealth and splendour; the poets broadcast the fame of our knowledge all around. In this way, between both of us, there is a great difference in view of honour and wealth. If you are reluctant to us, then we also are perfectly dispassionate towards you.

[It is also said:

vidvattvaṁ ca nṛpatvaṁ ca naiva tulyaṁ kadācana ।
svadeśe pūjyate rājā vidvān sarvatra pūjyate ॥ — *Pañcatantra* 2.59

Meaning: Kingship should never be compared with scholarship. Because a king is worshipped in his own country, while a scholar is revered in the whole world.

Bhartṛhari himself writes in his *Nītiśataka* 16:

harturyāti na gocaraṁ kimapi śaṁ puṣṇāti yatsarvadā
hyarthibhyaḥ pratipādyamānamaniśaṁ prāpnoti vṛddhiṁ parām ।
kalpānteṣvapi na prayāti nidhanaṁ vidyākhyamantardhanaṁ
yeṣāṁ tānprati mānamujjhata nṛpāḥ kastaiḥ saha spardhate ॥

Meaning: The secret wealth of knowledge remains invisible to a thief and always augments some unique indescribable happiness and welfare, largely increases even though constantly given to those who desire it and is not destroyed even at the time of universal of destruction. Oh Kings! cast off your pride before those who possess the secret treasure of wisdom. Who can ever compete with such scholarly persons, whose wealth is the knowledge?]

Purport — A prudent scholar is more honourable than a king. Because, a king can promote largely his own kingdom only, but a scholar does the welfare of the whole world with the knowledge acquired through his perseverance.

प्रभुत्व-जनित अहंकार की निन्दा

अभुक्तायां यस्यां क्षणमपि न जातं नृपशतै-
भुर्वस्तस्या लाभे क इव बहुमानः क्षितिभुजाम्[44]।
तदंशस्याप्यंशे तदवयवलेशेऽपि पतयो
विषादे कर्तव्ये विदधति जडाः प्रत्युत मुदम्॥ 25॥

अन्वय — नृपशतैः यस्याम् अभुक्तायां क्षणमपि न जातं, तस्याः भुवः लाभे क्षितिभुजां बहुमानः क इव। तदंशस्य अपि अंशे तदवयवलेशे अपि पतयो भवन्ति। विषादे कर्तव्ये, जडाः प्रत्युत मुदं विदधति।

जिस पृथ्वी को सैकड़ों राजाओं ने एक क्षण के लिए भी अभुक्त अर्थात् अशासित नहीं छोड़ा, फिर राजा लोग इसके स्वामी होने का अहंकार क्यों करते हैं? आश्चर्य यह है कि वे (अहंकारी लोग) छोटे से छोटे टुकड़े के भी स्वामी बनकर अभिमान के मारे फूले नहीं समाते। उन्हें प्रभुत्व की क्षणभंगुरता एवं अस्थिरता का बोध होना चाहिए और अस्थिर वस्तु पर आसक्ति दुःख का ही कारण होता है, न कि सुख का। परन्तु मन्दबुद्धि लोग दुर्भाग्य के कारण से (इस अस्थिरता को जानकर भी) आनन्दित होते हैं, यही चिन्ता का विषय है।

[कहा गया है —

यौवनं धनसम्पत्तिः प्रभुत्वमविवेकिता।
एकैकमप्यनर्थाय किमु यत्र चतुष्टयम्॥ — *हितोपदेशः* मित्रलाभः 11

अर्थात् यौवन, धन-दौलत, स्वामित्व एवं अविवेकिता इन चारों में से प्रत्येक अनर्थ के कारण होते हैं। जहाँ पर ये चारों साथ-साथ रहते हों, उनका तो कहना ही क्या!]

तात्पर्य — प्रभुत्व अस्थिर एवं अल्पावधि है। अतः प्रभुत्व पर अहंकार नहीं करना चाहिए।

Condemning Arrogance of Domination

abhuktāyāṁ yasyāṁ kṣaṇamapi na jātaṁ nṛpaśatai-
rbhuvastasyā lābhe ka iva bahumānaḥ kṣitibhujām।
tadaṁśasyāpyaṁśe tadavayavaleśe 'pi patayo
viṣāde kartavye vidadhati jaḍāḥ pratyuta mudam॥ 25॥

anvayaḥ — *nṛpaśataiḥ yasyām abhuktāyāṁ kṣaṇamapi na jātaṁ, tasyāḥ bhuvaḥ lābhe kṣitibhujāṁ bahumānaḥ ka iva*। *tadaṁśasya api aṁśe tadavayavaleśe api patayo bhavanti*। *viṣāde kartavye, jaḍāḥ pratyuta mudaṁ vidadhati*।

---

[44] क्षितिभृताम् — *GAV.1954.*

When the earth, which has not been left unacquired even for a moment by hundreds of rulers, why do the kings boast of being its masters? The wonder is that by procuring even the smallest piece of this earth, one does not get puffed up with pride. They should realize the impermanence and ephemerality of dominion and that attachment to a impermanent object is the cause of unhappiness, not happiness. But retarded people rejoice even on the cause of misfortune (even knowing this impermanence of dominion), this is a matter of concern.

[It is said:

yauvanaṁ dhanasampattiḥ prabhutvamavivekitā ।
ekaikamapyanarthāya kimu yatra catuṣṭayam ॥
— *Hitopadeśaḥ* Mitralābhaḥ 11

Meaning: Youth, wealth, possessiveness and indiscretion, each of these four causes disaster. Where all these four live together, what to say about them!]

Purport — Domination is unstable and transitory. Therefore, one should not be proud of dominance.

राजाओं से याचना की तुच्छता

मृत्पिण्डो जलरेखया वलयितः सर्वोऽप्ययं नन्वणुः
स्वांशीकृत्य[45] तमेव संयुगशतै[46] राज्ञां गणा भुञ्जते ।
[47]दद्युस्ते ददतोथवा [48]किमपरं क्षुद्रा दरिद्रा भृशं
धिग्धिक्तान्पुरुषाधमान्धनलवं[49] वाञ्छन्ति तेभ्योऽपि ये ॥ 26 ॥

अन्वय — अयं मृत्पिण्डो जलरेखया वलयितः, सर्वोऽपि अणुः ननु! तमेव (अणुमात्रं मृत्पिण्डं) संयुगशतैः स्वांशीकृत्य राज्ञां गणा भुञ्जते। ते (संयुगद्वारा प्राणघातकाः राजानः अस्य मृत्पिण्डस्य) अपरं किम् (मृद्भिन्नं) दद्युः अथवा ददतः? धिग्धिक् तान् पुरुषाधमान् ये क्षुद्रा दरिद्रा तेभ्योऽपि धनलवं भृशं वाञ्छन्ति।

---

45 भागीकृत्य — *JKM.1911.*

46 सङ्गरशतैः — *GAV.1954.*

47 तद्द्युः — *JKM.1911.*

48 न किमपि — *JKM.1911.*

49 धनकणं — *JKM.1911*, धनकणान् — *GAV.1954.*

यह पृथ्वी जो कि मिट्टी का एक पिण्ड मात्र है, जल की रेखा समुद्र से घिरी हुई है। उसी छोटे से मिट्टी के पिण्ड को सैकड़ों बार युद्ध आदि द्वारा दूसरों के प्राण लेकर, हिंसा करके, छोटे-छोटे अंशों में प्राप्त करके, राजागण बड़े अहंकार से भोग करते हैं। वे प्राणघातक अहंकारी राजागण जो युद्ध से प्राप्त इस मृत्पिण्ड के कुछ अंश को किसी और के लिए दान के रूप में दे भी दिए होंगे या दे रहे होंगे तब भी मिट्टी से भिन्न और क्या होगा जिसे वो दे रहे होंगे? परन्तु नीच हैं वे दरिद्र मनुष्य जो उन क्षुद्र राजाओं से तुच्छ धन लव की आशा से भीख माँगते हैं।

तात्पर्य — व्यक्ति को तृष्णा से प्रेरित होकर राजाओं से याचना करके अपने स्वाभिमान को नहीं खोना चाहिए। क्योंकि तृष्णा अकरणीय कार्य में प्रेरित करती है। कहा भी गया है — अकर्तव्येष्वसाध्वीव तृष्णा प्रेरयते जनम्।

Despicableness of Soliciting Before Kings

mṛtpiṇḍo jalarekhayā valayitaḥ sarvo 'pyayaṁ nanvaṇuḥ
svāṁśīkṛtya tameva saṁyugaśatai rājñāṁ gaṇā bhuñjate।
dadyuste dadatothavā kimaparaṁ kṣudrā daridrā bhṛśaṁ
dhigdhiktānpuruṣādhamāndhanalavaṁ vāñchanti tebhyo 'pi ye ॥ 26 ॥

anvayaḥ — *ayaṁ mṛtpiṇḍo jalarekhayā valayitaḥ, sarvo 'pi aṇuḥ nanu! tameva (aṇumātraṁ mṛtpiṇḍaṁ) saṁyugaśataiḥ svāṁśīkṛtya rājñāṁ gaṇā bhuñjate*। *te (saṁyugadvārā prāṇaghātakāḥ rājānaḥ asya mṛtpiṇḍasya) aparaṁ kim (mṛdbhinnaṁ) dadyuḥ athavā dadataḥ? dhigdhik tān puruṣādhamān ye kṣudrā daridrā tebhyo 'pi dhanalavaṁ bhṛśaṁ vāñchanti*।

The earth is a mere lump of clay rimmed by water. Even the whole of it is but an atom. To enjoy the same small lump of clay was partitioned into smaller parts and occupied by the arrogant kings through violences and hundreds of wars. Those arrogant kings who might have given some parts of it as a donation to some or may be giving to someone, even then what else would be different from the clay that they would be giving? But shame to those poor people who beg from these vindictive kings for the hope of immaterial money.

Purport — A person, inspired by thirst, should not lose his dignity by pleading with the kings. Because craving motivates to do the indefensible jobs. It has also been said: *akartavyeṣvasādhvīva tṛṣṇā prerayate janam.*

राजाओं की चाटुलालसापरता

न नटा न विटा न गायना[50] न च सत्येतरपक्षपातिनः[51] ।
[52]नृपमीक्षितुमत्र के वयं स्तनभारानमिता न योषितः ॥ 27 ॥

अन्वय — (वयं) नटाः न, विटाः न, (च) गायनाः (अपि) न , न च सत्येतरपक्षपातिनः, स्तनभारानमिता योषितः (अपि) न, अत्र नृपम् ईक्षितुं वयम् के?

न तो हम नट या बाज़ीगर हैं, न ही धूर्त हैं, और न हम गवैये हैं, न मिथ्या के पक्षपाती हैं और न हम उन्नत स्तनभार से अवनत स्त्रियां ही हैं; फिर हमारी पूछ राजाओं के यहाँ क्यों होने लगी? हम में इनमें से एक भी बात नहीं, फिर हमारा प्रवेश राजसभा में कैसे हो सकता है? वहाँ तो उनकी पूछ है — उन्हीं का आदर है — जो उस (राजा) की विषय-वासनाएं पूरी करते हैं।

[जैसा कि कवि कालिदास ने राजा दिलीप का चरित्र-वर्णन करते हुए एक निष्पक्ष, सत्यप्रिय एवं न्यायपर आदर्श राजा के चित्र का वर्णन किया है।

द्वेष्योऽपि सम्मतः शिष्टस्तस्यार्तस्य यथौषधम्।
त्याज्यो दुष्टः प्रियोऽप्यासीदङ्गुलीवोरगक्षता॥ — *रघुवंश* 1.28

अर्थ यह है कि जिस प्रकार रोगी कड़वी औषधि को भी "हितकर" समझकर अपनाता है, उसी प्रकार राजा दिलीप द्वेष करने के योग्य शत्रु भी सज्जन होने पर अपनाते थे एवं प्रियजन होते हुए भी दुर्जन को सांप से काटी हुई अंगुली की तरह त्याग देते थे।]

तात्पर्य — धर्माधिकारी राजाओं को चाटूक्ति से मोहित न होकर निष्पक्ष, सत्यप्रिय एवं न्यायपर होना चाहिए।

Sycophancy of Kings

na naṭā na viṭā na gāyanā na ca satyetarapakṣapātinaḥ ।
nṛpamīkṣitumatra ke vayaṁ stanabhārānamitā na yoṣitaḥ ॥ 27 ॥

---

50 न नटनविटनगायना — *Ms ORLS-3,* न नटा न विटा न गायकाः — *GAV.1954.*

51 न परद्रोहनिबद्धबुद्धयः — *Ms ORLS-3,* न च सभ्येतरवादचुञ्चवः — *GAV.1954.*

52 नृपसद्मनि नाम के वयं कुचभार — *Ms ORLS-3.*

anvayaḥ — *(vayaṁ) naṭāḥ na, viṭāḥ na, (ca) gāyanāḥ (api) na, na ca satyetarapakṣapātinaḥ, stanabhārānamitā yoṣitaḥ (api) na, atra nṛpam īkṣituṁ vayam ke?*

We are not actors, nor jesters, nor singers, nor are we partisans of falsehood, nor are we beautiful women, stooped down a little with the weight of lofty breasts; then how we wish to meet the king? We do not have even one of these things, then how can we enter the king's conclave? Only they are asked there and only they are respected there — who fulfil passions and desires of that (king).

[As poet Kālidāsa, while describing the character of King Dilīpa, has portrayed the picture of a fair, truthful and ideal king as follows:

dveṣyo 'pi sammataḥ śiṣṭastasyārtasya yathauṣadham ।
tyājyo duṣṭaḥ priyo 'pyāsīdaṅgulīvoragakṣatā ॥ — *Raghuvaṁśa* 1.28

Meaning: Just as a patient takes on bitter medicine considering it as "favourable", in the same way, King Dilīpa used to adopt even an enemy, worthy of hatred, if disciplined; and he abandoned even a dear one, if wicked, like a finger bitten by a snake.]

Purport — A king, who is the legislative, judiciary and executive head of the kingdom, should not be fascinated by sycophancy and should be fair, truthful and should practise justice.

गाली देने वाले की नीचता

ददतु ददतु गालीर्गालिमन्तो भवन्तो
वयमिह तदभावाद्गालिदानामसक्ताः ।
जगति विदितमेतद्दीयते विद्यमानं
ददतु शशविषाणं ये महात्यागिनोऽपि ॥ 28 ॥

अन्वय — ददतु ददतु गालीः गालिमन्तो भवन्तः, वयमिह तदभावाद् गालिदानामसक्ताः । जगति एतद् विदितं यद् विद्यमानं दीयते, ये महात्यागिनोपि (सन्ति, यैः अविद्यमानमपि दीयते, ते) शशविषाणं ददतु ।

आप लोगों के पास गालियां हैं इसीलिए आप लोग गालियां दे रहे हैं; क्योंकि आप लोगों के पास गालियों के सिवाय और कोई अच्छी वस्तु होती ना तब देते। हमारे पास गालियां

न होने से हम किसी को भी गाली नहीं दे सकते। क्योंकि संसार में यह सबको पता है कि जिसके पास जो होता है, वह वही दे सकता है। यदि ऐसा कोई महात्यागी है जो न होते हुए भी सब कुछ दे सकता है, तब वो खरगोश के सींग देकर दिखाए।

तात्पर्य — व्यक्ति को दूसरों के प्रति अच्छी भावना रखनी चाहिए एवं अच्छा व्यवहार करना चाहिए। क्योंकि अच्छी भावनाओं एवं अच्छे व्यवहारों से व्यक्ति के स्वयं का ही प्रतिबिम्बन होता है। कहा भी गया है — यादृशी भावना यस्य सिद्धिर्भवति तादृशी।

Abuser's Meanness

dadatu dadatu gālīrgālimanto bhavanto
vayamiha tadabhāvādgālidānāmasaktāḥ ।
jagati viditametaddīyate vidyamānaṁ
dadatu śaśaviṣāṇaṁ ye mahātyāgino 'pi ॥ 28 ॥

anvayaḥ — *dadatu dadatu gālīḥ gālimanto bhavantaḥ, vayamiha tadabhāvād gālidānāmasaktāḥ* । *jagati etad viditaṁ yad vidyamānaṁ dīyate, ye mahātyāginopi (santi, yaiḥ avidyamānamapi dīyate, te) śaśaviṣāṇaṁ dadatu* ।

You people own abuses and hence you are abusing; if you would have something else except abuses, then you could give that. Since we do not have abuses, we cannot abuse anyone. Because it is known to everyone in the world that one can award that only which he/she owns. If there are such great donors who can give everything even without possessing, then let one impart horns of the rabbit.

Purport — One should have good feelings towards others and should behave with others well. Because good feelings and good behaviour are the reflection of one's own personality. It has also been said: *yādṛśī bhāvanā yasya siddhirbhavati tādṛśī.*

विद्वत्ता से दुःखनाश

पुरा विद्वत्तासीदमलिनधियां[53] क्लेशहतये
गता कालेनाऽसौ विषयसुखसिद्ध्यै विषयिणाम्।

[53] उपशमवतां — *Ms ORLS-3.*

इदानीं [54]संप्रेक्ष्य क्षितितलभुजः शास्त्रविमुखा-
  नहो कष्टं साऽपि प्रतिदिनमधोऽधः प्रविशति ॥ 29 ॥

अन्वय — पुरा अमलिनधियां विद्वत्ता क्लेशहतये आसीत्, कालेन असौ (विद्वत्ता) विषयिणां विषयसुखसिद्ध्यै गता। इदानीं (तु) शास्त्रविमुखान् क्षितितलभुजः संप्रेक्ष्य कष्टम् (अनुभूयते)। अहो! सा (विद्वत्ता) अपि प्रतिदिनम् अधोऽधः प्रविशति ।

प्राचीन काल में विद्वत्ता निर्मल चित्त वालों की जन्म-मरण रूप सांसारिक दुःखों के नाश के लिए हुआ करती थी। परन्तु कालान्तर में यह विद्वत्ता इन्द्रिय-विषयासक्त लोगों द्वारा सेव्य होकर इन्द्रिय-सुखों की पूर्ति मात्र के लिए ही रह गई है। अब तो शास्त्रों से पराङ्मुख राजाओं को देखकर अत्यन्त कष्ट का अनुभव हो रहा है कि विद्वत्ता केवल इन्द्रिय-वासना की पूर्ति मात्र के लिए ही रह गई। अरे! दुर्भाग्य से, अब यही स्थिति आ चुकी है कि, वह विद्वत्ता भी प्रत्येक दिन कम और कम होती जा रही है।

[आसक्ति ही सुख एवं दुःख का मूल कारण है। आसक्ति से राग, भय, क्रोध आदि उत्पन्न होते हैं। मनुष्य अपने पारमार्थिक ज्ञान से आसक्ति-रहित होकर विभिन्न सांसारिक क्लेशों से मुक्त हो सकता है। विद्वत्ता या ज्ञान से राग, भय, क्रोध आदि को त्याग करके मनुष्य स्थितप्रज्ञ बन सकता है। अतएव कहा गया है –

दुःखेष्वनुद्विग्नमनाः सुखेषु विगतस्पृहः।
वीतरागभयक्रोधः स्थितधीर्मुनिरुच्यते ॥ — *श्रीमद्भगवद्गीता* II.56]

तात्पर्य — विद्वत्ता का वास्तविक उद्देश्य जन्म-मरण रूप सांसारिक दुःखों के नाश करने में है, न कि इन्द्रिय-सुखों की पूर्ति में।

Scholarship Destroys of Worldly Sorrows

purā vidvattāsīdamalinadhiyāṁ kleśahataye
  gatā kālenā 'sau viṣayasukhasiddhyai viṣayiṇām।
idānīṁ saṁprekṣya kṣititalabhujaḥ śāstravimukhā-
  naho kaṣṭaṁ sā 'pi pratidinamadho 'dhaḥ praviśati ॥ 29 ॥

anvayaḥ — *purā amalinadhiyāṁ vidvattā kleśahataye āsīt, kālena asau (vidvattā) viṣayiṇāṁ viṣayasukhasiddhyai gatā* । *idānīṁ (tu) śāstravimukhān kṣititalabhujaḥ saṁprekṣya kaṣṭam (anubhūyate)*। *aho! sā (vidvattā) api pratidinam adho 'dhaḥ praviśati*।

54 तु प्रेक्ष्य — *Ms ORLS-3*.

There was a time when the knowledge of immaculate and pure-minded scholars used to be for the destruction of sorrows, that came out of the cycle of birth and death. But in the course of time, the people attached to sense-objects, misused their knowledge for the fulfilment of sensual pleasures. Now, mind is inflicted with sorrows to see the kings who are ignorant of the scriptures. Hey! Unfortunately, it is such a strange situation that the scholarship is also depreciating lower and lower every day.

[Attachment is the root cause of happiness and sorrow. Attachment gives rise to fear, anger, etc. Man can become free from various worldly troubles by becoming free from attachment through his transcendental knowledge. By giving up fear, anger, etc. through scholarship or knowledge, a person can become *sthitaprajña* (situated in the transcendental bliss). Thus told:

duḥkheṣvanudvignamanāḥ sukheṣu vigataspṛhaḥ ।
vītarāgabhayakrodhaḥ sthitadhīrmunirucyate ॥
— *Śrīmadbhagavadgītā* II.56]

Purport — The real purpose of learning is in the destruction of worldly sorrows born out of birth and death, not in the fulfilment of sense-pleasures.

जन्म की सार्थकता का कारण

स जातः कोऽप्यासीन्मदनरिपुणा मूर्ध्नि धवलं
कपालं यस्योच्चैर्विनिहितमलङ्कारविधये ।
नृभिः प्राणत्राणप्रवणमतिभिः कैश्चिदधुना
नमद्भिः कः पुंसामयमतुलजन्म[55]ज्वरभरः ॥ 30 ॥

अन्वय — स कोऽपि जात आसीत् यस्य धवलं कपालं मदनरिपुणा (आत्मनः) अलङ्कारविधये मूर्ध्नि उच्चैः विनिहितम् । प्राणत्राणप्रवणमतिभिः कैश्चित् नमद्भिः नृभिः अधुना पुंसाम् अयम् अतुलजन्मज्वरभरः कः?

उनका जन्म वास्तव में सार्थक है, मृत्यु के पश्चात् भी जिनके सफेद कपालों (खोपड़ियों) को अलंकार बनाकर कामदेव के शत्रु शिव अपने सिर पर एक आभूषण के रूप में पहना करते हैं। परन्तु जो अपने जीवन की रक्षा के लिए शत्रु राजाओं के सामने अपना सिर

---

[55] दर्पज्वरभरः — *JKM.1911, GAV.1954.*

झुकाकर राजसिंहासन पर आरुढ़ होकर ही अपने जन्म को अतुल्य मानते हुए अभिमान के ज्वर (मद) से ग्रस्त हैं, उसका औचित्य क्या है?

[यहाँ ध्यान देने योग्य है कि कवि भर्तृहरि ने शिवजी के लिए मदनरिपु शब्द का प्रयोग किया है, मदनरिपु शब्द से भगवान् शिवजी का वैराग्य अभिव्यञ्जित है। अर्थात् वैरागी होते हुए भी स्वयं शिवजी उन महात्माओं के सम्मान हेतु उनके कपालों (खोपड़ियों) को माला बनाकर अपना शृंगार करते थे, जो महात्मा परोपकार की भावना से मृत्यु के पश्चात् भी दूसरों के काम में आते हैं। इससे उन महात्माओं के जन्म की सार्थकता द्योतित हो रही है।]

तात्पर्य — परार्थ के लिए प्रयुक्त जीवन की ही सार्थकता है। अतएव कहा गया है — "स्वार्थो यस्य परार्थ एव स पुमानेकः सतामग्रणीः" (परार्थ ही जिसका स्वार्थ है वही पुरुष सज्जनों का अग्रणी है)।

Reason for the Significance of Birth

sa jātaḥ ko 'pyāsīnmadanaripuṇā mūrdhni dhavalaṁ
kapālaṁ yasyoccairvinihitamalaṅkāravidhaye ।
nṛbhiḥ prāṇatrāṇapravaṇamatibhiḥ kaiścidadhunā
namadbhiḥ kaḥ puṁsāmayamatulajanmajvarabharaḥ ॥ 30 ॥

anvayaḥ — *sa ko 'pi jāta āsīt yasya dhavalaṁ kapālaṁ madanaripuṇā (ātmanaḥ) alaṅkāravidhaye mūrdhni uccaiḥ vinihitam* । *prāṇatrāṇapravaṇamatibhiḥ kaiścit namadbhiḥ nṛbhiḥ adhunā puṁsām ayam atulajanmajvarabharaḥkaḥ?*

His birth is worthwhile indeed, even after death, whose skull is used as an ornament to the head of Lord Śiva, the enemy of cupid. But what is the justification for those who have bowed down their heads in front of enemy kings, in order to save their lives and have ascended the throne out of others' mercy and show their arrogance, thinking their birth as incomparable.

[It is worth to note here that the poet Bhartṛhari has used the word Madanaripu for Lord Śiva. With the word Madanaripu serenity of Lord Śiva is expressed. That is, in spite of being a recluse, Lord Śiva used to adorn himself by making garlands of the skulls of those sages who serve others even after death with their spirit of charity.]

Purport —The significance of life lies in altruism only. Hence it is said: *svārtho yasya parārtha eva sa pumānekaḥ satāmagraṇīḥ* (only the altruist and selfless person is the best among gentlemen).

धनाढ्यों की वशवर्तिता की अस्वीकार्यता

अश्नीमहि वयं भिक्षामाशावासो वसीमहि।
शयीमहि महीपृष्ठे कुर्वीमहि किमीश्वरैः ॥ 31 ॥

अन्वय — वयं भिक्षाम् अश्नीमहि, आशावासो वसीमहि, महीपृष्ठे शयीमहि, ईश्वरैः किं कुर्वीमहि?

जब हम भिक्षान्न मात्र से उदरपूर्ति कर सकते हैं, वस्त्र की अपेक्षा किए बिना आकाश से ही अपना आवरण कर सकते हैं, धरती पर शयन कर सकते हैं तब धनाढ्यों के अधीन होकर उनके अविनय क्यों सहें?

[जब व्यक्ति अपने में ही सन्तुष्ट रहकर दूसरों से अपेक्षा नहीं रखेगा तब उसे किसी धन्याढ्य की वशवर्तिता स्वीकारने की आवश्यकता नहीं होगी। भगवान् श्रीकृष्ण *श्रीमद्भगवद्गीता* III.17 में यही उपदेश देते हुए कहते हैं —

यस्त्वात्मरतिरेव स्यादात्मतृप्तश्च मानवः।
आत्मन्येव च सन्तुष्टस्तस्य कार्यं न विद्यते॥

मनुष्य सुख की आशा से विभिन्न कर्मफलों से बँध जाता है। अतः *श्रीमद्भगवद्गीता* XIV.6 में कहा भी गया है —

तत्र सत्त्वं निर्मलत्वात्प्रकाशकमनामयम्।
सुखसङ्गेन बध्नाति ज्ञानसङ्गेन चानघ॥]

तात्पर्य — सुख-भोग के त्याग से स्वाभिमान की रक्षा एवं परिणामतः सन्तोष-प्राप्ति सम्भव है।

Abstaining from the Influence of the Rich

aśnīmahi vayaṁ bhikṣāmāśāvāso vasīmahi ।
śayīmahi mahīpṛṣṭhe kurvīmahi kimīśvaraiḥ ॥ 31 ॥

anvayaḥ — *vayaṁ bhikṣām aśnīmahi, āśāvāso vasīmahi, mahīpṛṣṭhe śayīmahi, īśvaraiḥ kiṁ kurvīmahi?*

When we can fill our stomach with alms, we can cover ourselves with the sky without expecting clothes, we can sleep on the earth without a bed, then why should we be subservient to the rich and suffer their humiliation?

[When a person will be satisfied with himself and will not expect anything from others, then he will not need to accept the subservience of any blessed person. In *Śrīmadbhagavadgītā* III.17, Lord Kṛṣṇa while giving this sermon says:

yastvātmaratireva syādātmatṛptaśca mānavaḥ ।
ātmanyeva ca santuṣṭastasya kāryaṁ na vidyate ॥

In the hope of material pleasure, man gets bound by the fruits of various actions, it has also been said in *Śrīmadbhagavadgītā* XIV.6:

tatra sattvaṁ nirmalatvātprakāśakamanāmayam ।
sukhasaṅgena badhnāti jñānasaṅgena cānagha ॥]

Purport — By renunciation of material pleasures one can achieve self-respect and satisfaction as a result.

भौतिक वैभव की तुच्छता

अर्थानामीशिषे त्वं वयमपि च गिरामीश्महे यावदिच्छं[56]
शूरस्त्वं वादिदर्पव्युपशमन[57]विधावक्षयं पाटवं नः ।
सेवन्ते त्वां धनान्धा[58] मतिमलहतये मामपि श्रोतुकामा
मय्यस्त्यास्था[59] न चेत्ते[60] त्वयि मम सुतरामेष राजन् गतोऽस्मि[61] ॥ 32 ॥

अन्वय — त्वम् अर्थानाम् ईशिषे, वयमपि च गिरां यावदिच्छं ईश्महे, त्वं शूरः, वादिदर्पव्युपशमनविधौ नः अक्षयं पाटवम् । त्वां धनान्धाः सेवन्ते, मामपि मतिमलहतये श्रोतुकामाः, मयि चेत् ते आस्था न, त्वयि मम सुतराम् (आस्था न), (अतः) हे राजन्! एष गतोस्मि ।

भौतिक वैभव से अहंकारी राजा से किसी निःस्पृह विद्वान् की उक्ति — "यदि तुम धन के स्वामी हो तो हम वाणी के स्वामी हैं। यदि तुम युद्ध करने में वीर हो तो हम अपने प्रतिपक्षियों (जो ईश्वर की सत्ता का विरोध करते हैं) से शास्त्रार्थ करके उनका मद-ज्वर तोड़ने में कुशल हैं। यदि तुम्हारी सेवा धनान्ध करते हैं, तो हमारी सेवा अज्ञान-अन्धकार का नाश चाहने वाले, शास्त्र सुनने के लिए करते हैं। यदि तुम्हें हमारे प्रति आस्था नहीं, तो हमें भी तुम्हारे प्रति कोई आदर नहीं है। अतः हे राजन्! हम आपके इस भौतिकवाद से कहीं दूर चल चुके हैं। [आदिशंकराचार्य ने कहा है —

---

56 यावदर्थं — *GAV.1954.*

57 ज्वरशमन — *JKM.1911.*

58 धनाढ्या — *JKM.1911, GAV.1954.*

59 मय्यप्यास्था — *JKM.1911.*

60 न चेत्तत् — *JKM.1911.*

61 राजन्ननास्था — *GAV.1954.*

मा कुरु धनजनयौवनगर्वं, हरति निमेषात्कालः सर्वम्।
मायामयमिदमखिलं हित्वा, ब्रह्मपदं त्वं प्रविश विदित्वा॥
— *भजगोविन्दस्तोत्रम्* 11

अर्थात् धन, शक्ति और यौवन पर गर्व मत करो। समय क्षण भर में इनको नष्ट कर देता है। इस विश्व को माया से घिरा हुआ जानकर तुम ब्रह्म पद में प्रवेश करो।]

तात्पर्य — निःस्पृह एवं वैरागी के लिए भौतिक वैभव तिनके की तरह तुच्छ है।

Insignificance of Material Wealth

arthānāmīśiṣe tvaṁ vayamapi ca girāmīśmahe yāvadicchaṁ
śūrastvaṁ vādidarpavyupaśamanavidhāvakṣayaṁ pāṭavaṁ naḥ ।
sevante tvāṁ dhanāndhā matimalahataye māmapi śrotukāmā
mayyastyāsthā na cette tvayi mama sutarāmeṣa rājan gato 'smi ॥ 32 ॥

anvayaḥ — *tvam arthānām īśiṣe, vayamapi ca girāṁ yāvadicchaṁ īśmahe, tvaṁ śūraḥ, vādidarpavyupaśamanavidhau naḥ akṣayaṁ pāṭavam*। *tvāṁ dhanāndhāḥ sevante, māmapi matimalahataye śrotukāmāḥ, mayi cet te āsthā na, tvayi mama sutarām (āsthā na), (ataḥ) he rājan! eṣa gatosmi*।

An austere scholar addresses a king who is proud of material wealth: "If you are the master of wealth, then we are the master of speech. If you are brave in fighting in the battle, then we are skilled in breaking the fever of our opponents (who reject the existence of God), by arguing with them. If you are served by the rich, while intents on learning the truth and willing to destroy their ignorance of mind, serve us to listen to the scriptures. If you do not have faith in us, then we also have no respect for you. That is why Oh king! we have gone far away from this materialism of yours."

[Thus told by Ādi-Śaṅkarācārya:

mā kuru dhanajanayauvanagarvaṁ,
harati nimeṣātkālaḥ sarvam ।
māyāmayamidamakhilaṁ hitvā,
brahmapadaṁ tvaṁ praviśa viditvā ॥
— *Bhajagovindastotram* 11

Meaning: Do not boast of wealth, friends and youth. Each one of these is destroyed within a minute by time. Free yourself from the illusion of the world of *māyā* and attain the timeless Truth.]

Purport — For an ascetic and renunciate, material splendour is as insignificant as a straw.

अल्पज्ञता से अहंकार

यदा किञ्चिज्ज्ञोऽहं द्विप इव मदान्धः समभवं
तदा सर्वज्ञोऽस्मीत्यभवदवलिप्तं मम मनः।
यदा किञ्चित् किञ्चिद्गुरुजन[62]सकाशादधिगतं
तदा मूर्खोऽस्मीति ज्वर इव मदो मे व्यपगतः ॥ 33 ॥

अन्वय — यदा अहं किञ्चिज्ज्ञ आसम् तदा द्विप इव मदान्धः समभवं, (तदा) सर्वज्ञोऽस्मि इति मम मनः अवलिप्तम् अभवत्। यदा किञ्चित् किञ्चिद् गुरुजनसकाशाद् अधिगतं तदा मूर्खोऽस्मि इति ज्वर इव मे मदो व्यपगतः।

जब मैं अल्पज्ञ था, तब मदान्ध हाथी के समान अहंकार से अन्धा था; और तब मैं सर्वज्ञ हूँ ऐसा समझते हुए मेरा मन अहंकार से चूर था। परन्तु जब मैंने विद्वान् गुरुजनों से थोड़ा-थोड़ा सीखा तब मुझे मेरी अज्ञता का परिचय हुआ तब मेरा झूठा मद, ज्वर की तरह उतर गया एवं तब मैंने समझा, कि मैं तो कुछ भी नहीं जानता।

["रिक्तो घटः घोषमुपैति नित्यम्" (खाली घड़ा हमेशा शोर मचाता है)। उसी तरह अल्प ज्ञान, घमण्ड और अहंकार को उपन्न करता है।]

तात्पर्य — अल्पज्ञता ही अहंकार का कारण है एवं तत्त्व-ज्ञान द्वारा व्यक्ति अहंकार-रहित एवं विनीत होता है।

Sciolism: The Source of Ego

yadā kiñcijjño 'haṁ dvipa iva madāndhaḥ samabhavaṁ
tadā sarvajño 'smītyabhavadavaliptaṁ mama manaḥ ।
yadā kiñcit kiñcidgurujanasakāśādadhigataṁ
tadā mūrkho 'smīti jvara iva mado me vyapagataḥ ॥ 33 ॥

anvayaḥ — *yadā ahaṁ kiñcijjña āsam tadā dvipa iva madāndhaḥ samabhavaṁ, (tadā) sarvajño 'smi iti mama manaḥ avaliptam abhavat* । *yadā*

62 बुधजन — *JKM.1911.*

kiñcit kiñcid gurujanasakāśād adhigataṁ tadā mūrkho 'smi iti jvara iva me mado vyapagataḥ ।

When I knew but a little, I was blinded by pride as an elephant in rut and my mind was puffed up with the thought that I were omniscient. When, however, I gradually gained knowledge through the contact of the wise, I learnt step by step and humbled with the thought that I was a fool, the ego vanished away like fever, with the idea that I knew nothing at all.

Purport — There is a proverb — "a little knowledge is dangerous". In other words, an empty pitcher sounds much. Likewise, partial knowledge creates vagueness and ego.

तप-साधन से परम श्रेय

मानेम्लायिनि[63] खण्डिते च वसुनि व्यर्थे[64] प्रयातेऽर्थिनि
क्षीणे बन्धुजने गते परिजने नष्टे शनैर्यौवने।
युक्तं केवलमेतदेव विदुषां[65] यज्जह्नुकन्यापयः-
पूतग्रावगिरीन्द्रगह्वरदरीकुञ्जे[66] निवासः क्वचित्॥ 34॥

अन्वय — माने म्लायिनि, वसुनि च खण्डिते, अर्थिनि व्यर्थे प्रयाते, बन्धुजने क्षीणे, परिजने गते, यौवने शनैः नष्टे। केवलम् एतदेव विदुषां युक्तं यत् क्वचिद् जह्नुकन्यापयःपूतग्रावगिरीन्द्रगह्वरदरीकुञ्जे निवासः (स्यात्)।

जब अपने प्रति लोगों का सम्मान घट जाए; धन नाश हो जाए; याचक अपनी इच्छा पूर्ण किए बिना लौट-लौटकर जाने लगे; भाई-बन्धु, स्त्री-पुत्र और सगे-सम्बन्धी कम हो जाएं; नौकर एवं सेवक वर्ग छोड़कर चले जाएं; यौवन धीरे-धीरे नष्ट होता रहे; तब बुद्धिमान को चाहिए कि किसी ऐसे पर्वत की गुफ़ा के कोने में जा बसे, जिसके पत्थर गंगाजी के जल से पवित्र हो रहे हों।

[जब लोगों में अपना मान न रहे, लोग नफ़रत की नज़र से देखने लगें; अपनी धन-दौलत जाती रहे; जो याचक पहले कुछ पाते थे, वे निर्धनता के कारण विमुख होकर लौट जाते हैं; भाई-बन्धु

---

63 म्लायति — *JKM.1911.*

64 व्यर्थं — *JKM.1911.*

65 सुधियां — *JKM.1911, GAV.1954.*

66 कन्दरतटीकुञ्जे — *JKM.1911, GAV.1954.*

और स्त्री-पुत्र प्रभृति नातेदार दूसरी दुनिया को चले गए हों, तब तो बुद्धिमान को चाहिए कि संसार को त्याग दे; इसमें मोह न रखे और किसी ऐसे पहाड़ की गुफ़ा में जाकर रहे, जिसके पत्थरों को पवित्र गंगाजल पखार-पखारकर पवित्र करता हो। ऐसी हालत में संसार में रहना वृथा समय खोना है। कम से कम उस समय तो बुद्धिमान एकान्त में बैठकर, सब तरह की आशा तृष्णा छोड़कर, भगवान् के चरणकमलों में मन लगाए।]

तात्पर्य — तपस्या ही परम श्रेय-प्राप्ति का अन्तिम एवं शाश्वत मार्ग है।

Penance: The Way to Achieve the Best

māne mlāyini khaṇḍite ca vasuni vyarthe prayāte 'rthini
kṣīṇe bandhujane gate parijane naṣṭe śanairyauvane ।
yuktaṁ kevalametadeva viduṣāṁ yajjahnukanyāpayaḥ-
pūtagrāvagirīndragahvaradarīkuñje nivāsaḥ kvacit ॥ 34 ॥

anvayaḥ — *māne mlāyini, vasuni ca khaṇḍite, arthini vyarthe prayāte, bandhujane kṣīṇe, parijane gate, yauvane śanaiḥ naṣṭe* । *kevalam etadeva viduṣāṁ yuktaṁ yat kvacid jahnukanyāpayaḥpūtagrāvagirīndragahvaradarīkuñje nivāsaḥ (syāt)* ।

When honour declines, riches get squandered away, mendicants start returning without fulfilling their wishes, the circle of friends dwindles, attendants leave and youthfulness starts reducing gradually, the wise have only one proper way left to follow — make a home somewhere on the side of a valley in the Himalayas, whose rocks have been made holy by the water of the Ganges.

[Whem people no longer respect you, start looking at you with hatred; your wealth and riches start slipping away; the beggars who used to get alms earilier turn away due to poverty; kins and relatives like brothers, wife and sons, daughters, etc. have died, then a wise person should renounce this world and should not be entangled to this mundane worldy illusion and go to a mountain cave whose stones are purified by the holy Gaṅgā water. Living in this condition in the world is a waste of time. At least at that time, the wise should sit in solitude, leave all kinds of hopes and desires and concentrate on the lotus feel of God.]

Purport — Austerity is the final and eternal path to attain ultimate success.

प्रसन्नता की आत्मनिष्ठता

परेषां चेतांसि प्रतिदिवसमाराध्य बहुधा
प्रसादं किं नेतुं विशसि हृदयक्लेशकलिलम्।
प्रसन्ने त्वय्येव स्वयमुदितचिन्तामणिगुणो[67]
विविक्तः[68] संकल्पः किमभिलषितं पुष्यति न ते ॥ 35 ॥

अन्वय — परेषां चेतांसि प्रतिदिवसम् आराध्य (तानि) प्रसादं नेतुं किं बहुधा हृदयक्लेशकलिलं विशसि। त्वयि प्रसन्ने एव स्वयमुदितचिन्तामणिगुणः संकल्पः विविक्तः (सन्) किं ते अभिलषितं न पुष्यति?

रे मन ! तू दूसरों के मनों को प्रसन्न करने के लिए स्वयं अपने हृदय को क्यों कष्ट पहुँचा रहे हो? तभी हम शुद्धचित्त और विमुक्तहृदय बन सकते हैं और अपने भीतर चिन्तामणि गुणों को प्राप्त कर सकते हैं, जब हम स्वयं से प्रसन्न हों। ऐसे में आपकी कौन सी इच्छा अधूरी रह जाएगी?

[*श्रीमद्भगवद्गीता* VI.5 में कहा गया है —

उद्धरेदात्मनात्मानं नात्मानमवसादयेत्।
आत्मैव ह्यात्मनो बन्धुरात्मैव रिपुरात्मनः ॥

अर्थात् मनुष्य को स्वयं ही स्वयं का उद्धार करना चाहिए। अतः ऐसा कार्य ही न करे जिससे स्वयं अधोगति को प्राप्त करे। जब व्यक्ति विवेकशील होकर सत्कर्म एवं सदाचार में प्रवण रहता है तब स्वयं ही स्वयं का मित्र बन जाता है, इसके विपरीत स्वयं ही स्वयं का शत्रु बनकर अधोगति को प्राप्त करता है। इस प्रकार व्यक्ति को विवेकशील होकर सत्कर्म एवं सदाचार-प्रवण रहते हुए स्वयं को सदा प्रसन्न रखना चाहिए, न कि दूसरों को प्रसन्न रखने के उपाय ढूँढ़ते हुए अपनी आत्मा को क्लेश एवं विपाक में डालता रहे। मन ही सब कामों का कर्ता है। सभी इन्द्रियां मन के ही अधीन हैं और मन की ही अनुगामिनी हैं। मन ही बन्धन और मोक्ष का कारण है। मनुष्य मन से ही पाप-पुण्य और सुख-दुःख प्रभृति का भागी होता है। मन ही मनुष्य को बुरा-भला, साधु-असाधु सब कुछ बना देता है। मन की वृत्ति सुधरने से ही, मन के वासनाहीन होने से ही, सब कुछ त्यागने से ही, वह आत्मसाक्षात्कार के योग्य हो जाता है। और कहा भी गया है —

मन एव मनुष्याणां कारणं बन्धमोक्षयोः।
बन्धाय विषयासङ्गि मुक्त्वा निर्विषयं मनः ॥ — *शाट्यायनीयोपनिषद्* 1

---

[67] गुणे — *JKM.1911*, गणो — *GAV.1954*.

[68] विमुक्तिः — *JKM.1911*.

अर्थात् मन ही सभी मनुष्यों के बन्धन एवं मोक्ष का प्रमुख कारण है। विषयों में आसक्त मन बन्धन का और कामना-संकल्प से रहित मन मोक्ष (मुक्ति) का कारण होता है।]

तात्पर्य — व्यक्ति को स्वयं में ही सुख का कारण ढूँढ़ना चाहिए।

Self: The Abode of Happiness

pareṣāṁ cetāṁsi pratidivasamārādhya bahudhā
prasādaṁ kiṁ netuṁ viśasi hṛdayakleśakalilam ।
prasanne tvayyeva svayamuditacintāmaṇiguṇo
viviktaḥ saṅkalpaḥ kimabhilaṣitaṁ puṣyati na te ॥ 35 ॥

anvayaḥ — *pareṣāṁ cetāṁsi pratidivasam ārādhya* (*tāni*) *prasādaṁ netuṁ kiṁ bahudhā hṛdayakleśakalilaṁ viśasi* । *tvayi prasanne eva svayamuditacintāmaṇiguṇaḥ saṅkalpaḥ viviktaḥ* (*san*) *kiṁ te abhilaṣitaṁ na puṣyati*?

Oh mind! why are you troubling your own heart to please the minds of others? You can become pure-minded as well as free-spirited and attain the *cintāmaṇi* qualities within yourself, only when you are happy with yourself. Then which of your wishes will be unfulfilled?

[Winning the favours of others is hard; why then does your heart seek to appease the minds of others? With inward tranquillity and abstaining from social intercourse, wise thought will arise in you spontaneously; and should you wish for anything that will you not acquire? As it is said in *Śrīmadbhagavadgītā* VI.5:

uddharedātmanātmānaṁ nātmānamavasādayet ।
ātmaiva hyātmano bandhurātmaiva ripurātmanaḥ ॥

An individual should be liberated only by himself. Therefore, do not do such works by which you yourself will get degraded. When a person is prudent and prone to good deeds and virtues, then he himself becomes his own friend; on the contrary, an individual becomes his own enemy and attains disgrace. In this way, by being prudent and being prone to good deeds and virtues, a person should always keep himself happy; instead of finding ways to keep others happy, he should put his soul in tribulation and misery. It is the mind that does all the work. All the senses are subordinate to the mind and followers of the mind. The mind is the cause of bondage and liberation. Man is a part of the nature of virtue–sin and happiness–sorrow from the mind itself. It is the mind that makes a man good or bad. It is only by improving the instinct of the mind, by the mind being devoid of desires, by relinquishing everything, that it becomes capable of self-realization. Thus it is said:

mana eva manuṣyāṇāṁ kāraṇaṁ bandhamokṣayoḥ ।
bandhāya viṣayāsaṅgi muktvā nirviṣayaṁ manaḥ ॥
— *Śāṭyāyanīyopaniṣad* 1

Meaning: The mind is the primary reason for the bondage or liberation of all entities. A mind attached to objects is the cause of bondage and a mind devoid of desire and determination is the cause of liberation.]

Purport — The reason for one's happiness lies within himself.

पश्चात्ताप मात्र से आत्मकल्याण की असाध्यता

अतिक्रान्तः कालो लटभललनाभोगसुभगो
भ्रमन्तः श्रान्ताः स्मः सुचिरमिह संसारसरणौ।
इदानीं स्वःसिन्धोस्तटभुवि समाक्रन्दनगिरः
सुतारैः फुत्कारैः शिव शिव शिवेति प्रतनुमः ॥ 36 ॥

अन्वय — लटभललनाभोगसुभगः कालः अतिक्रान्तः, इह संसारसरणौ सुचिरं भ्रमन्तः (वयं) श्रान्ताः स्मः। इदानीं स्वःसिन्धोः तटभुवि सुतारैः फुत्कारैः समाक्रन्दनगिरः शिव शिव शिवेति प्रतनुमः।

खुबसूरत स्त्रियों को भोगने-योग्य यौवन चला गया; और हम चिरकाल तक विषयों के पीछे दौड़ते-दौड़ते थक भी गए। अब हम जाह्नवी तट भूमि पर उच्च स्वर से शिव! शिव! शिव! इस प्रकार रोते हुए बीते समय के लिए पश्चात्ताप कर रहे हैं, जो कि निरर्थक है।

[भगवत्पाद आदि शंकराचार्य कहते हैं — बालक क्रीडा में आसक्त रहता है, युवा तरुणी स्त्री के प्रति आकर्षित रहता है, वृद्ध चिन्ताओं से घिरा रहता है, परन्तु प्रभु से कोई प्रेम नहीं करता। अतः हे मोहग्रस्त मानव! गोविन्द को भजो, गोविन्द का नाम लो, गोविन्द से प्रेम करो क्योंकि मृत्यु के समय व्याकरण के नियम याद रखने जैसे लौकिक कर्म मात्र से आपकी रक्षा नहीं हो सकती। जैसे कि —

बालस्तावत् क्रीडासक्तः, तरुणस्तावत् तरुणीसक्तः।
वृद्धस्तावच्चिन्तासक्तः, परे ब्रह्मणि कोऽपि न सक्तः ॥ — *मोहमुद्गरस्तोत्रम्* 7

भज गोविन्दम् भज गोविन्दम्, गोविन्दं भज मूढ़मते।
संप्राप्ते सन्निहिते काले, न हि न हि रक्षति डुकृञ् करणे ॥ — *मोहमुद्गरस्तोत्रम्* 1]

तात्पर्य — व्यक्ति को समय से ही आत्मकल्याण के लिए सजग होना चाहिए जिससे उसे पश्चात्ताप करना न पड़े।

Repentance for the Past cannot Reclaim the Virtue

atikrāntaḥ kālo laṭabhalalanābhogasubhago
bhramantaḥ śrāntāḥ smaḥ suciramiha saṁsārasaraṇau ।
idānīṁ svaḥ sindhostaṭabhuvi samākrandanagiraḥ
sutāraiḥ phutkāraiḥ śiva śiva śiveti pratanumaḥ ॥ 36 ॥

anvayaḥ — *laṭabhalalanābhogasubhagaḥ kālaḥ atikrāntaḥ, iha saṁsārasaraṇau suciraṁ bhramantaḥ (vayaṁ) śrāntāḥ smaḥ* । *idānīṁ svaḥsindhoḥ taṭabhuvi sutāraiḥ phutkāraiḥ samākrandanagiraḥ śiva śiva śiveti pratanumaḥ* ।

Gone is the youth that beautiful women can enjoy; and we got tired of running after the subjects of material pleasure for ever and ever. Now we chant Śiva! Śiva! Śiva! loudly on the shore of Jāhnavī. Thus crying and repenting for the past is futile.

[Bhagavatpāda Ādi-Śaṅkarācārya says — A child is engrossed in sports, a young man is attracted towards a young woman, an old man is surrounded by worries but no one loves God. Therefore, Oh deluded human being! worship Govinda, take the name of Govinda, love Govinda because at the time of death you cannot be saved by mere worldly deeds like remembering the rules of grammar. Thus told:

bālastāvat krīḍāsaktaḥ, taruṇastāvat taruṇīsaktaḥ ।
vṛddhastāvaccintāsaktaḥ, pare brahmaṇi ko 'pi na saktaḥ ॥
— *Mohamudgarastotram* 7

bhaja govindam bhaja govindam, govindaṁ bhaja mūḍhamate ।
saṁprāpte sannihite kāle, na hi na hi rakṣati ḍukṛñ karaṇe ॥
— *Mohamudgarastotram* 1]

Purport — A person should practise for self-welfare in time so that he/she will not have to repent.

परमात्मा ही अन्तिम आश्रय

नायातः[69] समयो रहस्यमधुना निद्राति नाद्यापि हि
स्थित्वा द्रक्ष्यति कुप्यति प्रभुरिति द्वारेषु येषां वचः ।

[69] नायं ते — *JKM.1911.*

चेतस्तानपहाय याहि पदवीं देवस्य विश्वेशितु-
निर्दौवारिकनिर्दयोक्तिपुरुषं[70] निःसीमसंवित्पदम्[71] ॥ 37 ॥

अन्वय — अधुना समयो न आयातः, अयम् अद्यापि रहस्यं निद्राति, हि (यदि) स्थित्वा न द्रक्ष्यति (तदा) प्रभुः कुप्यति, इति येषां द्वारेषु वचः, तान् अपहाय हे चेतः! विश्वेशितुः देवस्य पदवीं निर्दौवारिकनिर्दयोक्तिपुरुषं निःसीमसंवित्पदम् याहि।

हे चेतः! जिनके द्वार पर द्वारपाल लोगों से यह कहते हैं कि — "अभी स्वामी से मिलने का समय नहीं हुआ है, प्रभु इस समय एकान्त में सो रहे हैं, यदि तुम मिलने के लिए प्रतीक्षा नहीं करोगे तो प्रभु कुद्ध हो जाएंगे।" ऐसे मदोन्मत प्रभुओं को छोड़कर अनन्त आनन्द के स्रोत देवाधिदेव विश्वेश्वर की शरण जाओ जहाँ न कोई द्वारपाल रोकने वाला है, न कठोर वचन कहने वाला है।

तात्पर्य — परमात्मा ही अन्तिम आश्रय है जिसका द्वार सर्वदा सभी के लिए उन्मुक्त है।

God as the Ultimate Abode

nāyātaḥ samayo rahasyamadhunā nidrāti nādyāpi hi
sthitvā drakṣyati kupyati prabhuriti dvāreṣu yeṣāṁ vacaḥ ।
cetastānapahāya yāhi padavīṁ devasya viśveśitu-
rnirdauvārikanirdayoktipuruṣaṁ niḥsīmasaṁvitpadam ॥ 37 ॥

anvayaḥ — *adhunā samayo na āyātaḥ, ayam adyāpi rahasyaṁ nidrāti, hi (yadi) sthitvā na drakṣyati (tadā) prabhuḥ kupyati, iti yeṣāṁ dvāreṣu vacaḥ, tān apahāya he cetaḥ! viśveśituḥ devasya padavīṁ nirdauvārikanirdayoktipuruṣaṁ niḥsīmasaṁvitpadam yāhi* ।

Oh mind! there are the lords at whose door the porters warn the visitors: "It is not the time to meet the Lord, the Lord is sleeping alone now, if you enter without waiting, the Lord will become angry." Leave such intoxicated lords and surrender to the Supreme Power Godhead, who is the source of eternal happiness, where there is neither any porter to stop you nor anyone to say harsh words.

Purport — God is the ultimate shelter whose door is always open for all.

---

[70] अपरुषं — *JKM.1911.*

[71] निःसीमशर्मप्रदम् — *JKM.1911.*

काल का सर्वग्रासित्व

भ्रातः कष्टमहो गतः स नृपतिः[72] सामन्तचक्रं च तत्
पार्श्वे तस्य च सा विदग्धपरिषत्ताश्चन्द्रबिम्बाननाः।
उद्रिक्तः[73] स च राजपुत्रनिवहस्ते बन्दिनस्ताः कथाः
सर्वं यस्य वशादगात्स्मृतिपथं कालाय तस्मै नमः ॥ 38 ॥

अन्वय — भ्रातः! अहो कष्टम्! स नृपतिः गतः, तत्पार्श्वे च तत् सामन्तचक्रं (गतं), तस्य च सा विदग्धपरिषत् (साऽपि गता) ताः च चन्द्रबिम्बाननाः (गताः)। स च उद्रिक्तः राजपुत्रनिवहः (गतः) ते बन्दिनः, ताः कथाः, यस्य (कालस्य) वशात् सर्वं स्मृतिपथं (एव) अगात्, तस्मै कालाय नमः ॥

अरे भाई! कैसे कष्ट की बात है! वह राजा, उन सामन्तों का समूह, उनके विद्वानों की सभा, वे चाँद जैसी स्त्रियाँ, अहंकारी राजकुमारों का वह समूह, वे चारण, और उनकी वे कथाएं, जिस काल के कराल गह्वर में लीन होकर स्मृति मात्र में ही रह गए हैं। उस काल को हमारा प्रणाम।

[किसी सरोवर में खिले हुए प्रचुर कमल काल के वश से हिम के प्रभाव से नष्ट हो जाते हैं, उसी प्रकार संसार में सब कुछ अनित्य है। जैसे कि कहा गया है —

अत्रैव सरसि जातं विकसितमत्रैव निर्भरं नलिनैः।
कालवशागततुहिनैर्विलीनमत्रैव हा कष्टम् ॥ — *महासुभाषितसंग्रहः*]

तात्पर्य — संसार में सब कुछ अनित्य है एवं काल के कराल गह्वर में लीन हो जाता है।

All Gulping Nature of Time

bhrātaḥ kaṣṭamaho gataḥ sa nṛpatiḥ sāmantacakraṁ ca tat
pārśve tasya ca sā vidagdhapariṣattāścandrabimbānanāḥ ।
udriktaḥ sa ca rājaputranivahaste bandinastāḥ kathāḥ
sarvaṁ yasya vaśādagātsmṛtipathaṁ kālāya tasmai namaḥ ॥ 38 ॥

anvayaḥ — *bhrātaḥ! aho kaṣṭam! sa nṛpatiḥ gataḥ, tatpārśve ca tat sāmantacakraṁ (gataṁ), tasya ca sā vidagdhapariṣat (sā 'pi gatā) tāḥ ca candrabimbānanāḥ (gatāḥ)*। *sa ca udriktaḥ rājaputranivahaḥ (gataḥ) te bandinaḥ, tāḥ kathāḥ, yasya (kālasya) vaśāt sarvaṁ smṛtipathaṁ (eva) agāt, tasmai kālāya namaḥ*।

---

72 रम्या सा नगरी महान् स नृपतिः — *JKM.1911, GAV.1954.*

73 उद्धृत्तः — *GAV.1954.*

Oh brother what a pity! That king, that group of feudal lords, their gathering of scholars, those moon-like women, that group of arrogant princes, those bards and their stories are lost in the deep depths of that time and have remained only in memory. Our salute to that time.

[The abundant lotus flowers blooming in a lake are destroyed by the influence of snow in the course of time, similarly everything in the world is impermanent. As described below:

atraiva sarasi jātaṃ vikasitamatraiva nirbharaṁ nalinaiḥ ।
kālavaśāgatatuhinairvilīnamatraiva hā kaṣṭam ॥
— *Mahāsubhāṣitasaṁgrahaḥ*]

Purport — Everything in the world is impermanent and gets absorbed in the dark abyss of time.

संसार की नाशशीलता

वयं येभ्यो जाताश्चिरपरिगता[74] एव खलु ते
समं यैः संवृद्धाः स्मृतिविषयतां तेऽपि हि गताः[75] ।
इदानीमेते स्मः प्रतिदिवसमासन्नपतनां[76]
गतास्तुल्यावस्थां सिकतिलनदीतीरतरुभिः ॥ 39 ॥

अन्वय — वयं येभ्यो जाताः ते चिरपरिगता एव खलु, यैः समं संवृद्धाः तेऽपि हि स्मृतिविषयतां गताः । इदानीम् एते (वयं) सिकतिलनदीतीरतरुभिः प्रतिदिवसमासन्नपतनां तुल्यावस्थां गताः स्मः ।

जिनसे हमने जन्म लिया था, उन्हें इस दुनिया से गए बहुत दिन हो गए; जिनके साथ हम बड़े हुए थे, वे भी इस दुनिया को छोड़कर चले गए। अब हमारी दशा भी रेतीले नदी-किनारे के वृक्षों की सी हो रही है, जो दिन-प्रतिदिन जड़ छोड़ते हुए गिराऊ होते चले जा रहे हैं।

तात्पर्य — संसार का सब कुछ समय के साथ नाशशील है।

Transience of the World

vayaṁ yebhyo jātāściraparigatā eva khalu te
samaṁ yaiḥ saṁvṛddhāḥ smṛtiviṣayatāṁ te 'pi hi gatāḥ ।

---

[74] चिरमपगता — *JKM.1911.*

[75] तेऽपि गमिताः — *JKM.1911, GAV.1954.*

[76] पतनात् — *JKM.1911,* पतनाः — *GAV.1954.*

idānīmete smaḥ pratidivasamāsannapatanāṁ
gatāstulyāvasthāṁ sikatilanadītīratarubhiḥ ॥ 39 ॥

anvayaḥ *— vayaṁ yebhyo jātāḥ te ciraparigatā eva khalu, yaiḥ samaṁ saṁvṛddhāḥ te 'pi hi smṛtiviṣayatāṁ gatāḥ* । *idānīm ete (vayaṁ) sikatilanadītīratarubhiḥ pratidivasamāsannapatanāṁ tulyāvasthāṁ gatāḥ smaḥ* ।

Those who begot us have passed into eternity. Those with whom we grew up have also left this world. Now with every passing day our condition is akin to the trees, falling down day by day by leaving their roots, on the sandy banks of a river.

Purport — Everything belonging to this transient world is subject to decay in the course of time.

काल की परिवर्तनशील क्रीडा

यत्रानेकः[77] क्वचिदपि गृहे[78] तत्र तिष्ठत्यथैको
यत्राप्येकस्तदनु बहवस्तत्र चान्तेऽपि नैकः ।
इत्थं चेमौ रजनिदिवसौ [79]दोलयन्द्वाविवाक्षौ
कालः काल्या सह बहुकलः[80] क्रीडति प्राणिशारैः ॥ 40 ॥

अन्वय — यत्र क्वचिदपि गृहे अनेकः तत्र एक (एव) तिष्ठति, अथ यत्र एकः तदनु तत्र बहवः अन्तेऽपि च नैकः । इत्थं च इमौ रजनिदिवसौ द्वौ अक्षौ इव दोलयन् बहुकलः कालः काल्या सह प्राणिशारैः क्रीडति ।

जिस घर में पहले अनेक लोग थे, उसमें अब एक ही रह गया है। जिस घर में एक था, उसमें अनेक हो गए, परन्तु अन्त में एक भी न रहा। इससे मालूम होता है कि काल देवता, अपनी पत्नी काली के साथ, संसार-रूपी चौपड़ में, दिन–रात-रूपी पासों को लुढ़का-लुढ़काकर और इस जगत् के प्राणियों की गोटी बना-बनाकर, खेल रहा है।

तात्पर्य — काल की बदलती हुई क्रीडा में सब कुछ क्षणभंगुर है। अतः इस परिवर्तन में व्यक्ति को ना तो मोहग्रस्त और ना ही शोकग्रस्त होना चाहिए।

---

77 यत्रानेके — *JKM.1911.*

78 भवे — *Ms eG-2.*

79 लोलयन् — *GAV.1954.*

80 भुवनफलके — *JKM.1911*, कल्यो भुवनफ्लके — *GAV.1954.*

Changing Game of Time

yatrānekaḥ kvacidapi gṛhe tatra tiṣṭhatyathaiko
yatrāpyekastadanu bahavastatra cānte 'pi naikaḥ ।
ittham cemau rajanidivasau dolayandvāvivākṣau
kālaḥ kālyā saha bahukalaḥ krīḍati prāṇiśāraiḥ ॥ 40 ॥

anvayaḥ — *yatra kvacidapi gṛhe anekaḥ tatra eka (eva) tiṣṭhati, atha yatra ekaḥ tadanu tatra bahavaḥ ante 'pi ca naikaḥ* । *ittham ca imau rajanidivasau dvau akṣau iva dolayan bahukalaḥ kālaḥ kālyā saha prāṇiśāraiḥ krīḍati* ।

Where in some homes there were many occupants, now there is only one; where there was only one, became successively many, but none is left in the end. Thus does Time expertly play the game on the checker-board of this world, with creatures as the pieces to be moved and throwing the dice of days and nights.

Purport — Everything is fleeting in the changing game of time. Therefore, in this change, a person should neither be disillusioned nor bereaved.

आध्यात्मिक अनुभूति से शाश्वत सुख

तपस्यन्तः सन्तः किमधिनिवसामः सुरनदीं
गुणोदारान्दारानुत परिचरामः सविनयम् ।
पिबामः शास्त्रौघानुतविविधकाव्यामृतरसान्
न विद्मः किं कुर्मः कतिपयनिमेषायुषि जनौ ॥ 41 ॥

अन्वय — किं तपस्यन्तः सन्तः सुरनदीम् अधिनिवसामः, उत गुणोदारान् दारान् सविनयं परिचरामः । शास्त्रौघान् पिबामः उत विविधकाव्यामृतरसान् पिबामः? कतिपयनिमेषायुषि जनौ किं कुर्मः (इति) न विद्मः ।

हमारी समझ में नहीं आता है कि हम इस अल्पायु जीवन में क्या-क्या करें अर्थात् हम गंगा तट पर बसकर तपस्या करें अथवा गुणवती स्त्री की प्रेम-सहित यथायोग्य सेवा करें? वेदान्त शास्त्र का अमृत पिएं या काव्यरस-पान करें?

तात्पर्य — इस नश्वर संसार में परमार्थ चिन्तन एवं भगवत्सेवा सर्वोपरि है जो शाश्वत आनन्द-प्राप्ति की ओर ले जा सकते हैं।

Eternal Happiness through Spiritual Experience

tapasyantaḥ santaḥ kimadhinivasāmaḥ suranadīṁ
guṇodārāndārānuta paricarāmaḥ savinayam ।
pibāmaḥ śāstraughānutavividhakāvyāmṛtarasān
na vidmaḥ kiṁ kurmaḥ katipayanimeṣāyuṣi janau ॥ 41 ॥

anvayaḥ — *kiṁ tapasyantaḥ santaḥ suranadīm adhinivasāmaḥ, uta guṇodārān dārān savinayaṁ paricarāmaḥ* । *śāstraughān pibāmaḥ uta vividhakāvyāmṛtarasān pibāmaḥ? katipayanimeṣāyuṣi janau kiṁ kurmaḥ (iti) na vidmaḥ* ।

Shall we live ascetically on the banks of the heavenly river, or serve humbly our virtuous beloved wives? Shall we drink from the streams of scriptures or from the nectarine poetry? With a lifespan of a few eyewinks, we do not know what to do really!

Purport — In this mortal world, spiritual realization and service to God are paramount which can lead to attain eternal happiness.

सर्वत्र समभाव

अहौ वा हारे वा कुसुमशयने वा दृषदि[81] वा
मणौ वा लोष्ठे वा बलवति रिपौ वा सुहृदि वा।
तृणे वा स्त्रैणे वा मम समदृशो यान्तु दिवसाः
कदा पुण्येऽरण्ये शिव शिव शिवेति प्रलपतः ॥ 42 ॥

अन्वय — अहौ वा हारे वा, कुसुमशयने वा दृषदि वा, मणौ वा लोष्ठे वा बलवति रिपौ वा सुहृदि वा। तृणे वा स्त्रैणे वा कदा पुण्येरण्ये शिव शिव शिवेति प्रलपतः समदृशो मम दिवसाः यान्तु।

किसी वैरागी एवं तटस्थ व्यक्ति की उक्ति है — साँप हो या माला हो, फूलों की सेज हो या पत्थर का बिस्तर हो, कीमती हीरा हो या मिट्टी का ढेला हो, क्रूर शत्रु हो या मित्र हो, काँटों में रहना हो या स्त्रियों के मध्य हो, बस समदर्शी भाव से किसी पवित्र स्थान में रहकर शिव के मन्त्र का जप करते हुए मेरा जीवन व्यतीत हो।

तात्पर्य — परमार्थ चिन्तन एवं भगवद्भक्ति के लिए सुख, समृद्धि एवं अनुकूल साधन अपरिहार्य नहीं हैं।

---

81 दृशदि — *Ms ORLS-3.*

Equilibrium Everywhere

ahau vā hāre vā kusumaśayane vā dṛṣadi vā
maṇau vā loṣṭhe vā balavati ripau vā suhṛdi vā ।
tṛṇe vā straiṇe vā mama samadṛśo yāntu divasāḥ
kadā puṇye'raṇye śiva śiva śiveti pralapataḥ ॥ 42 ॥

anvayaḥ — *ahau vā hāre vā kusumaśayane vā dṛṣadi vā, maṇau vā loṣṭhe vā balavati ripau vā suhṛdi vā* । *tṛṇe vā straiṇe vā kadā puṇyeraṇye śiva śiva śiveti pralapataḥ samadṛśo mama divasāḥ yāntu* ।

This is the statement of a dispassionate and neutral individual: Be it a snake or a garland, a bed of flowers or that of stones, a precious diamond or a lump of clay, a cruel enemy or a friend, be it among thorns or be it among women that I may spend my life living in a holy place with an equanimous attitude and chanting the *mantra* of Śiva.

Purport — Happiness, prosperity and favourable means are not inevitable for spiritual thinking and devotion to God.

समाधि की स्थिति

गङ्गातीरे हिमगिरिशिलाबद्धपद्मासनस्य
ब्रह्मज्ञानाभ्यसन[82]विधिना योगनिद्रां गतस्य ।
किं तैर्भाव्यं मम सुदिवसैर्यत्र ते निर्विशङ्काः
कण्डूयन्ते जरठहरिणाः शृङ्गमङ्गे[83] मदीये ॥ 43 ॥

अन्वय — गङ्गातीरे हिमगिरिशिलाबद्धपद्मासनस्य ब्रह्मज्ञानाभ्यसनविधिना योगनिद्रां गतस्य मम किं तैः सुदिवसैः भाव्यं यत्र मदीये अङ्गे ते जरठहरिणाः निर्विशङ्काः शृङ्गं कण्डूयन्ते ।

गंगा के तट पर हिमालय के पत्थर पर कमल-आसन में बैठे; परमब्रह्म के ध्यान के अभ्यास से योग-निद्रा प्राप्त करते हुए; क्या मेरे ऐसे दिन होंगे जब वृद्ध और भयमुक्त हरिण अपने शरीर को मेरे शरीर से सहलाएंगे?

तात्पर्य — समाधि की अवस्था में व्यक्ति पूर्णतः निर्विकार होता है।

---

82 ब्रह्मध्यानाभ्यसन — *JKM.1911, GAV.1954.*

83 स्वाङ्गमङ्गे — *GAV.1954.*

The State of Meditative Consciousness

gaṅgātīre himagiriśilābaddhapadmāsanasya
brahmajñānābhyasanavidhinā yoganidrāṁ gatasya ।
kiṁ tairbhāvyaṁ mama sudivasairyatra te nirviśaṅkāḥ
kaṇḍūyante jaraṭhahariṇāḥ śṛṅgamaṅge madīye ॥ 43 ॥

anvayaḥ — *gaṅgātīre himagiriśilābaddhapadmāsanasya brahmajñānābhyasanavidhinā yoganidrāṁ gatasya mama kiṁ taiḥ sudivasaiḥ bhāvyaṁ yatra madīye aṅge te jaraṭhahariṇāḥ nirviśaṅkāḥ śṛṅgaṁ kaṇḍūyante* ।

Seated in the lotus-posture on a stone in the Himalayas on the banks of the Gaṅgā, attaining Yogic sleep by the practice of meditation on the Supreme Reality, will I have such days when the deer, old with age and free from fear, caressing their bodies against my body?

Purport — In the state of abstract meditation, an individual becomes completely free from perturbation.

अध्यात्म-साधना हेतु यत्न

स्फुरत्स्फारज्यौत्स्नि[84] धवलिततले क्वापि पुलिने
सुखासीनाः शान्तध्वनिषु रजनीषु द्युसरितः ।
भवाभोगोद्विग्नाः शिव शिव शिवेत्यात्तवचसः[85]
कदा स्यामो[86] हर्षोद्गतबहलबाष्पाकुलदृशः ॥ 44 ॥

अन्वय — क्वापि स्फुरत्स्फारज्यौत्स्नि द्युसरितः धवलिततले पुलिने शान्तध्वनिषु रजनीषु सुखासीनाः भवाभोगोद्विग्नाः कदा शिव शिव शिव इति आत्तवचसः हर्षोद्गतबहलबाष्पाकुलदृशः स्यामः?

[स्यामः –√ सो - अन्तकर्मणि + लटि + मस्-प्रत्यये = अन्तं (पञ्चत्वं) प्राप्स्यामः ।]

वह समय कब आएगा, संसार के विषय दुःखों से थककर, जब हम चाँदनी से धवलित पवित्र गंगा के तट पर सुख से बैठे होंगे और निःशब्द रात के समय, आनन्दाश्रुपूर्ण नेत्रों से, सर्वशक्तिमान शिव का नाम जपते हुए इस पार्थिव शरीर को त्यागकर पञ्चत्व को प्राप्त करेंगे?

---

84 ज्यौत्स्नाधवलिततले — *Ms ORLS-3, Ms eG-2, JKM.1911, GAV.1954.*

85 शिवेत्युच्चवचसा — *JKM.1911.*

86 स्यामानन्दोद्गतबहुलबाष्पाप्लुतदृशः — *JKM.1911*, यास्यामोन्तर्गतबहुलबाष्पाकुलदशाम् — *GAV.1954.*

तात्पर्य — संसार के मोहपाश में अपना जीवन वृथा खोने की अपेक्षा अलीक विषय-सुखों से दूर रहते हुए परम तत्त्व चिन्तन ही श्रेयस्कर है।

Endeavour for Spiritual Practice

sphuratsphārajyautsni dhavalitatale kvāpi puline
sukhāsīnāḥ śāntadhvaniṣu rajanīṣu dyusaritaḥ ।
bhavābhogodvignāḥ śiva śiva śivetyāttavacasaḥ
kadā syāmo harṣodgatabahalabāṣpākuladṛśaḥ ॥ 44 ॥

anvayaḥ — *kvāpi sphuratsphārajyautsni dyusaritaḥ dhavalitatale puline śāntadhvaniṣu rajanīṣu sukhāsīnāḥ bhavābhogodvignāḥ kadā śiva śiva śiva iti āttavacasaḥ harṣodgatabahalabāṣpākuladṛśaḥ syāmaḥ?*

Sitting peacefully on the banks of the celestial river, in the bright scattered glow of the moonlight, when silence pervades the nights, distressed by the thoughts of birth and death, when shall we leave this abode of material existence while reverberating the names of Śiva, with tears of ecstasy?

Purport — It is better to contemplate on the Ultimate Truth while staying away from other-worldly pleasures, than wasting one's life in the lure of the world.

इन्द्रिय-तृप्ति ही निराशा की जननी

अनन्तं जल्पन्तः कति बत गता नो यमपुरं
पुरस्तादस्माकं विधृतवदना व्यात्तनयनाः ।
प्रतीता अप्येवं न हि विजहितं[87] चेतसि वयं
वहामो हा मोहाद्विषयविषजातादवसिताः ॥ 45 ॥

अन्वय — अस्माकं पुरस्तात् विधृतवदना व्यात्तनयनाः अनन्तं जल्पन्तः नः कति यमपुरं गताः बत। हि (ते) एवं प्रतीताः अपि (तैः) न विजहितम्। हा विषयविषजातात् मोहात् चेतसि अवसिताः वयं (जीवनं) वहामः।

(प्रतीताः अपि = निजमरणे विश्वसिता अपि। न विजहितम् = अहंकारः न त्यक्तः।)

पता नहीं हम में से कितने ही लोग मुँह और आँखें खोलकर अनन्त बातें करते हुए हमारे सामने ही यमपुर चले गए हैं। अपनी मृत्यु पर विश्वास करते हुए भी उन्होंने अपना अहंकार

[87] निजहितं — *Ms ORLS-3.*

बखानना नहीं छोड़ा। दुःख यह है कि, हम इन्द्रिय-तृप्ति के विष से उत्पन्न मोह के कारण निराश होते हुए अपना जीवन व्यतीत कर रहे हैं।

तात्पर्य — इन्द्रियों की तृप्ति में आसक्ति ही निराशा को जन्म देती है।

Sense Gratification: The Cause of Frustration

anantaṁ jalpantaḥ kati bata gatā no yamapuraṁ
purastādasmākaṁ vidhṛtavadanā vyāttanayanāḥ ।
pratītā apyevaṁ na hi vijahitaṁ cetasi vayaṁ
vahāmo hā mohādviṣayaviṣajātādavasitāḥ ॥ 45 ॥

anvayaḥ — *asmākaṁ purastāt vidhṛtavadanā vyāttanayanāḥ anantaṁ jalpantaḥ naḥ kati yamapuraṁ gatāḥ bata* । *hi (te) evaṁ pratītāḥ api (taiḥ) na vijahitam* । *hā viṣayaviṣajātāt mohāt cetasi avasitāḥ vayaṁ (jīvanaṁ) vahāmaḥ* ।

We do not know how many of us have gone to the abode of Yama or the city of death in front of us, talking endlessly with their mouths and eyes open. Despite believing in their death, they did not restrain from showing off their arrogance. Alas! we are passing our lives with disappointment due to the attachment caused by the poison of sense gratification.

Purport — Attachment to sense gratification only gives frustration.

अविचारित कर्म ही पतन का कारण

शिरः शार्वं स्वर्गात् पशुपतिशिरस्तः क्षितिधरं
गिरीन्द्रा[88]दुत्तुङ्गादवनिमवनेश्चापि जलधिम्।
अधोऽधो गङ्गावद्वयमुपगता नूनमथवा[89]
विवेकभ्रष्टानां भवति विनिपातः शतमुखः ॥ 46 ॥

अन्वय — स्वर्गात् शार्वं शिरः, पशुपतिशिरस्तः क्षितिधरं, उत्तुङ्गाद् गिरीन्द्राद् अवनिम्, अवनेश्चापि जलधिम्। (एवं) गङ्गावद् वयम् अधोऽधः उपगताः, अथवा विवेकभ्रष्टानां शतमुखः विनिपातः भवति।

गंगाजी स्वर्ग से शिवजी के सिर पर आई; उनके सिर से हिमालय पर्वत पर; हिमालय से पृथ्वी पर; और पृथ्वी से समुद्र में पहुँची। इससे मालूम होता है, कि विवेकहीनों का पद-पद पर सैकड़ों प्रकार से पतन होता है।

---

[88] महीध्रा — *Ms ORLS-3, JKM.1911.*

[89] गङ्गेयं पदमुपगता स्तोकमथवा — *JKM.1911.*

[जो विचारपूर्वक काम नहीं करते, उनका बार बार अधःपतन होता है यह बात यहाँ गंगा के दृष्टान्त से बताई गई है। गंगा को बड़ा घमण्ड था, तब उसका गर्व खत्म करने के लिए ब्रह्मा ने उसे अपने कमण्डलु में भर लिया। तब गंगा का मस्तक नीचे हो गया। फिर भी, उसने घमण्ड न छोड़ा, तब शिवजी ने उसे अपनी जटाओं में रोक लिया। महाराज भगीरथ ने शिवजी की जटाओं से गंगा को पृथ्वी पर लाने हेतु घोर तप किया, तो शिवजी ने उसे छोड़ा। शिवजी के सिर से वह हिमालय पर आई और वहाँ से बहती-बहती समुद्र में जा गिरी। अतः मनुष्य को भूलकर भी घमण्ड नहीं करना चाहिए और खूब विचारकर कार्य करना चाहिए।]

तात्पर्य — विचारपूर्वक कार्य नहीं करने से एवं अहंकार से व्यक्ति का पुनः-पुनः पतन होता है। अतः किसी भी कार्य से पहले सभी लाभ और क्षति के बारे में सोचना बुद्धिमानी है।

Lack of Discernment Causes of Downfall

śiraḥ śārvaṁ svargāt paśupatiśirastaḥ kṣitidharaṁ
girīndrāduttuṅagādavanimavaneścāpi jaladhim ।
adho 'dho gaṅgāvadvayamupagatā nūnamathavā
vivekabhraṣṭānāṁ bhavati vinipātaḥ śatamukhaḥ ॥ 46 ॥

anvayaḥ — *svargāt śārvaṁ śiraḥ, paśupatiśirastaḥ kṣitidharaṁ, uttuṅagād girīndrād avanim, avaneścāpi jaladhim* । *(evaṁ) gaṅgāvad vayam adho 'dhaḥ upagatāḥ, athavā vivekabhraṣṭānāṁ śatamukhaḥ vinipātaḥ bhavati* ।

River Gaṅgā fell from heaven on Lord Śiva's head; from his head to the Himalayan mountains; from the Himalayas to the earth; and from the earth into the sea. From this example, it becomes clear that due to the lack of discernment, an individual falls in hundreds of ways at every stage.

[There would be a gradual degradation, this has been explained here with the example of River Gaṅgā. Lord Brahmā when found River Gaṅgā very arrogant, to end her ego, filled her in his *kamaṇḍalu* (water pot). By this, Gaṅgā's head became lowered. Still, she did not give up her ego, then Lord Śiva concealed her in his clotted hairs. When King Bhagīratha performed severe penance to bring Gaṅgā to the earth with the help of Lord Śiva's hair, Lord Śiva released her from his clotted hairs. From Lord Śiva's head River Gaṅgā fell on the Himalayas and from there it flowed into the sea. This way there was a gradual degradation of River Gaṅgā. Therefore, a person should not be arrogant even by mistake and should work with proper discernment.]

Purport — By arrogance and without discernment, a person falls down again and again. Therefore, it is wise to think all pros and cons before an action.

शाश्वत सुख का रहस्य

महादेवो देवः सरिदपि च सैवामरसरिद्
गुहा चैवागारं वसनमपि ता एव हरितः।
सुहृद्वा कायोऽयं[90] व्रतमिदमदैन्यव्रतमियत्
कियद्वा वक्षामो वटविटप एवास्तु दयितः[91] ॥ 47 ॥

अन्वय — महादेवो देवः, सा अमरसरिद् एव सरित्, गुहा एव च अगारं, ता हरितः एव अपि वसनम् । अयं कायः सुहृद् वा, इयत् इदम् अदैन्यव्रतम् (एव) व्रतम्, कियद् वा वक्षामो, वटविटप एव दयितः अस्तु।

महादेव ही एक हमारा देव हो, जाह्नवी ही हमारी नदी हो, एक गुफ़ा ही हमारा घर हो, दिशा ही हमारे वस्त्र हों, स्वयं का शरीर ही हमारा मित्र हो, इसी प्रकार किसी के सामने दीन न होना ही हमारा व्रत हो, अधिक क्या कहें, वट-वृक्ष ही हमारी अर्धांगिनी हो।

[मनुष्य की प्राथमिक आवश्यकताएं खाद्य, वस्त्र एवं आवास होते हैं। आराध्य देव, मित्र एवं पत्नी जीवन-यात्रा में परम सहायक होते हैं। परन्तु यदि ये सभी बिना किसी अपेक्षा से केवल प्रकृति से ही निर्भर होकर व्यक्ति पूरा कर लेता है, तब वही व्यक्ति संसार में सबसे सुखी होता है। दूसरों की अपेक्षा के बिना अपने में ही सन्तुष्ट रहने वाला व्यक्ति ही भगवान् श्रीकृष्ण का प्रिय होता है ऐसा उन्होंने भी *गीता* XII.16 में कहा है —

अनपेक्षः शुचिर्दक्ष उदासीनो गतव्यथः।
सर्वारम्भपरित्यागी यो मद्भक्तः स मे प्रियः ॥]

तात्पर्य — अन्य व्यक्ति एवं वस्तुओं पर अपेक्षा के बिना सन्तुष्ट रहना ही परम सुख है।

The Secret of Perpetual Happiness

mahādevo devaḥ saridapi ca saivāmarasarid
guhā caivāgāraṁ vasanamapi tā eva haritaḥ ।
suhṛdvā kāyo 'yaṁ vratamidamadainyavratamiyat
kiyadvā vakṣāmo vaṭaviṭapa evāstu dayitaḥ ॥ 47 ॥

---

[90] कालोयं — *JKM.1911.*

[91] दयिता — *JKM.1911.*

anvayaḥ — *mahādevo devaḥ, sā amarasarid eva sarit, guhā eva ca agāraṁ, tā haritaḥ eva api vasanam। ayaṁ kāyaḥ suhṛd vā, iyat idam adainyavratam (eva) vratam, kiyad vā vakṣāmo, vaṭaviṭapa eva dayitaḥ astu।*

May Lord Śiva be our only God, River Gaṅgā should be our river, a cave should be our home, directions should be our clothes, our own body should be our friend, thus our vow should not be dejected in front of anyone, what should I say more, the banyan tree should be our better half.

[The primary needs of humans are food, clothing and shelter. Adorable God, friends and wife are the ultimate helpful in the journey of life. But if a person accomplishes all these without expecting anything from anyone and relying only on Nature, then that person is the happiest in the world. Only the person who is satisfied within himself without expecting anything from others is dear to Lord Kṛṣṇa, this is also said in *Gītā* XII.16:

> *anapekṣaḥ śucirdakṣa udāsīno gatavyathaḥ।*
> *sarvārambhaparityāgī yo madbhaktaḥ sa me priyaḥ॥*]

Purport — Being content without expectations from other people and things is the ultimate happiness.

आशा ही दुःखों का कारण

> आशा नाम नदी मनोरथजला तृष्णातरङ्गाकुला
> रागग्राहवती वितर्कविहगा धैर्यद्रुमध्वंसिनी।
> मोहावर्तसुदुस्तरातिगहना प्रोत्तुङ्गचिन्तातटा
> तस्याः पारगता विशुद्धमनसो नृत्यन्ति[92] योगीश्वराः ॥ 48 ॥

अन्वय — आशा नाम नदी मनोरथजला तृष्णातरङ्गाकुला रागग्राहवती वितर्कविहगा धैर्यद्रुमध्वंसिनी। मोहावर्तसुदुस्तरातिगहना प्रोत्तुङ्गचिन्तातटा तस्याः पारगता विशुद्धमनसः योगीश्वराः नृत्यन्ति।

आशा एक नदी है, जिसमें इच्छा-रूपी जल है; तृष्णा उस नदी की तरंगें हैं, प्रीति उसके मगरमच्छ हैं, तर्क-वितर्क उसके पक्षी हैं, जो मोह-रूपी भँवर से दुस्तर है; चिन्ता ही उसके ऊँचे किनारे हैं। वह आशा नदी धैर्यरूपी वृक्ष को गिराने वाली है; इस कारण उसके पार होना बड़ा कठिन है। जो शुद्ध-चित्त योगीश्वर उसके पार चले जाते हैं; वे बड़ा आनन्द उपभोग करते हैं।

---

[92] नन्दन्ति — *JKM.1911, GAV.1954.*

तात्पर्य — आशा ही मोह, चिन्ता, आदि समस्त दुःखों का कारण है। समस्त आशाओं का त्याग ही परम सुख है।

Desire: The Cause of Sorrow

āśā nāma nadī manorathajalā tṛṣṇātaraṅgākulā
rāgagrāhavatī vitarkavihagā dhairyadrumadhvaṁsinī ।
mohāvartasudustarātigahanā prottuṅgacintātaṭā
tasyāḥ pāragatā viśuddhamanaso nṛtyanti yogīśvarāḥ ॥ 48 ॥

anvayaḥ — *āśā nāma nadī manorathajalā tṛṣṇātaraṅgākulā rāgagrāhavatī vitarkavihagā dhairyadrumadhvaṁsinī । mohāvartasudustarātigahanā prottuṅgacintātaṭā tasyāḥ pāragatā viśuddhamanasaḥ yogīśvarāḥ nṛtyanti ।*

Hope, like a river, with fantasies as water, agitated by waves of desires; attachments to various objects as the objects of seizing; abounding in thoughts of greed like birds; destroying the foes of courage; surrounded by eddies of ignorance deep and difficult to cross; with precipitous banks of anxiety. This is such a river, that can be crossed over perversely. The pure-minded sages can cross it and enjoy the beatitude.

Purport — Desire is the cause of all sorrows like attachment and worry. Renunciation of all desires is the ultimate happiness.

मन की चञ्चलता

आसंसारं त्रिभुवनमिदं चिन्वतां तात तादृक्
नैवास्माकं नयनपदवीं श्रोत्रवर्त्मागतोऽपि ।
योऽयं धत्ते विषयकरिणीगाढगूढानुराग-[93]
क्षीबस्यान्तःकरणकरिणः संयमालानलीलाम् ॥ 49 ॥

अन्वय — हे तात! आसंसारम् इदं त्रिभुवनं चिन्वताम् अस्माकं नयनपदवीं श्रोत्रवर्त्म अपि तादृक् नैव आगतः, योऽयं विषयकरिणीगाढगूढानुरागक्षीबस्य अन्तःकरणकरिणः संयमालानलीलां धत्ते।

रे पुत्र! मैं सारे संसार में घूमा और तीनो भुवनों में मैंने खोज की; परन्तु ऐसा मनुष्य मैंने ना देखा और ना सुना, जो अपनी कामेच्छा पूर्ण करने के लिए हथिनी के पीछे दौड़ते हुए मदोन्मत्त हाथी के समान मन को संयम-रूपी आलान-स्तम्भ से नियन्त्रित कर सकता हो।

---

[93] गाढरूढानुराग — *Ms ORLS-3*, गाढरूढाभिमान — *JKM.1911.*

[अर्जुन भी श्रीकृष्ण से मन की चञ्चलता के बारे में *गीता* VI.34 में कहते हैं —

चञ्चलं हि मनः कृष्ण प्रमाथि बलवद्दृढम्।
तस्याहं निग्रहं मन्ये वायोरिव सुदुष्करम्॥

अर्थात् हे कृष्ण! क्योंकि मन अति चञ्चल, अशान्त, हठी और बलवान् है। मुझे वायु की तरह मन को वश में करना अत्यन्त कठिन लगता है।

मन इतना दृढ़ और जिद्दी है कि कभी-कभी यह बुद्धि पर हावी हो जाता है, हालाँकि मन को बुद्धि के अधीन माना जाता है। व्यावहारिक जगत् में जिस मनुष्य को इतने सारे विरोधी तत्त्वों से लड़ना पड़ता है, उसके लिए मन को नियन्त्रित करना निश्चित रूप से बहुत कठिन है। कृत्रिम रूप से कोई भी व्यक्ति मित्र और शत्रु दोनों के प्रति मानसिक सन्तुलन स्थापित कर सकता है, परन्तु अन्ततः कोई भी सांसारिक व्यक्ति ऐसा नहीं कर सकता, क्योंकि यह प्रचण्ड हवा को नियन्त्रित करने से भी अधिक कठिन है।]

तात्पर्य — इस संसार में मन ही अत्यन्त चञ्चल एवं दृढ़ है जिसे नियन्त्रित करना सबसे कठिन है।

Restlessness of Mind

āsaṁsāraṁ tribhuvanamidaṁ cinvatāṁ tāta tādṛk
naivāsmākaṁ nayanapadavīṁ śrotravartmāgato 'pi ।
yo 'yaṁ dhatte viṣayakariṇīgāḍhagūḍhānurāga-
kṣībasyāntaḥkaraṇakariṇaḥ saṁyamālānalīlām ॥ 49 ॥

anvayaḥ — *he tāta! āsaṁsāram idaṁ tribhuvanaṁ cinvatām asmākaṁ nayanapadavīṁ śrotravartma api tādṛk naiva āgataḥ, yo 'yaṁ viṣayakariṇīgāḍhagūḍhānurāgakṣībasya antaḥkaraṇakariṇaḥ saṁyamālānalīlāṁ dhatte* ।

Oh my son! since creation, in our search in all the three worlds, we have not seen nor heard anything that can act like a tying post to control the mind, deeply and inexplicably infatuated with sensuality, like an elephant wildly excited by the female elephant.

[Arjuna also tells Śrī Kṛṣṇa about the restlessness of the mind in *Gītā* VI.34:

cañcalaṁ hi manaḥ kṛṣṇa pramāthi balavaddṛḍham ।
tasyāhaṁ nigrahaṁ manye vāyoriva suduṣkaram ॥

Meaning: The mind is restless, turbulent, obstinate and very strong, Oh Kṛṣṇa! and to subdue it, I think, is more difficult than controlling the wind.

The mind is so strong and obstinate that it sometimes overcomes the intelligence, although the mind is supposed to be subservient to the intelligence. For a man in the practical world, who has to fight so many opposing elements, it is certainly difficult to control the mind. Artificially, one may establish a mental equilibrium towards both friend and enemy, but ultimately no worldly man can do so, for this is more difficult than controlling the raging wind.]

Purport — The mind itself is very fickle and strong. It is the most difficult to be controlled.

विषय-वासना से निवृत्ति

ये वर्धन्ते धनपतिपुरः प्रार्थनादुःखभाजो
ये चाल्पत्वं दधति विषयाक्षेपपर्यस्तबुद्धेः ।
तेषामन्तःस्फुरितहसितं वासराणां स्मरेयं
ध्यानच्छेदे शिखरिकुहरग्रावशय्यानिषण्णः ॥ 50 ॥

अन्वय — ये धनपतिपुरः प्रार्थनादुःखभाजो वर्धन्ते, ये च विषयाक्षेपपर्यस्तबुद्धेः अल्पत्वं दधति, शिखरिकुहरग्रावशय्यानिषण्णः (अहं) ध्यानच्छेदे तेषां वासराणाम् अन्तःस्फुरितहसितं स्मरेयम्।

वे दिन जो धन के लिए धनवानों की प्रार्थना करने के दुःख से बड़े मालूम होते थे और वे दिन जो विषयासक्ति में विपर्यस्त बुद्धि होने के कारण छोटे लगते थे; उन दोनों प्रकार के दिनों को मैं पर्वत की एकान्त गुफ़ा में, पत्थर की शिला पर बैठे हुए आत्मध्यान में मग्न होकर, ध्यान भंग होने पर अन्तःकरण में हँसते हुए याद करुँगा।

[न केवल विषयों के उपभोग से ही, अपितु विषय-भोग की इच्छा से भी विषयों में प्रवृत्ति होती है। उभय ही दुःख के कारण होते हैं। *गीता* III.6 में भी कहा गया है —

कर्मेन्द्रियाणि संयम्य य आस्ते मनसा स्मरन् ।
इन्द्रियार्थान्विमूढात्मा मिथ्याचारः स उच्यते ॥

अर्थात् जो अपनी कर्मेन्द्रियों के बाह्य घटकों को तो नियन्त्रित करते हैं लेकिन मन से इन्द्रियों के विषयों का चिन्तन करते हैं, वे निःसन्देह स्वयं को धोखा देते हैं और पाखण्डी कहलाते हैं।]

तात्पर्य — मन एवं कर्म उभय से विषयों के प्रति अनासक्ति ही परम सुख एवं परम श्रेय का द्वार है।

Restricting of Sense Gratification

ye vardhante dhanapatipuraḥ prārthanāduḥkhabhājo
ye cālpatvaṁ dadhati viṣayākṣepaparyastabuddheḥ ।
teṣāmantaḥsphuritahasitaṁ vāsarāṇāṁ smareyaṁ
dhyānacchede śikharikuharagrāvaśayyāniṣaṇṇaḥ ॥ 50 ॥

anvayaḥ — *ye dhanapatipuraḥ prārthanāduḥkhabhājo vardhante, ye ca viṣayākṣepaparyastabuddheḥ alpatvaṁ dadhati, śikharikuharagrāvaśayyāniṣaṇṇaḥ (ahaṁ) dhyānacchede teṣāṁ vāsarāṇām antaḥsphuritahasitaṁ smareyam* ।

Those days which seemed bigger due to the sorrow of grovelling for money before the rich and those days which seemed shorter due to the mind being distorted in sensual pleasures; may I recall both those of days of plight with an inner smile, while lying down on a stone-bed in a mountain-cave, during the lulls in-between meditation.

[Not only the enjoyments of objects, but also desire to enjoy the objects, both are the causes of sorrow. Thus it is cited in *Gītā* III.6:

karmendriyāṇi saṁyamya ya āste manasā smaran ।
indriyārthān vimūḍhātmā mithyācāraḥ sa ucyate ॥

Meaning: He who, restraining the organs of action, sits thinking of the sense-objects in his mind, he, of deluded understanding, is called a hypocrite.]

Purport — Detachment from the objects of both mind and action is the door to ultimate happiness.

वैराग्य का छल ही आत्म-वञ्चना का प्रतिरूप

विद्या नाधिगता कलङ्करहिता वित्तं न चोपार्जितं
शुश्रूषापि समाहितेन मनसा पित्रोर्न सम्पादिता ।
आलोलायतलोचना युवतयः स्वप्नेऽपि नालिङ्गिताः
कालोऽयं परपिण्डलोलुभतया[94] काकैरिव प्रेरितः ॥ 51 ॥

---

[94] लोलुपतया — *JKM.1911, GAV.1954.*

अन्वय — कलङ्करहिता विद्या नाधिगता, वित्तं च न उपार्जितं, पित्रोः शुश्रूषापि समाहितेन मनसा न सम्पादिता, आलोलायतलोचना युवतयः स्वप्नेऽपि न आलिङ्गिताः, अयं कालः परपिण्डलोलुभतया काकैः इव प्रेरितः।

ना तो हमने निष्कलंक विद्या पढ़ी और ना धन कमाया; ना हमने शान्त-चित्त से माता-पिता की सेवा ही की और न स्वप्न में भी दीर्घनयनी कामिनियों को गले से ही लगाया। पूरा जीवन लोभी कौवों की तरह दूसरों की अधीनता में व्यतीत हो गया।

[परमात्मा एवं परम तत्त्व से प्रेम हुए बिना, मनुष्य के मन की चञ्चलता नहीं जाती और स्थिरता नहीं होती। मन के स्थिर हुए बिना परमानन्द-प्राप्ति का द्वार नहीं खुलता। जो लोग गेरुआ वस्त्र धारण करके साधु हो जाते हैं और भगवान् में मन नहीं लगाते — वे लोग पेट के लिए दर-दर चीख-चिल्लाकर अपना दुर्लभ मनुष्य जीवन वृथा ही गँवाते हैं। वे इस बात को नहीं समझते, कि यह मनुष्य जन्म बड़ी कठिनाई से मिला है। इससे तो यही अच्छा होता, कि वे संसार-त्यागी बनने का ढोंग ना रचकर, संसारी या गृहस्थ ही बने रहते। संसारी बने रहने से वे इस दुनिया के मिथ्या सुख-भोग तो भोग लेते। परन्तु ऐसे ढोंगी दोनों तरफ से जाते हैं।]

तात्पर्य — उदर-पोषणार्थ या कर्मभीरुता के कारण वैराग्य के अभिनय से परमार्थ-प्राप्ति नहीं होती।

Hoax of Renunciation Is Self-deprivation

vidyā nādhigatā kalaṅkarahitā vittaṁ na copārjitaṁ
śuśrūṣāpi samāhitena manasā pitrorna sampāditā ।
ālolāyatalocanā yuvatayaḥ svapne 'pi nāliṅgitāḥ
kālo 'yaṁ parapiṇḍalolubhatayā kākairiva preritaḥ ॥ 51 ॥

anvayaḥ — *kalaṅkarahitā vidyā nādhigatā, vittaṁ ca na upārjitaṁ, pitroḥ śuśrūṣāpi samāhitena manasā na sampāditā, ālolāyatalocanā yuvatayaḥ svapne 'pi na āliṅgitāḥ, ayaṁ kālaḥ parapiṇḍalolubhatayā kākaiḥ iva preritaḥ* ।

Faultless knowledge has not been gained, nor riches acquired; nor served the parents devotedly; nor, even in dreams, embraced the beloved ones with dancing eyes; whole life has been spent, like greedy crows, in subordination to others.

[Without love for God and the Supreme Being, the restlessness of the human mind never vanishes and there is no stability. Without the mind becoming stable, the door to attaining bliss does not open.

Those people who wear saffron clothes and act to become sages and do not concentrate on God, they waste their rare human life by crying out for food. They do not understand that this human birth has been achieved with great difficulty. It would have been better if they had remained a householder instead of pretending to renounce the world. By remaining worldly, they would have enjoyed the false pleasures of this world. But such hypocrites are lost from both sides.]

Purport — Pretending as a recluse due to hunger for nourishment or desisting from action does not lead to spiritual attainment.

दासत्व की निन्दा

खड्गाग्रैर्न विदारिताः करिघटा नोद्वेजिता वैरिण-
स्तन्वङ्ग्या विपुले नितम्बपुलिने[95] नो क्रीडितं लीलया।
नो जुष्टं गिरिराजनिर्झररणज्झङ्कारि गाङ्गं पयः
कालोऽयं परपिण्डलोलुभतया काकैरिव प्रेरितः ॥ 52 ॥

अन्वय — खड्गाग्रैः करिघटाः न विदारिताः, वैरिणः न उद्वेजिताः, तन्वङ्ग्याः विपुले नितम्बपुलिने लीलया न क्रीडितं, गिरिराजनिर्झररणज्झङ्कारि गाङ्गं पयः न जुष्टं, अयं कालः परपिण्डलोलुभतया काकैः इव प्रेरितः।

न तो हमने खड्गों के अग्र भागों से हाथियों को विदीर्ण किया, न ही शत्रुओं को त्रस्त किया, न तो कामिनी के स्थूल नितम्ब तट पर लीला से काम-क्रीडा की और न ही हिमालय के झरने के झंकृत गंगा के तट पर तपस्या की। पूरा जीवन लोभी कौवों की तरह दूसरों की अधीनता में व्यतीत हो गया।

[धर्म, अर्थ, काम एवं मोक्ष ये चतुर्वर्ग ही मनुष्य जीवन के साध्य हैं। यदि किसी ने अपने जीवन में इन चतुर्वर्गों की प्राप्ति हेतु यत्न नहीं किया तो मनुष्य जीवन आहार, निद्रा, भय और मैथुन में ही व्यतीत करने वाले पशुतुल्य है। जैसे कि कहा गया है —

आहारनिद्राभयमैथुनानि समानि चैतानि नृणां पशूनाम्।
ज्ञाने नराणामधिको विशेषो ज्ञानेन हीना पशुभिः समानाः ॥ — *चाणक्यनीतिः* 7.17]

तात्पर्य — धर्म, अर्थ, काम एवं मोक्ष, इन चतुर्वर्ग में से कोई भी जीवन का साध्य होना चाहिए, अन्यथा जीवन निष्फल होता है।

---

[95] नितम्बफलके — *Ms ORLS-3.*

Reproaching Enslavement

khaḍgāgrairna vidāritāḥ karighaṭā nodvejitā vairiṇa-
stanvaṅgyā vipule nitambapuline no krīḍitaṁ līlayā ।
no juṣṭaṁ girirājanirjhararaṇajjhaṅkāri gāṅgaṁ payaḥ
kālo 'yaṁ parapiṇḍalolubhatayā kākairiva preritaḥ ॥ 52 ॥

anvayaḥ — *khaḍgāgraiḥ karighaṭāḥ na vidāritāḥ, vairiṇaḥ na udvejitāḥ, tanvaṅgyāḥ vipule nitambapuline līlayā na krīḍitaṁ, girirājanirjhararaṇa-jjhaṅkāri gāṅgaṁ payaḥ na juṣṭaṁ, ayaṁ kālaḥ parapiṇḍalolubhatayā kākaiḥ iva preritaḥ* ।

Neither did we dismember the elephants with the points of the swords, nor did we persecute the enemies, neither did we play around with the rounded hips of beautiful women, nor did we do penance on the banks of the Gaṅgā, whumming with the waterfalls of the Himalayas, Whole life has been spent, like greedy crows, in subordination to others.

[*Dharma* = Doing duty as per the Sanātana Dharma, *artha* = ultimate divine wealth, *kāma* = spiritual passion, *mokṣa* = divine liberation, there are the four *puruṣārtha*s (four ways or human efforts of life). If someone does not make efforts to attain these four human efforts of life, then he is like an animal who spends his life in food, sleep, fear and sex. As stated:

āhāranidrābhayamaithunāni samāni caitāni nṛṇāṁ paśūnām ।
jñāne narāṇāmadhiko viśeṣo jñānena hīnā paśubhiḥ samānāḥ ॥
— *Cāṇakyanītiḥ* 7.17]

Purport — Life should have a goal to achieve, that is either *dharma* = righteousness, *artha* = ultimate divine wealth, *kāma* = spiritual passion and *mokṣa* = divine liberation. Without these goals, the life is meaningless.

संसार की सारहीनता

वितीर्णे सर्वस्वे तरुणकरुणापूर्णहृदयाः
स्मरन्तः संसारं विगुणपरिणामावधिगतम्[96] ।

96 संसारे विगुणपरिणामा विधिगतीः — *JKM.1911*, संसारे विगुणपरिणामां विधिगतिं — *GAV.1954.*

वयं पुण्येऽरण्ये[97] परिणतशरच्चन्द्रकिरणा-
  स्त्रियामा[98] नेष्यामो हरचरणचिन्तैकशरणाः[99] ॥ 53 ॥

अन्वय — सर्वस्वे वितीर्णे (सति) तरुणकरुणापूर्णहृदयाः हरचरणचिन्तैकशरणाः विगुणपरिणामावधिगतं संसारं स्मरन्तः वयं पुण्ये अरण्ये (कदा) परिणतशरच्चन्द्रकिरणाः त्रियामाः नेष्यामः?

(विगुणपरिणामावधिगतं = विगुणपरिणामौ + अधिगतं)

सर्वस्व त्यागकर अत्यन्त करुणापूर्ण हृदय से, संसार के अन्त (परिणाम) को सारहीन समझकर, केवल शिव-चरणों के ध्यान को ही अपना शरण समझते हुए, हम शरद् ऋतु के पूर्ण चन्द्र की चाँदनी में, किसी पवित्र वन में बैठे हुए कब रातें बिताएंगे?

तात्पर्य — संसार में जो सुख के साधन दिख रहे हैं, वास्तव में उनका परिणाम सारहीन है। अतः संसार की सारहीनता को समझते हुए चिदानन्द शाश्वत सत्य की उपासना करनी चाहिए।

Intangibility of the World

vitīrṇe sarvasve taruṇakaruṇāpūrṇahṛdayāḥ
  smarantaḥ saṁsāraṁ viguṇapariṇāmāvadhigatam ।
vayaṁ puṇye 'raṇye pariṇataśaraccandrakiraṇā-
  striyāmā neṣyāmo haracaraṇacintaikaśaraṇāḥ ॥ 53 ॥

anvayaḥ — *sarvasve vitīrṇe (sati) taruṇakaruṇāpūrṇahṛdayāḥ haracaraṇa-cintaikaśaraṇāḥ viguṇapariṇāmāvadhigataṁ saṁsāraṁ smarantaḥ vayaṁ puṇye araṇye (kadā) pariṇataśaraccandrakiraṇāḥ triyāmāḥ neṣyāmaḥ?*

Forsaking all, with the heartful of the most tender compassion, considering the end of the world as immaterial, let us spend the nights in holy forests, in the glow of the autumnal moonbeams, meditating on Śiva's feet, our sole shelter.

Purport — The visible material means of happiness in the world are immaterial. Therefore, understanding the intangibility of the world, one should worship the eternal truth, leading to experience the pure consciousness.

---

97 पुण्यारणे — *JKM.1911, GAV.1954.*

98 त्रियामां — *JKM.1911.*

99 हरचरणचित्तैकशरणाः — *JKM.1911.*

तृष्णा ही दरिद्रता है : सन्तोष ही सम्पन्नता

वयमिह परितुष्टा वल्कलैस्त्वं च लक्ष्म्या[100]
सम इह परितोषो निर्विशेषोऽपि शेषः ।
स तु भवतु दरिद्रो यस्य तृष्णा विशाला
मनसि तु परितुष्टे कोऽर्थवान्को दरिद्रः ॥ 54 ॥

अन्वय — इह वयं वल्कलैः परितुष्टाः, त्वं च लक्ष्म्या (परितुष्टः)। इह परितोषः समः, निर्विशेषः अपि शेषः। स तु दरिद्रो भवतु यस्य तृष्णा विशाला। मनसि परितुष्टे तु कः अर्थवान् कः (च) दरिद्रः?

हम वृक्षों की छाल पहनकर सन्तुष्ट हैं; आप लक्ष्मी से सन्तुष्ट हो। हम दोनों का सन्तोष समान है जिसमें कोई भेद न होते हुए भी भेद है, जैसे कि वह दरिद्र है, जिसके मन में तृष्णा है। मन में सन्तोष होने पर कौन धनी और कौन निर्धन है? अर्थात् सन्तोष ही सम्पन्नता एवं असन्तोष ही दारिद्र्य है।

[धनी व्यक्ति धन से भले ही सम्पन्न हो परन्तु उसकी तृष्णा ही अपने दारिद्र्य का बोध कराती है, जो कभी घटती नहीं। इसके विपरीत जो धन-हीन होते हुए भी सन्तुष्ट है, तृष्णा के अभाव से उसे कभी किसी वस्तु की कमी का अनुभव नहीं होता एवं वह सदैव सम्पन्नता का अनुभव करता है। इस प्रकार धनी और निर्धन दोनों में सन्तोष समान होते हुए भी भिन्न है।]

तात्पर्य — तृष्णा ही दरिद्रता एवं सन्तोष ही सम्पन्नता।

Desire Is Poverty: Contentment Is Prosperity

vayamiha parituṣṭā valkalaistvaṁ ca lakṣmyā
sama iha paritoṣo nirviśeṣo 'pi śeṣaḥ ।
sa tu bhavatu daridro yasya tṛṣṇā viśālā
manasi tu parituṣṭe ko 'rthavānko daridraḥ ॥ 54 ॥

anvayaḥ — *iha vayaṁ valkalaiḥ parituṣṭāḥ, tvaṁ ca lakṣmyā (parituṣṭaḥ)* । *iha paritoṣaḥ samaḥ* । *nirviśeṣaḥ api śeṣaḥ* । *sa tu daridro bhavatu yasya tṛṣṇā viśālā* । *manasi parituṣṭe tu kaḥ arthavān kaḥ (ca) daridraḥ?*

We are content to wear tree-barks for clothes, and you with rich dresses; although the contentment is alike, indifferent, still there is a difference. As he, whose desires are numerous, is indeed poor. If contentment is in the mind, then who is rich or poor?

---

[100] दुकूलैः — *JKM.1911, GAV.1954.*

[A rich person may be rich in wealth but his passion itself makes him aware of his poverty, which never decreases. On the contrary, the one who is content despite not having wealth, due to devoid of thirst, he never experiences lack of anything and he always experiences prosperity. Thus, substantially, there is a great difference in between those, although the satisfaction of the rich and the poor is the same.]

Purport — Desire is poverty and contentment is prosperity.

तपस्या का परिणाम

यदेतत्स्वच्छन्दं विहरणमकार्पण्यमशनं
सहार्यैः संवासः श्रुतमुपशमैकव्रतफलम्।
मनो मन्दस्पन्दं बहिरिति[101] चिरस्यापि विमृशन्
न जाने कस्यैषा परिणतिरुदारस्य तपसः ॥ 55 ॥

अन्वय — यदेतत्स्वच्छन्दं विहरणम्, अकार्पण्यम् अशनं, आर्यैः सह संवासः, उपशमैकव्रतफलं श्रुतं, मनो बहिः अपि मन्दस्पन्दं, इति चिरस्य विमृशन् न जाने कस्य उदारस्य तपसः एषा परिणतिः ।

यह जो स्वतन्त्र विहरण, शुद्ध एवं पवित्र भोजन, अभिजात व्यक्तियों की संगति, आत्म निरोध के व्रत का उपदेश देने वाला शास्त्र ज्ञान, अन्तःकरण एवं बाहर भी मन्द एवं संयमित प्रतिक्रिया — दीर्घ चिन्तन के बाद भी मैं यह नहीं समझ पाता कि वह कौन-सी उच्च तपस्या होनी चाहिए जिसके फलस्वरूप ये सब प्राप्त हुए।

तात्पर्य — स्वच्छन्दता, पवित्रता, आत्म निरोध एवं संयमित प्रतिक्रिया — ये सब तप आचरण के लक्षण हैं।

Result of Austerity

yadetatsvacchandaṁ viharaṇamakārpaṇyamaśanaṁ
sahāryaiḥ saṁvāsaḥ śrutamupaśamaikavrataphalam ।
mano mandaspandaṁ bahiriti cirasyāpi vimṛśan
na jāne kasyaiṣā pariṇatirudārasya tapasaḥ ॥ 55 ॥

anvayaḥ — *yadetatsvacchandaṁ viharaṇam, akārpaṇyam aśanaṁ, āryaiḥ saha saṁvāsaḥ, upaśamaikavrataphalaṁ śrutaṁ, mano bahiḥ api mandaspandaṁ, iti cirasya vimṛśan na jāne kasya udārasya tapasaḥ eṣā pariṇatiḥ* ।

---

101 बहिरपि — *JKM.1911, GAV.1954.*

The vows of roaming freely, eating pure food, associating with holy persons and cultivating spiritual wisdom leading to cessation of worries, a restrained antiphon or response inside and out — what should be the lofty austerity that resulted in these, I fail to understand even after a prolonged contemplation.

Purport — Independency, purity, self-control and restrained reaction — all these are characteristics of ascetic conduct.

संन्यासियों की महिमा

पाणिः पात्रं पवित्रं भ्रमणपरिगतं भैक्षमक्षय्यमन्नं
विस्तीर्णं वस्त्रमाशादशकमपमलं[102] तल्पमस्वल्पमुर्वी।
येषां निःसङ्गताङ्गीकरणपरिणतिः[103] स्वान्तसंतोषिणस्ते
धन्याः संन्यस्तवृत्ति[104] व्यतिकरनिकराः कर्म निर्मूलयन्ति ॥ 56 ॥

अन्वय — ते स्वान्तसंतोषिणः संन्यस्तवृत्तिव्यतिकरनिकराः धन्याः कर्म निर्मूलयन्ति येषां निःसङ्गताङ्गीकरणपरिणतिः पाणिः पवित्रं पात्रं, भ्रमणपरिगतं भैक्षम् अक्षय्यम् अन्नं, विस्तीर्णं आशादशकम् अपमलं वस्त्रं, उर्वी (च) अस्वल्पं तल्पम् ।

जिन्हें अपनी आत्मा में ही सन्तोष रहता है, संन्यास वृत्ति का अवलम्बन करते हुए कर्म का नाश करते रहते हैं, परिग्रह-त्याग-रूप परिणति वाले हाथ ही जिनके पवित्र पात्र हैं, सदा भ्रमण करते हुए प्राप्त भिक्षा ही जिनका अक्षय अन्न है, विस्तीर्ण दश दिशाएं जिनके निर्मल वस्त्र हैं, सम्पूर्ण पृथ्वी ही जिनकी शय्या है, ऐसे महात्मा लोग धन्य हैं।

[जिन्होंने सबसे मन हटाकर, सब तरह के विषयों को त्यागकर, संसारी मायाजाल काटकर अपनी आत्मा में ही सन्तोष कर लिया है; जो किसी भी वस्तु की आकांक्षा नहीं रखते, यहाँ तक कि जल पीने को भी कोई बर्तन पास नहीं रखते; अपने हाथों से ही बर्तन का काम लेते हैं; खाने के लिए घर में सामान नहीं रखते, कल के भोजन की फ़िक्र नहीं करते, आज इस गाँव में माँगकर पेट भर लेते हैं तो कल दूसरे गाँव में जा माँगते हैं, एक गाँव में दो रात नहीं बिताते; जो शरीर ढकने के लिए वस्त्रों की भी जरुरत नहीं रखते, दशों दिशाओं को ही अपना वस्त्र समझते हैं; जो पलंग-तोशक, गद्दे-तकियों की आवश्यकता नहीं समझते, जो किसी का संग नहीं करते, अकेले रहते हैं, वैराग्य में ही परमानन्द समझते हैं; जो किसी के सामने दीनता नहीं करते और अपने स्वरूप में ही मगन

---

102 अचपलं — *GAV.1954.*

103 निःसङ्गतान्तःकरणपरिणतिः स्वात्मसंतोषिणस्ते — *JKM.1911.*

104 संन्यस्तदैन्य — *Ms ORLS-3, JKM.1911, GAV.1954.*

रहते हैं, वे पुरुष वास्तव में ही महापुरुष हैं। ऐसे पुरुष-रत्न धन्य हैं ! उन्होंने निश्चय ही कर्मबन्धन काट दिया है । वे ही सच्चे त्यागी और संन्यासी हैं।

वही संन्यासी परमेश्वर को प्रिय है। जैसा कि भगवान् श्रीकृष्ण ने *गीता* XII.16 में कहा है —

अनपेक्षः शुचिर्दक्ष उदासीनो गतव्यथः ।
सर्वारम्भपरित्यागी यो मद्भक्तः स मे प्रियः ॥

वे जो सांसारिक प्रलोभनों से उदासीन रहते हैं बाह्य और आन्तरिक रूप से शुद्ध, निपुण, चिन्तारहित, कष्टरहित और सभी कार्य-कलापों में स्वार्थरहित रहते हैं, मेरे ऐसे भक्त मुझे अतिप्रिय हैं।]

तात्पर्य — संन्यास ही परमानन्द के मार्ग पर उत्कृष्ट साधना है।

Glory of Monks

pāṇiḥ pātraṁ pavitraṁ bhramaṇaparigataṁ bhaikṣama-
kṣayyamannaṁ
vistīrṇaṁ vastramāśādaśakamapamalaṁ talpamasvalpamurvī ।
yeṣāṁ niḥsaṅgatāṅgīkaraṇapariṇatiḥ svāntasaṁtoṣiṇaste
dhanyāḥ saṁnyastavṛttivyatikaranikarāḥ karma nirmūlayanti ॥ 56 ॥

anvayaḥ — *te svāntasaṁtoṣiṇaḥ saṁnyastavṛttivyatikaranikarāḥ dhanyāḥ karma nirmūlayanti yeṣāṁ niḥsaṅgatāṅgīkaraṇapariṇatiḥ pāṇiḥ pavitraṁ pātraṁ, bhramaṇaparigataṁ bhaikṣam akṣayyam annaṁ, vistīrṇaṁ āśādaśakam apamalaṁ vastraṁ, urvī* (*ca*) *asvalpaṁ talpam* ।

Blessed are such great people, who remain content in their own soul, who keep destroying the *karma* by relying on the attitude of renunciation, whose hands are the sacred vessels leading to renunciation, whose inexhaustible food is the alms obtained while strolling, who have the vast expanse of the ten directions as clothes.

[Those, who have renounced all kinds of subjects of sensual pleasure, have cut off the web of worldly illusion and have become content in their soul; who do not aspire to anything; who do not even expect any vessel for drinking water and utensils to eat; who do not worry about tomorrow's food; who do not even need clothes to cover their body, who consider only ten directions as their clothes; who do not need beds, covers, mattresses and pillows; who do not associate with anyone; who live alone and contemplate only in renunciation, are truly blessed great men. They have definitely cut off the bondage of *karma*. They are the true renunciant and ascetics.

He is the monk dear to God. As said by Lord Śrīkṛṣṇa in *Śrīmadbhagavadgītā* XII.16:

anapekṣaḥ śucirdakṣa udāsīno gatavyathaḥ ।
sarvārambhaparityāgī yo madbhaktaḥ sa me priyaḥ ॥

Meaning: He who is free from wants, pure, expert, unconcerned, and free from pain, renouncing all undertakings and commencements, he who is devoted to me is dear to me.]

Purport — Renunciation is the sublime practice on the path to Supreme Bliss.

धन-संग्रह की अनावश्यकता

भिक्षा कामदुघा धेनुः कन्था शीतनिवारिणी ।
अचला च शिवे भक्तिर्विभवैः किं प्रयोजनम् ॥ 57 ॥

अन्वय — भिक्षा कामदुघा धेनुः, कन्था शीतनिवारिणी, शिवे च अचला भक्तिः, विभवैः किं प्रयोजनम्?

भिक्षा ही कामधेनु की तरह जिसकी आवश्यकता को पूर्ण करने वाली है, जीर्ण वस्त्र ही जिसके शीत एवं आतप आदि का निवारण करने वाला है, भगवान् शिव में जिसकी स्थिर भक्ति है, उसके लिए धन-सम्पत्ति का प्रयोजन क्या है?

[व्यक्ति अपनी अनपेक्षित एवं अतिरेक तृष्णा की पूर्ति हेतु धन इकट्ठा करना चाहता है। तृष्णा एवं वासना से रहित व्यक्ति के लिए धन-सम्पत्ति संग्रह करने की आवश्यकता ही क्या है? *श्रीमद्भागवत पुराण* 7.14.8 में भगवान् व्यास देव ने कहा है —

यावद् भ्रियेत जठरं तावत् स्वत्वं हि देहिनाम् ।
अधिकं योऽभिमन्येत स स्तेनो दण्डमर्हति ॥

अर्थात् लोगों को केवल उतने पर ही अधिकार है जिससे उनकी उदर-पूर्ति जैसी मूलभूत आवश्यकताएं पूरी हो सकें। इससे अधिक की कामना जो करता है वह चोर है और दण्ड का पात्र है।]

तात्पर्य — तृष्णा एवं वासना से रहित व्यक्ति के लिए धन-सम्पत्ति संग्रह करने की आवश्यकता नहीं है। अतः धन-संग्रह की स्पृहा अनुचित है।

Abdication of Yearning for Wealth

bhikṣā kāmadughā dhenuḥ kanthā śītanivāriṇī ।
acalā ca śive bhaktirvibhavaiḥ kiṁ prayojanam ॥ 57 ॥

anvayaḥ — *bhikṣā kāmadughā dhenuḥ, kanthā śītanivāriṇī, śive ca acalā bhaktiḥ, vibhavaiḥ kiṁ prayojanam?*

Who depends on alms only like Kāmadhenu to fulfil his/her needs, who relies on old and torn-out clothes only to get relief from cold and heat, etc. and who has steadfast devotion towards Lord Śiva, then what is the purpose of wealth for him/her?

[A person wants to collect money only to satisfy his unexpected and excessive rapacity. For a person who is free from thirst and lust, what is the need to accumulate wealth? Śrī Vyāsa Deva has rightly said in *Śrīmadbhāgavata Purāṇa* 7.14.8:

> *yāvad bhriyeta jaṭharaṁ tāvat svatvaṁ hi dehinām* ।
> *adhikaṁ yo 'bhimanyeta sa steno daṇḍamarhati* ॥

Meaning: One may claim proprietorship to as much wealth as required to maintain body and soul together, but one, who desires proprietorship over more than that, must be considered a thief, and he deserves to be punished by the laws of Nature.]

Purport — There is no need to accumulate wealth for a person who is free from thirst and lust. Therefore, the desire to accumulate wealth is inappropriate.

तपोमार्ग ही परम श्रेय का द्वार

> दुराराधा[105]श्चामी तुरगचलचित्ताः क्षितिभुजो
> वयं च स्थूलेच्छाः सुमहति फले[106] बद्धमनसः ।
> जरा देहं मृत्युर्हरति दयितं[107] जीवितमिति
> सखे नान्यच्छ्रेयो जगति विदुषोऽन्यत्र तपसः ॥ 58 ॥

अन्वय — अमी क्षितिभुजो दुराराधाः तुरगचलचित्ताः च, वयं च स्थूलेच्छाः सुमहति फले बद्धमनसः । हे सखे! जरा देहं, मृत्युः दयितं जीवितं हरति इति जगति विदुषः तपसः अन्यत्र अन्यत् श्रेयः न ।

राजाओं के चित्त तो घोड़े की गति की तरह चञ्चल हैं अतः उनको प्रसन्न रखना कठिन है। हमारे मन में भी ऊँचे-ऊँचे पद पाने की लालसा है। इधर शरीर को वृद्धावस्था और प्रिय

---

105 दुराराध्याः — *JKM.1911, GAV.1954.*

106 पदे — *Ms ORLS-3.*

107 सकलं — *JKM.1911.*

जीवन को मृत्यु हर लेती है। ऐसे में लगता है कि विवेकवान और विद्वान् पुरुषों के लिए तपोबल के अलावा अन्य कोई श्रेय का मार्ग नहीं है।

[इच्छाएं अनन्त हैं और इनका कहीं अन्त नहीं है। आदमी अपने भौतिक लक्ष्यों की पूर्ति में लगा रहता कि उसे बुढ़ापा घेर लेता है। ऐसे में तो केवल एक ही बात उचित लगती है कि अपना समय सत्संग, भक्ति तथा आध्यात्मिक ज्ञान ग्रहण करने में बिताना चाहिए जिससे तत्त्व ज्ञान होने पर इस संसार में दुःख तथा मानसिक सन्ताप से छुटाकारा पाया जा सके।]

तात्पर्य — भौतिक इच्छाएं, जागतिक वासनाएं, शरीर एवं जीवन आदि समस्त ऐहिक श्रेय नाशशील हैं। अतः केवल तपोमार्ग से ही पारमार्थिक श्रेय-प्राप्ति का प्रयास करना चाहिए।

Path of Penance: The Gateway to the Ultimate Virtue

durārādhāścāmī turagacalacittāḥ kṣitibhujo
vayaṁ ca sthūlecchāḥ sumahati phale baddhamanasaḥ ।
jarā dehaṁ mṛtyurharati dayitaṁ jīvitamiti
sakhe nānyacchreyo jagati viduṣo 'nyatra tapasaḥ ॥ 58 ॥

anvayaḥ — *amī kṣitibhujo durārādhāḥ turagacalacittāḥ ca, vayaṁ ca sthūlecchāḥ sumahati phale baddhamanasaḥ* । *he sakhe! jarā dehaṁ, mṛtyuḥ dayitaṁ jīvitaṁ harati iti jagati viduṣaḥ tapasaḥ anyatra anyat śreyaḥ na* ।

These rulers of the world have minds restless like a horse and (therefore) are difficult to be pleased, while we are ambitious with minds pitched on vast gain; age steals away bodily strength and death cuts short this dear life. Oh friend!, nothing is good for the wise in this world except the practice of austerities!

[Desires are infinite and have no end. While an individual is busy in achieving his material goals, old age overtakes him. Therefore, one should spend one's time in the devotion, acquiring spiritual knowledge and association of nobles; so that by having the knowledge of the superconsciousness, one can get relief from sorrow and mental anguish in this world.]

Purport — All worldly happinesses, such as material desires, passions, the body and the life, are perishable. Therefore, one should strive to attain the transcendental good only through the path of penance.

योग-साधना से ही ध्येय-प्राप्ति

भोगा मेघवितानमध्यविलसत्सौदामिनी[108]चञ्चला
आयुर्वायुविघट्टिताब्ज[109]पटलीलीनाम्बुवद्भङ्गुरम्।
लोला यौवनलालना[110]स्तनुभृतामित्याकलय्य द्रुतं
योगे [111]ध्येयसमाधिसिद्धिसुभगे बुद्धिं विदध्वं बुधाः ॥ 59 ॥

अन्वय — भोगाः मेघवितानमध्यविलसत्सौदामिनीचञ्चलाः, आयुः वायुविघट्टिताब्जपटलीलीनाम्बुवद्भङ्गुरम्। तनुभृतां यौवनलालनाः लोला इति आकलय्य हे बुधाः! ध्येयसमाधिसिद्धिसुभगे योगे द्रुतं बुद्धिं विदध्वम्।

देहधारियों के भोग-विषय सुख-रूपी सघन बादलों में चमकने वाली बिजली की तरह चञ्चल हैं; मनुष्यों की आयु या उम्र हवा से कम्पमान कमल के जल के समान क्षणस्थायी या नाशमान है और जवानी की उमंग भी स्थिर नहीं है। इसलिए बुद्धिमानों! धैर्य से चित्त को एकाग्र करके उसे ध्येय-प्राप्ति हेतु योग-साधना में लगाओ।

[विषय-भोग, आयु और यौवन को अनित्य और क्षणभंगुर समझकर इनमें आसक्ति न रखते हुए और मन को एकाग्र करके प्रत्येक क्षण परमात्मा का भजन करें तो जन्म-मरण से छुटकारा मिल सकता है और परमानन्द की प्राप्ति हो सकती है। *सुभाषितावली* में लिखा है —

चला विभूतिः क्षणभंगि यौवनं कृतान्तदन्तान्तरवर्ति जीवितम्।
तथाप्यवज्ञा परलोकसाधने नृणामहो विस्मयकारि चेष्टितम्॥

विभूति चञ्चल है, यौवन क्षणभंगुर है, जीवन काल के दाँतों में है; तो भी लोग परलोक साधन की परवाह नहीं करते। मनुष्यों की यह चेष्टा विस्मयकारक है!]

तात्पर्य — अस्थिर संसार में चित्त को योग-साधना द्वारा स्थिर करके ध्येय-प्राप्ति हेतु प्रयत्न करना चाहिए।

Attainment of Supreme Consciousness Through the Practice of Equanimity

bhogā meghavitānamadhyavilasatsaudāminīcañcalā
āyurvāyuvighaṭṭitābjapaṭalīlīnāmbuvadbhaṅguram ।

108 सौदामनी — *Ms ORLS-3.*

109 अभ्र — *JKM.1911.*

110 लालसा — *GAV.1954.*

111 धैर्य — *JKM.1911, GAV.1954.*

lolā yauvanalālanāstanubhṛtāmityākalayya drutaṁ
yoge dhyeyasamādhisiddhisubhage buddhiṁ vidadhvaṁ budhāḥ ॥ 59 ॥

anvayaḥ — *bhogāḥ meghavitānamadhyavilasatsaudāminīcañcalāḥ, āyuḥ vāyuvighaṭṭitābjapaṭalīlīnāmbuvadbhaṅguram* । *tanubhṛtāṁ yauvanalālanāḥ lolā iti ākalayya he budhāḥ! dhyeyasamādhisiddhisubhage yoge drutaṁ buddhiṁ vidadhvam* ।

Sensual pleasures are as fickle as the flash of lightning in the clouds. Life can collapse as easily as the drop of water on the edge of a lotus leaf swayed by the wind. Fickle are the longings in youth. Quickly realizing this, let the wise ones engage their minds in equanimity, attained easily by courage.

[Considering sensual pleasures, age and youth as impermanent and transitory, without having any attachment to them and concentrating the mind and worshipping God persistently, one can get relieved from the cycle of birth and death to attain bliss. Thus, it is stated in *Subhāṣitāvalī*:

calā vibhūtiḥ kṣaṇabhaṅgi yauvanaṁ
kṛtāntadantāntaravarti jīvitam ।
tathāpyavajñā paralokasādhane nṛṇāmaho
vismayakāri ceṣṭitam ॥

Prosperity and power are fickle, youth is fleeting, life is in the teeth of time; still, it is astonishing that people do not care about the afterlife. This effort of humans is surprising!]

Purport — One should endeavour to attain supreme consciousness through the practice of equanimity.

बन्धुओं में याचना की निन्दा

पुण्ये ग्रामे वने वा महति सितपटच्छन्नपालीं कपाली-
मादाय न्यायगर्भद्विजहुतहुतभुग्धूमवर्णोपकण्ठम्[112] ।
द्वारं द्वारं प्रवृत्तो वरमुदरदरीपूरणाय क्षुधार्तो
मानी प्राणैः सनाथो[113] न पुनरनुदिनं तुल्यकुल्येषु दीनः ॥ 60 ॥

112 धूमधुम्रोपकण्ठम् — *JKM.1911*, धूमधुम्रोपकण्ठे — *GAV.1954.*

113 प्राणी स्वदेशे — *JKM.1911.*

अन्वय — क्षुधार्तो मानी प्राणैः सनाथो उदरदरीपूरणाय पुण्ये ग्रामे महति वने वा सितपटच्छन्नपालीं कपालीम् आदाय न्यायगर्भद्विजहुतहुतभुग्धूमवर्णोपकण्ठं द्वारं द्वारं प्रवृत्तो वरमु, न पुनः अनुदिनं तुल्यकुल्येषु दीनः (वरम्)।

वह क्षुधार्त किन्तु स्वाभिमानी पुरुष, जो अपने पेट-रूपी खड्डे को भरने के लिए हाथ में सफेद कपड़े से ढका हुआ भीख का कटोरा लेकर वन-वन और गाँव-गाँव घूमता है और उनके दरवाज़े पर जाते हुए अच्छा समझता है, जिनकी द्वारदेश न्यायतः विद्वान् ब्राह्मणों द्वारा कराए हुए हवन के धुँए से मलिन हो रही है, अच्छा है; किन्तु वह समान कुल वालों के यहाँ जाकर भीख माँगना पसन्द नहीं करता।

तात्पर्य — बन्धुओं में याचना से स्वाभिमान नष्ट हो जाता है जो कि मृत्यु से भी अधिक दुःखदायी है।

Censuring Entreaty Among Compeers

puṇye grāme vane vā mahati sitapaṭacchannapālīṁ kapālī-
mādāya nyāyagarbhadvijahutahutabhugdhūmavarṇopa-
kaṇṭham ।
dvāraṁ dvāraṁ pravṛtto varamudaradarīpūraṇāya kṣudhārto
mānī prāṇaiḥ sanātho na punaranudinaṁ tulyakulyeṣu
dīnaḥ ॥ 60 ॥

anvayaḥ — *kṣudhārto mānī prāṇaiḥ sanātho udaradarīpūraṇāya puṇye grāme mahati vane vā sitapaṭacchannapālīṁ kapālīm ādāya nyāyagarbhadvijahutahutabhugdhūmavarṇopakaṇṭhaṁ dvāraṁ dvāraṁ pravṛtto varamu, na punaḥ anudinaṁ tulyakulyeṣu dīnaḥ (varam)* ।

Wandering in holy places or extensive forests, whose outskirts are grey with smoke of fires tended by priests who are experts in rituals; a begging bowl in hand covered with a white cloth; going from door to door to appease the distressing hunger by filling the stomach and sustaining the energy, is preferred by a self-respecting person to being a beggar among his compeers every day.

Purport — Imploringness among brothers destroys one's self-respect, which is more painful than death.

स्तुति और निन्दा में समभाव ही संन्यास

चण्डालः किमयं द्विजातिरथवा शूद्रोऽथ किं[114] तापसः
किं वा तत्त्वविशेष[115]पेशलमतिर्योगीश्वरः कोऽपि वा।
इत्युत्पन्नविकल्पजल्पमुखरैः संभाष्यमाणा जनैः
नो क्रुद्धाः पथि नैव तुष्टमनसो यान्ति स्वयं योगिनः ॥ 61 ॥

अन्वय — किम् अयं चण्डालः अथवा द्विजातिः, किं शूद्रः अथ तापसः, किं वा तत्त्वविशेषपेशलमतिः कोऽपि योगीश्वरः वा? इति उत्पन्नविकल्पजल्पमुखरैः जनैः संभाष्यमाणाः योगिनः स्वयं नो क्रुद्धाः नैव तुष्टमनसः (सन्तः) पथि यान्ति।

यह चाण्डाल है या ब्राह्मण? यह शूद्र है या तपस्वी? क्या यह तत्त्वविद् योगीश्वर है? लोगों की ऐसी अनेक प्रकार की संशय और विकल्पयुक्त बातें सुनकर योगी लोग न क्रुद्ध होते हैं और न ही प्रसन्न होते हैं; अपितु वे अपनी राह चले जाते हैं ।

[*श्रीमद्भगवद्गीता* XII.19 में कहा गया है कि निन्दा एवं स्तुति उभय में समान भाव रखने वाला व्यक्ति ईश्वर का प्रिय होता है। जैसे कि —

तुल्यनिन्दास्तुतिर्मौनी संतुष्टो येन केनचित्।
अनिकेतः स्थिरमतिर्भक्तिमान्मे प्रियो नरः ॥

जो निन्दा-स्तुति को समान समझने वाला, मननशील और जिस किसी प्रकार से भी शरीर का निर्वाह होने में सदा ही सन्तुष्ट है और रहने के स्थान में ममता और आसक्ति से रहित है — वह स्थिरबुद्धि भक्तिमान् पुरुष मुझको प्रिय है।]

तात्पर्य — सुख एवं दुःख, मान एवं अपमान आदि द्वन्द्वों में समभाव बनाए रखना ही वास्तविक योग है।

Renunciation Is Equanimity between Praise and Criticism

caṇḍālaḥ kimayaṁ dvijātirathavā śūdro 'tha kiṁ tāpasaḥ
kiṁ vā tattvaviśeṣapeśalamatiryogīśvaraḥ ko 'pi vā ।
ityutpannavikalpajalpamukharaiḥ saṁbhāṣyamāṇā janaiḥ
no kruddhāḥ pathi naiva tuṣṭamanaso yānti svayaṁ yoginaḥ ॥ 61 ॥

anvayaḥ — *kim ayaṁ caṇḍālaḥ athavā dvijātiḥ, kiṁ śūdraḥ atha tāpasaḥ, kiṁ vā tattvaviśeṣapeśalamatiḥ ko 'pi ryogīśvaraḥ vā? iti utpannavikalpajalpa-*

[114] वा — *Ms ORLS-3.*

[115] विवेक — *JKM.1911, GAV.1954.*

mukharaiḥ janaiḥ saṁbhāṣyamāṇāḥ yoginaḥ svayaṁ no kruddhāḥ naiva tuṣṭamanasaḥ (santaḥ) pathi yānti ।

"Is this person an outcaste? or a brāhmaṇa? or a śūdra? or an ascetic? or else a master *yogī* with the mind filled with philosophical discernment?" When people address the ascetic thus, doubting and debating garrulously, the *yogī*s themselves walk away, neither angry nor pleased.

[It is said in *Śrīmadbhagavadgītā* XII.19 that a person who has equal feelings towards praise and criticism is loved by God. Thus cited below:

> *tulyanindāstutirmaunī saṅtuṣṭo yena kenacit* ।
> *aniketaḥ sthiramatirbhaktimānme priyo naraḥ* ॥

He who is neutral in censure and praise, he who is silent, content with anything (in the world), does not claim any residence as his home, he who is steady-minded, full of devotion; that man is dear to Me.]

Purport — Real *yoga* (ascetism) is to maintain equanimity in conflicts like happiness and sorrow, respect and humility.

परमानन्द-प्राप्ति के मार्ग

> एतस्माद्विरमेन्द्रियार्थगहनादायासकादाश्रय-
> श्रेयोमार्गमशेषदुःखदहन[116]व्यापारदक्षं क्रमात्[117] ।
> स्वास्थ्यं तावदपेहि[118] संत्यज निजां कल्लोललोलां गतिं
> मा भूयो भज भङ्गुरां भवरतिं चेतः प्रसीदाधुना ॥ 62 ॥

अन्वय — एतस्माद् आयासकात् इन्द्रियार्थगहनात् क्रमात् विरम। अशेषदुःखदहनव्यापारदक्षम् आश्रयश्रेयोमार्गम् भज। तावत् स्वास्थ्यम् अपेहि, निजां कल्लोललोलां गतिं संत्यज, भङ्गुरां भवरतिं भूयो मा भज। चेतः! अधुना प्रसीद।

हे चित्त! इन्हीं इन्द्रियों के विषय जो कि परिणामतः अत्यधिक दुःख देने वाले हैं, उनसे धीरे-धीरे दूरी बना लो। अनन्त पीड़ा को दग्ध करने में कुशल आश्रय और श्रेय के उस

---

116 शमन — *JKM.1911, GAV.1954.*

117 क्षणात् — *JKM.1911, GAV.1954.*

118 शान्तं भावमुपैहि — *JKM.1911,* स्वात्मीभावमुपैहि — *GAV.1954.*

मार्ग की पूजा करो। इन्द्रियार्थों की सेवा से उत्पन्न सन्तोष का त्याग करो। तरंग के समान चञ्चल चाल को छोड़ दो; नाशमान संसारी पदार्थों में पुनः अनुराग रखना छोड दो। बहुत कहना व्यर्थ है, अब तुम अपने आप में ही प्रसन्न रहो।

तात्पर्य — अनन्त दुःखों के कारण सांसारिक सुखों के प्रति आसक्ति से दूर रहते हुए ही स्वयं के अन्तःकरण में सत् चित् एवं आनन्द का अनुभव करना चाहिए।

Way to Ultimate Happiness

etasmādviramendriyārthagahanādāyāsakādāśraya-
śreyomārgamaśeṣaduḥkhadahanavyāpāradakṣaṁ kramāt ।
svāsthyaṁ tāvadapehi saṁtyaja nijāṁ kallolalolāṁ gatiṁ
mā bhūyo bhaja bhaṅgurāṁ bhavaratiṁ cetaḥ prasīdādhunā ॥ 62 ॥

anvayaḥ — *etasmād āyāsakāt indriyārthagahanāt kramāt virama* । *aśeṣa-duḥkhadahanavyāpāradakṣam āśrayaśreyomārgam bhaja* । *tāvat svāsthyam apehi, nijāṁ kallolalolāṁ gatiṁ saṁtyaja, bhaṅgurāṁ bhavaratiṁ bhūyo mā bhaja* । *cetaḥ! adhunā prasīda* ।

Oh mind! gradually distance yourself from the perilous maze of sense-objects which result in immense suffering. Worship that path of shelter and ultimate goodness, skilled in burning infinite suffering. Give up the satisfaction arising out of enjoying the senses. Abandon the wavelike agitation and change. Do not cling to the transitory joys of the world. Stop having attachment to perishable and fragile worldly objects. Now seek the tranquillity of the mind and reach the state of your True Self.

Purport — One should experience true consciousness and joy within oneself while staying away from attachment to worldly pleasures leading to infinite sorrows.

वैराग्य से संसार पर विजय

पुण्यैर्मूलफलैः प्रियां प्रणयिनीं[119] वृत्तिं कुरुष्वाधुना
भूःशय्यातृणवल्कलैरकृपणै[120]रुत्तिष्ठ यामो वनम्।

[119] प्रियैश्च सलिलैः — *JKM.1911*, तथा प्रणयिनीं — *GAV.1954.*

[120] भूशय्यानववल्कलैरकरुणै — *JKM.1911.*

क्षुद्राणामविवेकमूढमनसां यत्रेश्वराणां नहि[121]
वित्तव्याधिविकारविह्वलधियां[122] नामापि न श्रूयते ॥ 63 ॥

अन्वय — अधुना पुण्यैः अकृपणैः मूलफलैः भूः-शय्या-तृणवल्कलैः प्रियां प्रणयिनीं वृत्तिं कुरुष्व, उत्तिष्ठ वनं यामः, यत्र अविवेकमूढमनसां क्षुद्राणां नहि, वित्तव्याधिविकारविह्वलधियाम् ईश्वराणाम् अपि नाम न श्रूयते।

हे चित्त! अब तू पवित्र एवं पर्याप्त फल-मूलों से अपनी गुज़र कर; बनी-बनाई भूमि-शय्या और वृक्षों की छाल के वस्त्रों से अपना निर्वाह कर। उठ, हम तो वन में जाते हैं, जहाँ उन मूर्ख और विचार-बुद्धिहीन और धन की व्याधि से विकृत बुद्धि वालों का नाम भी नहीं सुनाई देता।

तात्पर्य — धन की गर्मी से पीड़ित लोगों पर विजय पाने का सबसे अच्छा साधन संन्यास ही है।

Conquer the World Through Renunciation

puṇyairmūlaphalaiḥ priyāṁ praṇayinīṁ vṛttiṁ kuruṣvādhunā
bhūḥśayyātṛṇavalkalairakṛpaṇairuttiṣṭha yāmo vanam ।
kṣudrāṇāmavivekamūḍhamanasāṁ yatreśvarāṇāṁ nahi
vittavyādhivikāravihvaladhiyāṁ nāmāpi na śrūyate ॥ 63 ॥

anvayaḥ — *adhunā puṇyaiḥ akṛpaṇaiḥ mūlaphalaiḥ bhūḥ-śayyā-tṛṇavalkalaiḥ priyāṁ praṇayinīṁ vṛttiṁ kuruṣva, uttiṣṭha vanaṁ yāmaḥ, yatra avivekamūḍhamanasāṁ kṣudrāṇāṁ nahi, vittavyādhivikāravihvaladhiyām īśvarāṇām api nāma na śrūyate* ।

Oh mind! now maintain yourself lovingly with the sacred roots and fruits for sustenance and the earth covered with fresh leaves of branches for a bed. Let us go forth to the forest, where people whose minds are mean and devoid of discretion, and who always talk excruciatingly of the afflictions of wealth are not even heard of.

Purport — The best way to conquer over the people afflicted by the warmth of wealth is renunciation.

---

[121] सदा — *Ms ORLS-3, JKM.1911, GAV.1954.*

[122] गिरां — *JKM.1911, GAV.1954.*

परम तत्त्व का आसंग

मोहं [123]मार्जयतामुपार्जय रतिं चन्द्रार्धचूडामणौ
चेतः स्वर्गतरङ्गिणीतटभुवामासङ्गमङ्गीकुरु[124]।
को वा वीचिषु बुद्बुदेषु च तडिल्लेखासु च स्त्रीषु[125] च
ज्वालाग्रेषु च पन्नगेषु च सरिद्दुर्गेषु[126] च प्रत्ययः ॥ 64 ॥

अन्वय — हे चेतः! मोहं मार्जयतां स्वर्गतरङ्गिणीतटभुवाम् आसङ्गम् अङ्गीकुरु, चन्द्रार्धचूडामणौ रतिम् उपार्जय। वीचिषु, बुद्बुदेषु च, तडिल्लेखासु च, स्त्रीषु च, ज्वालाग्रेषु च, पन्नगेषु च, सरिद्दुर्गेषु च, को वा प्रत्ययः?

हे चित्त! तू मोह को नष्ट करने वाले गंगा किनारे के वृक्षों के नीचे विश्राम ले और शिर पर अर्द्धचन्द्र धारण करने वाले भगवान् शिव से प्रीति कर। देख! पानी की लहरों, पानी के बुलबुलों, बिजली की चमक, लक्ष्मी या धन-दौलत पर आग की लौ, स्त्री, सर्प और नदी के प्रवाह की स्थिरता पर कोई विश्वास नहीं करना चाहिए; क्योंकि ये सातों चञ्चल हैं।

तात्पर्य — व्यक्ति को अस्थिर संसार का भ्रम त्यागकर परम तत्त्व पर ध्यान केन्द्रित करना चाहिए जिससे इहलोक एवं परलोक में अनन्त सुख की प्राप्ति हो।

Focusing on the Reality

mohaṁ mārjayatāmupārjaya ratiṁ candrārdhacūḍāmaṇau
cetaḥ svargataraṅgiṇītaṭabhuvāmāsaṅgamaṅgīkuru ।
ko vā vīciṣu budbudeṣu ca taḍillekhāsu ca strīṣu ca
jvālāgreṣu ca pannageṣu ca sariddūrgeṣu ca pratyayaḥ ॥ 64 ॥

anvayaḥ — *he cetaḥ! mohaṁ mārjayatāṁ svargataraṅgiṇītaṭabhuvām āsaṅgam aṅgīkuru, candrārdhacūḍāmaṇau ratim upārjaya* । *vīciṣu, budbudeṣu ca, taḍillekhāsu ca, strīṣu ca, jvālāgreṣu ca, pannageṣu ca, saridvargeṣu ca, ko vā pratyayaḥ?*

Oh mind! you take rest under the trees on the banks of Gaṅgā, which destroys all delusion, worship and love Lord Śiva, who wears the crescent moon on his head. See, one should not believe

---

123 मार्जय तां — *JKM.1911, GAV.1954.*

124 संसर्गमङ्गीकुरु — *Ms ORLS-3.*

125 श्रीषु — *GAV.1954.*

126 सरिद्दुर्गेषु — *Ms ORLS.3*, सरिद्वेगेषु — *JKM.1911, GAV.1954.*

in the waves of water, the water acacias, the flash of lightning, wealth, the flame of fire, women, snakes and the stability of the flow of the river; because all seven are fickle.

Purport — An individual should give up the illusion of the unstable world and concentrate on the Supreme Truth so that he/she can attain eternal happiness in this world and the next.

सांसारिक आसक्तियों की लम्पटता

अग्रे गीतं सरसकवयः पार्श्वयोर्दाक्षिणात्याः
पृष्ठे[127] लीलावलयरणितं चामरग्राहिणीनाम्।
यद्यस्त्येवं कुरु भवरसास्वादने लम्पटत्वं
नो चेच्चेतः प्रविश सहसा निर्विकल्पे समाधौ ॥ 65 ॥

अन्वय — अग्रे गीतं, पार्श्वयोः दाक्षिणात्याः सरसकवयः, पृष्ठे चामरग्राहिणीनां लीलावलयरणितम्। यदि एवम् अस्ति भवरसास्वादने लम्पटत्वं कुरु, नो चेत् हे चेतः! सहसा निर्विकल्पे समाधौ प्रविश।

हे मन! तेरे सामने चतुर गवैये गाते हों, दाहिने-बाएं दक्षिण देश के दक्ष कवि सरस काव्य सुनाते हों, तेरे पीछे चामर ढोलने वाली सुन्दर स्त्रियों के कंकणों की मधुर झंकार होती हो, यदि ऐसे उपभोग के अवसर हों, तो तुम संसार के रसास्वादन में लम्पटता करो; नहीं तो सब कुछ छोड़कर निर्विकल्प समाधि में लीन हो जाओ।

तात्पर्य — क्षणिक सुख-प्राप्ति हेतु सांसारिक आसक्ति-रूप लम्पटता को त्यागकर अनन्त सुख की प्राप्ति हेतु निर्विकल्प समाधि में लीन होना ही उचित है।

Dissoluteness of Worldly Attachments

agre gītaṁ sarasakavayaḥ pārśvayordākṣiṇātyāḥ
pṛṣṭhe līlāvalayaraṇitaṁ cāmaragrāhiṇīnām ।
yadyastyevaṁ kuru bhavarasāsvādane lampaṭatvaṁ
no ceccetaḥ praviśa sahasā nirvikalpe samādhau ॥ 65 ॥

anvayaḥ — *agre gītaṁ, pārśvayoḥ dākṣiṇātyāḥ sarasakavayaḥ, pṛṣṭhe cāmaragrāhiṇīnāṁ līlāvalayaraṇitam* । *yadi evam asti bhavarasāsvādane lampaṭatvaṁ kuru, no cet he cetaḥ! sahasā nirvikalpe samādhau praviśa* ।

---

[127] पश्चात् — *GAV.1954.*

If there be music playing in front of you, by your side expert poets from the south and behind you the courtesans waving fans and shaking their bracelets with a clinking sound, then undergo the dissoluteness to indulge unstintingly in these worldly pleasures. Otherwise, oh mind! enter the realm of beatitude by renouncing all attachments and delusion.

Purport — It is wise to give up worldly attachments and lustfulness to attain momentary happiness to get absorbed in *nirvikalpa saṃādhi* or undeviating meditation to attain eternal happiness.

कामासक्ति की नरकोन्मुखता

विरमत बुधा योषित्सङ्गात्सुखात्क्षणभङ्गुरात्
कुरुत करुणाप्रज्ञामैत्रीवधूजनसङ्गमम्।
न खलु नरके हाराक्रान्तं घनं स्तनमण्डलं
शरणमथवा श्रोणीबिम्बं रणन्मणिमेखलम्॥ 66॥

अन्वय — हे बुधाः ! क्षणभङ्गुरात् योषित्सङ्गात् सुखात् विरमत। करुणाप्रज्ञामैत्रीवधूजनसङ्गमं कुरुत। नरके हाराक्रान्तं घनं स्तनमण्डलं अथवा रणन्मणिमेखलं श्रोणीबिम्बं न खलु शरणम्।

हे बुद्धिमानों! स्त्री के संग से बचो, क्योंकि उनके संग से जो सुख मिलता है, वह क्षणिक है। आप करुणा-रूपी मित्र की संगति करो और प्रज्ञा-रूपी वधू के साथ संगम करो। जिस समय नरक में सजा मिलेगी, उस समय युवतियों के हारों से शोभित स्थूल स्तनद्वय और घुँघरूदार करधनियों से सुशोभित कमर तुम्हारी सहायता नहीं करेगी।

तात्पर्य — नरकोन्मुखी क्षणिक स्त्री-संग से बचकर करुणा को मित्र और प्रज्ञा को वधू रूप में अपनाकर परम सन्तोष एवं शाश्वत सुख का अनुभव करना चाहिए।

Hellishness of Lust

viramata budhā yoṣitsaṅgātsukhātkṣaṇabhaṅgurāt
kuruta karuṇāprajñāmaitrīvadhūjanasaṅgamam ।
na khalu narake hārākrāntaṁ ghanaṁ stanamaṇḍalaṁ
śaraṇamathavā śroṇībimbaṁ raṇanmaṇimekhalam ॥ 66 ॥

anvayaḥ — *he budhāḥ! kṣaṇabhaṅgurāt yoṣitsaṅgāt sukhāt viramata* । *karuṇāprajñāmaitrīvadhūjanasaṅgamaṁ kuruta* । *narake hārākrāntaṁ ghanaṁ stanamaṇḍalaṁ athavā raṇanmaṇimekhalaṁ śroṇībimbaṁ na khalu śaraṇam* ।

Oh wise ones! avoid the company of women, because the happiness you get from their company is temporary. You should be in the company of a friend in the form of compassion and mate with a bride in the form of wisdom. At the time when you will be punished in hell, the big breasts adorned with necklaces and the hip adorned with curly girdles will not salvage you.

Purport — One should avoid temporary company of women that leads to hell. Rather, one should experience ultimate satisfaction and eternal happiness by adopting compassion as friend and wisdom as bride.

कल्याण के मार्ग

प्राण्याघातान्निवृत्तिः[128] परधनहरणे संयमः सत्यवाक्यं
काले शक्त्या प्रदानं युवतिजनकथामूकभावः परेषाम् ।
तृष्णास्रोतोविभङ्गो गुरुषु च विनयः सर्वभूतानुकम्पा
सामान्यः सर्वशास्त्रेष्वनुपहतगतिः[129] श्रेयसामेष पन्थाः ॥ 67 ॥

अन्वय — प्राण्याघातात् निवृत्तिः, परधनहरणे संयमः, सत्यवाक्यं, काले शक्त्या प्रदानं, परेषां युवतिजनकथामूकभावः । तृष्णास्रोतोविभङ्गो, गुरुषु च विनयः, सर्वभूतानुकम्पा, सर्वशास्त्रेषु अनुपहतगतिः, श्रेयसाम् एष सामान्यः पन्थाः ।

किसी भी जीव की हिंसा न करना, पराया धन न चुराना, सत्य बोलना, समय पर सामर्थ्यानुसार दान करना, पर-स्त्रियों की चर्चा में मौन रहना, लालच के स्रोत को तोड़ देना, गुरुजनों के सामने नम्र रहना, सब प्राणियों पर दया करना और भिन्न-भिन्न शास्त्रों में समान विश्वास रखना — ये सब श्रेय-प्राप्ति के अचूक रास्ते हैं ।

तात्पर्य — अहिंसा, अस्तेय, सत्यवादिता, दानशीलता, अपरिग्रह, विनय, दया एवं शास्त्र-व्यसन ये सभी कल्याण के मार्ग हैं ।

Paths to Welfare

prāṇyāghātānnivṛttiḥ paradhanaharaṇe saṁyamaḥ satyavākyaṁ
kāle śaktyā pradānaṁ yuvatijanakathāmūkabhāvaḥ pareṣām ।

---

[128] प्राणाघातान्निवृत्तिः — *JKM.1911.*

[129] अनुपहतविधिः — *JKM.1911.*

tṛṣṇāsrotovibhaṅgo guruṣu ca vinayaḥ sarvabhūtānukampā
sāmānyaḥ sarvaśāstreṣvanupahatagatiḥ śreyasāmeṣa panthāḥ ॥ 67 ॥

anvayaḥ — *prāṇyāghātāt nivṛttiḥ, paradhanaharaṇe saṁyamaḥ, satya-vākyaṁ, kāle śaktyā pradānaṁ, pareṣāṁ yuvatijanakathāmūkabhāvaḥ* । *tṛṣṇāsrotovibhaṅgo, guruṣu ca vinayaḥ, sarvabhūtānukampā, sarvaśāstreṣu anupahatagatiḥ, śreyasām eṣa sāmānyaḥ panthāḥ* ।

Not doing violence to any living being, not stealing someone else's money, truthfulness, donating as per one's capacity at the right time, undertaking silence about other women, eliminating sources of greed, being humble in front of teachers, being kind to all living beings and others, having equal faith in every scripture — all these are sure ways to welfare.

Purport — Non-violence, selflessness, truthfulness, charity, non-possessiveness, modesty, kindness and devotion to scriptures are the paths to welfare.

निःस्पृह व्यक्ति के लिए धन की तुच्छता

मातर्लक्ष्मि भजस्व कञ्चिचिदपरं[130] मत्प्रार्थिनी मा स्म भूः
भोगेभ्यः स्पृहयालवो न हि वयं का निःस्पृहाणा[131]मसि ।
सद्यःस्यूतपलाशपत्रपुटिकापात्रे पवित्रीकृते
भिक्षासक्तु[132]भिरेव सम्प्रति वयं वृत्तिं समीहामहे ॥ 68 ॥

अन्वय — हे मातः! लक्ष्मि कञ्चिदपरं भजस्व, मत्प्रार्थिनी मा स्म भूः, हि वयं भोगेभ्यः न स्पृहयालवः, (त्वं) निःस्पृहाणां का असि? वयं पवित्रीकृते सद्यःस्यूतपलाशपत्रपुटिकापात्रे भिक्षासक्तुभिरेव सम्प्रति वृत्तिं समीहामहे ।

हे माँ लक्ष्मी! अब किसी और को खोज, मेरी इच्छा न कर; अब मुझे विषय-भोगों की चाह नहीं है; मेरे जैसे निःस्पृह (इच्छा-रहितों) के सामने तू तुच्छ है। क्योंकि अब मैंने पलाश के पत्तों के दोनों में भिक्षा के सत्तू से अपना निर्वाह करने का संकल्प कर लिया है।

तात्पर्य — कामनाओं की पूर्ति हेतु धन की आवश्यकता होती है। परन्तु निष्काम व्यक्ति के लिए तो धन-दौलत तुच्छ ही है।

---

130 कच्चिदपरं — *Ms ORLS.3.*

131 निस्पृहाणाम् — *JKM.1911.*

132 वस्तु — *GAV.1954.*

Insignificance of Wealth to a Recluse

mātarlakṣmi bhajasva kañcicidaparaṁ matprārthinī mā sma bhūḥ
bhogebhyaḥ spṛhayālavo na hi vayaṁ kā niḥspṛhāṇāmasi ।
sadyaḥsyūtapalāśapatraputikāpātre pavitrīkṛte
bhikṣāsaktubhireva samprati vayaṁ vṛttiṁ samīhāmahe ॥ 68 ॥

anvayaḥ — *he mātaḥ! lakṣmi kañcidaparaṁ bhajasva, matprārthinī mā sma bhūḥ, hi vayaṁ bhogebhyaḥ na spṛhayālavaḥ, (tvaṁ) niḥspṛhāṇāṁ kā asi? vayaṁ pavitrīkṛte sadyaḥsyūtapalāśapatraputikāpātre bhikṣāsaktubhireva samprati vṛttiṁ samīhāmahe* ।

Oh Mother Lakṣmī! devote yourself to someone else! Do not long for me! Those who covet pleasures are under your sway; what are you to us who are dispassionate? Now, we want to subsist on alms gathered and purified in a bowl instantly made from the leaves of *palāśa* tree.

Purport — Wealth is required to fulfil wordly desires. But for a recluse with no desires, wealth is worthless.

विषयासक्ति ही भेद का कारण

यूयं वयं वयं यूयमित्यासीन्मतिरावयोः
किं जातमधुना येन यूयं यूयं वयं वयम् ॥ 69 ॥

अन्वय — यूयं वयं वयं यूयम् इति आवयोः मतिः आसीत्। अधुना किं जातं, येन यूयं यूयं वयं वयम्?

पहले हमारा आपका इतना गाढ़ सम्बन्ध था कि, आप थे सो मैं था और मैं था सो आप थे। अब क्या फर्क हो गया है, कि मैं, मैं ही हूँ और आप, आप ही हैं?

तात्पर्य — जिस व्यक्ति के पास कोई कामुकता नहीं है, उसके लिए सब कुछ और हर कोई समान दिखता है। लेकिन अपनी इन्द्रियों की सन्तुष्टि में लिप्त व्यक्ति व्यक्ति-व्यक्ति के बीच भेदभाव पाता है।

Hedonism Causes Discrimination

yūyaṁ vayaṁ vayaṁ yūyamityāsīnmatirāvayoḥ ।
kiṁ jātamadhunā yena yūyaṁ yūyaṁ vayaṁ vayam ॥ 69 ॥

anvayaḥ — *yūyaṁ vayaṁ vayaṁ yūyam iti āvayoḥ matiḥ āsīt* । *adhunā kiṁ jātaṁ, yena yūyaṁ yūyaṁ vayaṁ vayam?*

Earlier we had such a deep relationship with you that you were there, so I was there and I was there, so you were there. What is the difference now, that I am only me and you are only you?

Purport — For an individual having no sensuality everything and everybody looks equal. But an individual indulged in the gratification of his senses finds discrimination between person to person.

विषमता की जननी विषय-वासना

वयमेव पुरा यूयं यूयमेव पुरा वयम्।
इदानीमथ सम्बन्धाद्यूयं यूयं वयं वयम्॥ 70॥

अन्वय — वयमेव पुरा यूयं यूयमेव पुरा वयम् अथ इदानीं सम्बन्धाद् यूयं यूयं वयं वयम्।

पहले हम ही आप थे और आप ही हम थे। परन्तु अभी ऐसा क्या हो गया कि आप, आप हो गए और हम, हम हो गए।

तात्पर्य — विषय-वासना विषमता की जनयित्री है।

Sensuality: The Source of Inequality

vayameva purā yūyaṁ yūyameva purā vayam ।
idānīmatha sambandhādyūyaṁ yūyaṁ vayaṁ vayam ॥ 70 ॥

anvayaḥ — *vayameva purā yūyaṁ yūyameva purā vayam atha idānīṁ sambandhād yūyaṁ yūyaṁ vayaṁ vayam* ।

Earlier we were you and you were us. But what happened now that you became you and we became us.

Purport — Sensuality is the source of inequality.

विनाशोन्मुखी संसार का त्याग

रम्यं हर्म्यतलं न किं वसतये श्रव्यं[133] न गेयादिकं
किं वा प्राणसमासमागमसुखं नैवाधिक[134]प्रीतये।

---

[133] श्राव्यं — *GAV.1954.*

[134] नैवाधिकं — *Ms ORLS-3, JKM.1911.*

किन्तु भ्रान्त[135]पतङ्गपक्षिपवनव्यालोलदीपानल-
ज्वालाचञ्चलमाकलय्य सकलं सन्तो वनान्तं गताः ॥ 71 ॥

अन्वय — किं रम्यं हर्म्यतलं वसतये न? गेयादिकं किं श्रव्यं न? (किं) वा प्राणसमासमागमसुखं अधिकप्रीतये नैव?। किंतु सकलं भ्रान्तपतङ्गपक्षिपवनव्यालोलदीपानलज्वालाचञ्चलम् आकलय्य सन्तो वनान्तं गताः।

क्या सन्तों के रहने के लिए उत्तमोत्तम महल न थे, क्या सुनने के लिए श्रुतिमधुर गान न थे, क्या प्यारी-प्यारी स्त्रियों के संगम का सुख न था, जो वे लोग वनों में रहने को गए? हाँ, सब कुछ था; परन्तु उन्होंने इस जगत् को उड़ते हुए पतंगों के पंखों से उत्पन्न हवा से हिलते हुए दीपक की ज्वाला के समान अथवा भ्रमित पतंगे के फड़फड़ाते पंखों पर टिमटिमाती लौ की छाया की तरह चञ्चल समझकर छोड़ दिया; संसार को अपना नाश करते देखकर संसार को छोड़ दिया।

[जिस तरह पतंगा नहीं समझता कि दीपक से प्रेम करने में मेरी जान चली जाएगी; उसी तरह संसारी आदमी नहीं समझते, कि इन संसारी विषय-वासनाओं में फँसकर, इनसे प्रेम करके हम अपना नाश स्वयं करा बैठेंगे। जो बुद्धिमान और विचारवान हैं, वे इस बात को समझते हैं; अतः संसारी पदार्थों से मोह नहीं करते और अपने नाश से बचते हैं। वे संसार को अनित्य और नाश की निशानी समझकर, इससे मन हटाकर परमात्मा में मन लगाते हैं।]

तात्पर्य — सन्त एवं संन्यासी अपने विवेक से विनाशोन्मुखी एवं अस्थिर संसार के प्रति आसक्ति-रहित होते हैं।

Abandonment of a Doomed World

ramyaṁ harmyatalaṁ na kiṁ vasataye śravyaṁ na geyādikaṁ
kiṁ vā prāṇasamāsamāgamasukhaṁ naivādhikaprītaye ।
kintu bhrāntapataṅgapakṣipavanavyāloladīpānala-
jvālācañcalamākalayya sakalaṁ santo vanāntaṁ gatāḥ ॥ 71 ॥

anvayaḥ — *kiṁ ramyaṁ harmyatalaṁ vasataye na? geyādikaṁ kiṁ śravyaṁ na? (kiṁ) vā prāṇasamāsamāgamasukhaṁ adhikaprītaye naiva?* । *kiṅtu sakalaṁ bhrāntapataṅgapakṣipavanavyāloladīpānalajvālācañcalam ākalayya santo vanāntaṁ gatāḥ* ।

Is living in a palace not pleasant? Or is listening to music with its accompaniments not pleasant? Or is the company of women

[135] उद्भ्रान्तपततपतङ्गपवनव्यालोलदीपाङ्कुरच्छाया — *JKM.1911*, उद्भ्रान्तपततपतङ्गपक्षपवनव्यालोल-दीपाङ्कुरच्छाया — *GAV.1954.*

is not pleasurable? But, in spite of all those amenities available, wise persons have taken to the forest life, having realized that these are as fickle as the shadow of a flickering flame on the fluttering wings of a delirious moth.

[Just as the kite does not understand that loving the lamp will cost it its life; in the same way, worldly people do not understand that by getting entangled in these worldly objects and desires and by loving them, they will destroy themselves. Those who are intelligent and thoughtful, understand this; therefore, do not get attached to worldly things and avoid self-destruction. They consider the world as a sign of impermanence and destruction, and turn their mind away from it and concentrate on God.]

Purport — Saints and ascetics, by their conscience, are free from attachment to the destructive and unstable world.

धन-मत्तों के सामने दीनता की निन्दा

किं कन्दाः कन्दरेभ्यः प्रलयमुपगता निर्झरा वा गिरिभ्यः
प्रध्वस्ता वा तरुभ्यः सरसफलभृतो वल्कलिन्यश्च शाखाः।
वीक्ष्यन्ते यन्मुखानि प्रसभमुपहत[136]प्रश्रयाणां खलानां
दुःखोपात्ताल्पवित्तस्मयवशपवनानर्तितभ्रूलतानाम्[137] ॥ 72 ॥

अन्वय — किं कन्दरेभ्यः कन्दाः प्रलयमुपगताः? (किं) गिरिभ्यः निर्झराः (प्रलयमुपगताः) वा? तरुभ्यः सरसफलभृतः वल्कलिन्यः शाखाः च प्रध्वस्ता वा? यत् दुःखोपात्ताल्पवित्तस्मयवशपवनानर्तितभ्रूलतानाम् उपहतप्रश्रयाणां खलानां मुखानि प्रसभं वीक्ष्यन्ते।

क्या पहाड़ों की गुफ़ाओं में कन्द-मूल और उनकी चट्टानों में पानी के झरने नहीं रहे, क्या छाल वाले वृक्षों में रसीली फलवती शाखाएं नहीं रहीं, जो लोग उन अभिमानी और नीचों के सामने दीनता करते हैं, जिनकी भौंहें अभिमान से भरी चढ़ी रहती हैं और जिन्होंने बड़े कष्ट से थोड़ा सा धन जमा कर लिया है?

[जब प्रकृति से ही मनुष्य की मूलभूत आवश्यकताएं सुलभता से पूर्ण हो जाती हैं फिर भी लोग उन धनियों की कुटिल भृकुटियों को क्यों देखते हैं, जिनकी आँखें उस थोड़े से धन के मद से नहीं

---

136 प्रसभमपगत — *JKM.1911, GAV.1954.*

137 भ्रूलतानि — *JKM.1911, GAV.1954.*

खुलती, जो उन्होंने बड़े-बड़े कष्टों से येन-केन-प्रकारेण जमा कर लिया है! ऐसे नीच अभिमानियों से अपमानित होने की अपेक्षा पहाड़ों में रहना और फल-मूल तथा शीतल जल पर गुज़ारा करना भला।]

तात्पर्य — अत्यधिक अभाव में भी धन-मत्तों के सामने अपना दैन्य व्यक्त नहीं करना चाहिए।

Denunciation of Humility before the People Infatuated with Wealth

kiṁ kandāḥ kandarebhyaḥ pralayamupagatā nirjharā vā giribhyaḥ
pradhvastā vā tarubhyaḥ sarasaphalabhṛto valkalinyaśca śākhāḥ ।
vīkṣyante yanmukhāni prasabhamupahatapraśrayāṇāṁ khalānāṁ
duḥkhopāttālpavittasmayavaśapavanānartitabhrūlatānām ॥ 72 ॥

anvayaḥ — *kiṁ kandarebhyaḥ kandāḥ pralayamupagatāḥ? (kiṁ) giribhyaḥ nirjharāḥ (pralayamupagatāḥ) vā? tarubhyaḥ sarasaphalabhṛtaḥ valkalinyaḥ śākhāḥ ca pradhvastā vā? yat duḥkhopāttālpavittasmaya-vaśapavanānartitabhrūlatānām upahatapraśrayāṇāṁ khalānāṁ mukhāni prasabhaṁ vīkṣyante* ।

Have the roots and herbs from the caves gone out of existence, or have the streams disappeared from the mountains, or have the trees yielding succulent fruits on their branches and barks from their trunks been destroyed for one to fall down before those proud and mean people, whose eyebrows are raised with pride and have accumulated a little wealth with great difficulty? [When the basic needs of people are easily fulfilled by Nature itself, then why do people look at the crooked eyebrows of those rich people, whose eyes do not open due to arrogance of having little wealth accumulated through great hardships and by all means? It would be better to survive on fruits and cool water of the mountains than to be insulted by such lowly and arrogant people.]

Purport — One should not express one's plight in front of rich people even in extreme circumstances.

राजाओं के सामने दीनता की निन्दा

किं शाका न वसन्ति भूधरसरित्कुञ्जेषु मूलानि वा
किं वा जीवनमेतदेव विहितं याच्ञैव नान्यत्क्वचित्।

येन श्रीमदमोहमूढमनसां स्थित्वाऽग्रतो भूभुजां
श्वासोत्कम्पकदर्थिताक्षरपदा देहीति वागुच्यते ॥ 73 ॥

अन्वय — किं भूधरसरित्कुञ्जेषु शाका मूलानि वा न वसन्ति? किं वा जीवनम् एतदेव विहितं (येन) याच्ञा एव, अन्यत्क्वचित् न? येन श्रीमदमोहमूढमनसां भूभुजाम् अग्रतः स्थित्वा श्वासोत्कम्पकदर्थिताक्षरपदा देही इति वाक् उच्यते।

क्या पर्वत और नदी तट के कुञ्जों में शाक-सब्जी नहीं उगते? क्या जीवन इतना ही सीमित है कि माँगने के अलावा और और कहीं आश्रय या वृत्ति-निर्वाह नहीं हो सकता? जिससे धन के अहंकार और मोह से मूढ़ व्यक्तियों के सामने रहकर रोते हुए कम्पित स्वर से याचना करनी पड़ती है?

तात्पर्य — अपनी आजीविका हेतु केवल राजाओं से याचना ही एकमात्र स्रोत नहीं है। प्रकृति में उपलब्ध संसाधनों से सन्तुष्ट रहकर व्यक्ति को याचना-विमुख होना चाहिए।

Reproofing Humility before the Arrogant Kings

kiṁ śākā na vasanti bhūdharasaritkuñjeṣu mūlāni vā
kiṁ vā jīvanametadeva vihitaṁ yācñaiva nānyatkvacit ।
yena śrīmadamohamūḍhamanasāṁ sthitvā 'grato bhūbhujāṁ
śvāsotkampakadarthitākṣarapadā dehīti vāgucyate ॥ 73 ॥

anvayaḥ — *kiṁ bhūdharasaritkuñjeṣu śākā mūlāni vā na vasanti? kiṁ vā jīvanam etadeva vihitaṁ (yena) yācñā eva, anyatkvacit na? yena śrīmadamohamūḍhamanasāṁ bhūbhujām agrataḥ sthitvā śvāsotkampakadarthitākṣarapadā dehī iti vāk ucyate* ।

Do vegetables not grow in the groves of mountains and river-banks? Is life so limited that there cannot be shelter or livelihood anywhere else except by begging? Due to which one has to cry and plead with trembling voice in front of people who are duped by arrogance and addiction to money?

Purport — Begging from kings is not the only source of one's livelihood. To devoid solicitations, an individual should be satisfied with the resources available in the Nature.

पराश्रय ही अपमान का कारण

गङ्गातरङ्गभरशीकर[138]शीतलानि
विद्याधराध्युषितधामशिलातलानि[139] ।
स्थानानि किं हिमवतो विलये[140] गतानि
येनावमानपरपिण्डरता मनुष्याः ॥ 74 ॥

अन्वय — गङ्गातरङ्गभरशीकरशीतलानि विद्याधराध्युषितधामशिलातलानि हिमवतः स्थानानि किं विलये गतानि येन मनुष्याः अवमानपरपिण्डरताः (सन्ति)?

क्या गंगा की लहरों के जल-कणों से अतिशय शीतल हिमालय पर्वतमालाएं और (विद्याधरों) पर्वतीय संगीतकारों द्वारा बसाए गए सुन्दर चट्टानी पठार विघटित और लुप्त हो गए हैं, जो लोगों को अपनी आजीविका के लिए दूसरों पर निर्भर होकर स्वयं को अपमानित करने के लिए प्रेरित करते हैं?

तात्पर्य — पराश्रित होकर तिरस्कृत होने की अपेक्षा वनवास करना अधिक संगत एवं उचित है।

Dependency Results in Affront

gaṅgātaraṅgabharaśīkaraśītalāni
vidyādharādhyuṣitadhāmaśilātalāni ।
sthānāni kiṁ himavato vilaye gatāni
yenāvamānaparapiṇḍaratā manuṣyāḥ ॥ 74 ॥

anvayaḥ — *gaṅgātaraṅgabharaśīkaraśītalāni vidyādharādhyuṣita-dhāmaśilātalāni himavataḥ sthānāni kiṁ vilaye gatāni yena manuṣyāḥ avamānaparapiṇḍaratāḥ* (*santi*)?

Have the Himalayan ranges, cooled by the fine spray from the waves of the Ganges, and with the beautiful rocky plateaus habited by celestial musicians, dissolved and disappeared, that prompting people to disgrace themselves by depending on others for their livelihood?

Purport — It is more appropriate to live in the forest than to become dependent and despised.

---

138 हिमशीकर — *JKM.1911*, कणशीकर — *GAV.1954.*

139 चारुशिलातलानि — *JKM.1911, GAV.1954.*

140 प्रलयं — *Ms ORLS-3, JKM.1911, GAV.1954.*

जीवन की चञ्चलता

यदा[141] मेरुः श्रीमान्निपतति युगान्ताग्न्यभिहतः[142]
समुद्राः शुष्यन्ति प्रवरमकरग्राहकलिलाः[143] ।
धरा गच्छत्यन्तं धरणिधरपादैरपि धृता
शरीरे का वार्ता करिकलभकर्णाग्रचपले ॥ 75 ॥

अन्वय — यदा युगान्ताग्न्यभिहतः श्रीमान् मेरुः निपतति, प्रवरमकरग्राहकलिलाः समुद्राः शुष्यन्ति, धरणिधरपादैः अपि धृता धरा अन्तं गच्छति, करिकलभकर्णाग्रचपले शरीरे का वार्ता?

जब प्रलय की अग्नि के मारे सुन्दर सुमेरु पर्वत गिर पड़ता है; विशालकाय मगरमच्छों के रहने के स्थान समुद्र भी सूख जाते हैं; पर्वतों के पैरों से दबी हुई पृथ्वी भी नाश हो जाती है; तब हाथी के कान की कोर के समान चञ्चल मनुष्य की क्या गिनती?

तात्पर्य — मनुष्य का जीवन अत्यन्त क्षणस्थायी है, अतः जीवन में किसी भी भौतिक पदार्थ से आसक्त नहीं होना चाहिए।

Transience of Life

yadā meruḥ śrīmānnipatati yugāntāgnyabhihataḥ
samudrāḥ śuṣyanti pravaramakaragrāhakalilāḥ ।
dharā gacchatyantaṁ dharaṇidharapādairapi dhṛtā
śarīre kā vārtā karikalabhakarṇāgracapale ॥ 75 ॥

anvayaḥ — *yadā yugāntāgnyabhihataḥ śrīmān meruḥ nipatati, pravaramakaragrāhakalilāḥ samudrāḥ śuṣyanti, dharaṇidharapādaiḥ api dhṛtā dharā antaṁ gacchati, karikalabhakarṇāgracapale śarīre kā vārtā?*

When the beautiful Sumeru mountain falls due to the fire of destruction, the seas which are home to giant crocodiles also dry up, the earth pressed under the feet of mountains also gets destroyed, then what is the account of a man who is as fickle as the ear of an elephant?

Puport — Human life is very momentary, hence one should not be attached to any material thing in life.

---

141 यतो — *GAV.1954.*

142 युगान्ताग्निनिहतः — *JKM.1911*, युगान्ताग्निवलितः — *GAV.1954.*

143 प्रचुरनिकरग्राहनिलयाः — *JKM.1911.*

आसक्ति-रहित कर्मोपासना

एकाकी निःस्पृहः शान्तः पाणिपात्रो दिगम्बरः।
कदा शम्भो भविष्यामि कर्मनिर्मूलनक्षमः ॥ 76 ॥

अन्वय — हे शम्भो! (अहम्) एकाकी निःस्पृहः शान्तः पाणिपात्रो दिगम्बरः (सन्) कदा कर्मनिर्मूलनक्षमः भविष्यामि?

हे शिव! मैं कब अकेला, इच्छारहित और शान्त होऊँगा? कब हाथ ही मेरा पात्र होगा और कब दिशाएं मेरे वस्त्र होंगे? मैं कब कर्मों की जड़ उखाड़ने में समर्थ होऊँगा?

[यदि मनुष्य यश और अपयश, सफलता और असफलता, सुख और दुःख दोनों को समान रूप से भगवान् की इच्छा मानते हुए ग्रहण करना सीख लेता है तभी उसके भीतर समभाव विकसित होता है, और वह सभी कर्मों की सेवा निःस्पृह होकर कर सकता है। जैसे कि *श्रीमद्भगवद्गीता* II.48 में कहा गया है —

योगस्थः कुरु कर्माणि सङ्गं त्यक्त्वा धनञ्जय।
सिद्ध्यसिद्ध्योः समो भूत्वा समत्वं योग उच्यते ॥

हे अर्जुन! सफलता और असफलता की आसक्ति को त्यागकर तुम दृढ़ता से अपने कर्त्तव्य का पालन करो। यही समभाव योग कहलाता है।]

तात्पर्य — सुख-प्राप्तीच्छा-रहित होकर निष्काम कर्म करना ही वास्तव में योग है। यही संन्यास तथा परमतत्त्व-सान्निध्य का मार्ग है।

Non-attachment to Karma

ekākī niḥspṛhaḥ śāntaḥ pāṇipātro digambaraḥ ।
kadā śambho bhaviṣyāmi karmanirmūlanakṣamaḥ ॥ 76 ॥

anvayaḥ — *he śambho*! (*aham*) *ekākī niḥspṛhaḥ śāntaḥ pāṇipātro digambaraḥ* (*san*) *kadā karmanirmūlanakṣamaḥ bhaviṣyāmi*?

When shall I be free from the roots of action, leading a life of solitude, dispassion, serenity, with my hands serving as a bowl and the sky for clothing?

[If an individual learns to accept fame and infamy, success and failure, happiness and sorrow equally as the will of God, then only equanimity develops within him, and he can serve all actions without attachment. *Śrīmadbhagavadgītā* II.48 states:

yogasthaḥ kuru karmāṇi saṅgaṁ tyaktvā dhanañjaya ।
siddhyasiddhyoḥ samo bhūtvā samatvaṁ yoga ucyate ॥

Oh Arjuna! perform action, being steadfast in *yoga*, abandoning attachment and balanced in success and failure; evenness of mind is called *yoga*.]

Purport — Action without the desire to attain happiness is really *yoga* and the path to renunciation leading to attain Eternal Bliss in the Self.

तत्त्व-ज्ञान से ही शान्ति

प्राप्ताः श्रियः सकलकामदुघास्ततः किं
दत्तं[144] पदं शिरसि विद्विषतां ततः किं।
सन्तर्पिताः[145] प्रणयिनो विभवैस्ततः किं
कल्पं स्थितं[146] तनुभृतां तनुभिस्ततः किम्॥ 77॥

अन्वय — सकलकामदुघाः श्रियः प्राप्ताः, ततः किं? विद्विषतां शिरसि पदं दत्तं, ततः किं? विभवैः प्रणयिनः सन्तर्पिताः, ततः किं? तनुभृतां तनुभिः कल्पं स्थितं, ततः किम्?

यदि मनुष्यों को सब इच्छाओं को पूर्ण करने वाली लक्ष्मी मिल गई तो क्या हुआ? यदि शत्रुओं को पदानत कर दिया तो क्या हुआ? यदि धन से मित्रों को तृप्त कर दिया तो क्या हुआ? यदि इसी देह से इस जगत् में एक कल्प तक भी रहे तो भी क्या हो गया?

[चाहे जितना वैभव, समृद्धि और दीर्घ जीवन प्राप्त हो गया हो, परन्तु यदि अन्तःकरण में संसार बन्धन को मुक्त करने वाली आत्म-ज्ञान की ज्योति न जगी, तो कुछ भी नहीं पाया और कुछ भी नहीं किया। अर्थात् सारे संसार के राज्य-वैभव अथवा त्रिभुवन के अधिपति होने में भी जो आनन्द नहीं है, वह आत्म-ज्ञान या ब्रह्म-ज्ञान में है। आत्म-ज्ञान होने से ही मनुष्य, जीवन–मरण के कष्ट से छुटकारा पाकर, परम शान्ति प्राप्त करता है। जैसे कि भगवान् श्रीकृष्ण ने *श्रीमद्भगवद्गीता* V.29 में कहा है —

भोक्तारं यज्ञतपसां सर्वलोकमहेश्वरम्।
सुहृदं सर्वभूतानां ज्ञात्वा मां शान्तिमृच्छति॥

---

144 न्यस्तं — *GAV.1954.*

145 सम्मानिताः — *JKM.1911*, सम्पादिताः — *GAV.1954.*

146 स्थिताः — *GAV.1954.*

अर्थात् सब यज्ञों और तपों का भोक्ता सम्पूर्ण लोकों का महान् ईश्वर तथा सम्पूर्ण प्राणियों का सुहृद् (स्वार्थरहित दयालु और प्रेमी) मुझे जानकर भक्त शान्ति को प्राप्त करता है।]

तात्पर्य — मनुष्य भले ही सभी प्रकार के भौतिक सुख और सुविधाओं को प्राप्त कर ले परन्तु जब तक परम तत्त्व की अनुभूति नहीं होती तब तक शाश्वत शान्ति नहीं मिल सकती।

Peace through Spiritual Knowledge Only

prāptāḥ śriyaḥ sakalakāmadughāstataḥ kiṁ
dattaṁ padaṁ śirasi vidviṣatāṁ tataḥ kiṁ ।
santarpitāḥ praṇayino vibhavaistataḥ kiṁ
kalpaṁ sthitaṁ tanubhṛtāṁ tanubhistataḥ kim ॥ 77 ॥

anvayaḥ — *sakalakāmadughāḥ śriyaḥ prāptāḥ, tataḥ kiṁ? vidviṣatāṁ śirasi padaṁ dattaṁ, tataḥ kiṁ? vibhavaiḥ praṇayinaḥ santarpitāḥ, tataḥ kiṁ? tanubhṛtāṁ tanubhiḥ kalpaṁ sthitaṁ, tataḥ kim?*

What if one acquires wealth that will fulfil all desires, even stomping on the enemies' heads with one's feet, or if riches bring friends, or even if one's body lasts till the end of time?

[No matter how much glory, prosperity and long life one has achieved, if the light of self-knowledge that frees one from the bondage of the world is not awakened in one's heart, then nothing has been achieved. Self-knowledge or experiencing the reality is the only way by which an individual attains ultimate peace by getting rid of the pain of life and death. *Śrīmadbhagavadgītā* V.29 says:

bhoktāraṁ yajñatapasāṁ sarvalokamaheśvaram ।
suhṛdaṁ sarvabhūtānāṁ jñātvā māṁ śāntimṛcchati ॥

Meaning: Having realized Me as the enjoyer of all sacrifices and austerities, the Supreme Lord of all the worlds and the selfless friend of all living beings, My devotee attains peace.]

Purport — An individual may attain all kinds of material comforts and facilities, but he/she cannot attain eternal peace unless he/she realizes the ultimate essence.

वैराग्य का स्वरूप

भक्तिर्भवे मरणजन्मभयं हृदिस्थं
स्नेहो न बन्धुषु न मन्मथजा विकाराः ।

संसर्गदोषरहिता[147] विजना वनान्ता
वैराग्यमस्ति किमितः[148] परमर्थनीयम् ॥ 78 ॥

अन्वय — भवे भक्तिः, हृदिस्थं मरणजन्मभयं, बन्धुषु स्नेहो न, मन्मथजा विकाराः न। संसर्गदोषरहिता विजनाः वनान्ताः, इतः परं किं वैराग्यम् अर्थनीयम् अस्ति?

सदाशिव में भक्ति हो, हृदय में जन्म-मरण का भय हो, बन्धुओं सें स्नेह न हो, मन में काम-विकार न हों और संसर्ग-दोष से रहित होकर जनशून्य वन में वास हो — अगर हम में ये गुण हों तब और कौन सा वैराग्य चाहिए?

तात्पर्य — शरीर, मन और अन्तःकरण से सांसारिक तृष्णाओं को दूर करते हुए परमात्मा के प्रति आत्मसमर्पण ही वैराग्य है।

Characteristics of Renunciation

bhaktirbhave maraṇajanmabhayaṁ hṛdisthaṁ
sneho na bandhuṣu na manmathajā vikārāḥ ।
saṁsargadoṣarahitā vijanā vanāntā
vairāgyamasti kimitaḥ paramarthanīyam ॥ 78 ॥

anvayaḥ — *bhave bhaktiḥ, hṛdisthaṁ maraṇajanmabhayaṁ, bandhuṣu sneho na, manmathajā vikārāḥ na* । *saṁsargadoṣarahitā vijanāḥ vanāntāḥ, itaḥ paraṁ kiṁ vairāgyam arthanīyam asti*?

If there be devotion to Lord Śiva in the heart and the fear of death and birth, no ties to family, nor agitation by passions; when there is the solitude of uninhabited forests, if we have these qualities then what other renunciation or dispassion is required?

Purport — Renunciation is surrender to God while renouncing all the worldly desires from body, mind and conscience.

ब्रह्म-तत्त्व के चिन्तन की श्रेष्ठता

तस्मादनन्तमजरं परमं विकासि
तद्ब्रह्म चिन्तय किमेभिरसद्विकल्पैः।

---

147 संसारदोषरहिता — *Ms ORLS-3.*

148 किमतः — *Ms ORLS-3, JKM.1911.*

यस्यानुषङ्गिण इमे भुवनाधिपत्य-
भोगादयः कृपणलोकमता भवन्ति ॥ 79 ॥

अन्वय — तस्मात् अनन्तम् अजरं परमं विकासि तद् ब्रह्म चिन्तय, एभिः असद्विकल्पैः किम्। इमे भुवनाधिपत्यभोगादयः कृपणलोकमता यस्य अनुषङ्गिणः भवन्ति।

इसलिए, अनन्त, अनादि, सर्वोच्च, प्रकाशमान शाश्वत ब्रह्म-तत्त्व का ध्यान करें। असत् पदार्थों के बारे में चिन्तन ही क्यों? दुनिया पर सम्प्रभुता, उसके साथ जुड़े सुखों के साथ, ब्रह्म-तत्त्व के साक्षात्कार की तुलना में क्षुद्र दिमाग की इच्छाओं के रूप में तुच्छ दिखाई देती हैं।

तात्पर्य — ब्रह्म-तत्त्व के चिन्तन से अनुभूत शाश्वत आनन्द की अपेक्षा सांसारिक सुख अत्यन्त तुच्छ है।

Superiority of Contemplation of Supreme Consciousness

tasmādanantamajaraṁ paramaṁ vikāsi
tadbrahma cintaya kimebhirasadvikalpaiḥ ।
yasyānuṣaṅgiṇa ime bhuvanādhipatya-
bhogādayaḥ kṛpaṇalokamatā bhavanti ॥ 79 ॥

anvayaḥ — *tasmāt anantam ajaraṁ paramaṁ vikāsi tad brahma cintaya, ebhiḥ asadvikalpaiḥ kim* । *ime bhuvanādhipatyabhogādayaḥ kṛpaṇalokamatā yasya anuṣaṅgiṇaḥ bhavanti* ।

Therefore, meditate on the infinite, ageless, supreme, luminous Reality. Why these false thoughts about the unreal? The sovereignty over the world, with its accompanying pleasures, appear as the desires of the petty-minded when compared to the pursuit of Reality.

Purport — Worldly happiness is quite insignificant in comparison to the eternal joy experienced by contemplation of *brahma-tattva* (Supreme Consciousness).

आनन्द की आत्मनिष्ठता

पातालमाविशसि यासि नभो विलङ्घ्य
दिङ्मण्डलं भ्रमसि मानसचापलेन।

भ्रान्त्यापि जातु विमलं कथमात्मनिष्ठं[149]
तद्ब्रह्म न स्पृशसि[150] निर्वृतिमेषि येन ॥ 80 ॥

अन्वय — मानसचापलेन पातालम् आविशसि, नभो विलङ्घ्य यासि, दिङ्मण्डलं भ्रमसि। (परं) भ्रान्त्या अपि जातु विमलम् आत्मनिष्ठं तद् ब्रह्म कथं न स्पृशसि येन निर्वृतिम् एषि।

हे चित्त! तू अपनी चञ्चलता के कारण पाताल में प्रवेश करता है, आकाश से भी परे जाता है, दशों दिशाओं में घूमता है; परन्तु भूल से भी तू उस विमल परम ब्रह्म की याद नहीं करता, जो तेरे हृदय में ही विद्यमान है, जिसके याद करने से ही तुझे परमानन्द (मोक्ष) मिल सकता है!

तात्पर्य — मनुष्य अपनी चञ्चलता के कारण सुख-प्राप्ति हेतु आकाश और पाताल जैसे दूर-दूर तक भटकता रहता है, जबकि आनन्द तो स्वयं के अन्तःकरण में ही विद्यमान ब्रह्म-तत्त्व के निदिध्यासन से प्राप्त हो सकता है।

Self as the Domain of Bliss

pātālamāviśasi yāsi nabho vilaṅghya
diṅmaṇḍalaṁ bhramasi mānasacāpalena ।
bhrāntyāpi jātu vimalaṁ kathamātmaniṣṭhaṁ
tadbrahma na spṛśasi nirvṛtimeṣi yena ॥ 80 ॥

anvayaḥ — *mānasacāpalena pātālam āviśasi, nabho vilaṅghya yāsi, diṅmaṇḍalaṁ bhramasi* । *(paraṁ) bhrāntyā api jātu vimalam ātmaniṣṭhaṁ tad brahma kathaṁ na spṛśasi yena nirvṛtim eṣi* ।

With such a fickle mind, you do enter *pātāla* (netherworld) one moment, fly to the limits of the sky, or wander in all directions. But, why, even by mistake, do you not meditate on that Transcendent Truth (Supreme *Brahman*), who is present within you only, by remembering whom only you can get bliss/ salvation?

Purport — Due to fickleness, an individual keeps wandering to such distant places as the sky and the underworld to attain happiness, whereas happiness can be attained only by meditating on the *brahma-tattva* present in one's self.

---

149 कथामात्मनीनं — *JKM.1911, GAV.1954.*

150 न ब्रह्म संस्मरसि — *GAV.1954.*

मोह ही अज्ञान का जनक

रात्रिः सैव पुनः स एव दिवसो मिथ्यामुदा[151] जन्तवो
धावन्त्युद्यमिनस्तथैव निभृतप्रारब्धतत्तत्क्रियाः ।
व्यापारैः पुनरुक्तदोषविषयैरित्थंविधेनामुना[152]
संसारेण कदर्थिताः कथमहो[153] मोहान्न लज्जामहे ॥ 81 ॥

अन्वय — सा एव रात्रिः स एव पुनः दिवसो, (तथापि) निभृतप्रारब्धतत्तत्क्रियाः उद्यमिनः जन्तवो मिथ्यामुदा तथैव धावन्ति। पुनरुक्तदोषविषयैः व्यापारैः इत्थंविधेन अमुना संसारेण कदर्थिताः (भवन्ति) अहो मोहात् कथं न लज्जामहे!

वही पूर्वानुभूत रात्रि है और वही पूर्वानुभूत दिवस है, इस बात को संसारी अच्छी तरह जानते हैं फिर भी पहले से प्रारब्ध कर्म को पूर्ण करने के लिए लोग उन्हीं व्यापारों को करने में लीन रहा करते हैं जिनको कि वे पहले से करते आए हैं। इस प्रकार के इस संसार से निन्दा के पात्र हम अज्ञान के कारण लज्जित नहीं हो रहे हैं?

तात्पर्य — व्यक्ति का निरर्थक संसार से इतना मोह हो जाता है कि वह शाश्वत एवं नित्य ब्रह्म-तत्त्व को भूल जाता है।

Delusion Causes Ignorance

rātriḥ saiva punaḥ sa eva divaso mithyāmudā jantavo
dhāvantyudyaminastathaiva nibhṛtaprārabdhatattatkriyāḥ ।
vyāpāraiḥ punaruktadoṣaviṣayairitthaṁvidhenāmunā
saṁsāreṇa kadarthitāḥ kathamaho mohānna lajjāmahe ॥ 81 ॥

anvayaḥ — *sā eva rātriḥ sa eva punaḥ divaso,* (*tathāpi*) *nibhṛtaprārabdhatattatkriyāḥ udyaminaḥ jantavo mithyāmudā tathaiva dhāvanti* । *punaruktadoṣaviṣayaiḥ vyāpāraiḥ itthaṁvidhena amunā saṁsāreṇa kadarthitāḥ* (*bhavanti*) *aho mohāt kathaṁ na lajjāmahe*!

Watching the night following the day, creatures still vainly persist in running busily with various actions motivated by desires. Such repetitious actions, alas! born of desires bring us

---

151 मत्वा बुधा — *JKM.1911, GAV.1954.*

152 पुनरुक्तभुक्तविषयैरेवंविधेनामुना — *JKM.1911*, पुनरुक्तमुक्तविषयैरेवंविधेनामुना — *GAV.1954.*

153 वयमहो — *GAV.1954.*

no shame, keeping us deluded in the revolving cycles of births and deaths.

Purport — Man becomes so attached to the meaningless world that he forgets the eternal and infinite *Brahman*.

वैराग्य से ही परम सुख

महीशय्याशायी[154] विपुलमुपधानं भुजलता
  वितानं चाकाशं व्यजनमनुकूलोऽयमनिलः ।
स्फुरद्दीपश्चन्द्रो[155] विरतिवनितासङ्गमुदितः
  सुखं[156] शान्तः शेते मुनिरतनुभूतिर्नृप इव ॥ 82 ॥

अन्वय — महीशय्याशायी, भुजलता विपुलमुपधानं, आकाशं च वितानं, अयम् अनुकूलः अनिलः व्यजनं, चन्द्रः स्फुरद्दीपः । विरतिवनितासङ्गमुदितः शान्तः मुनिः अतनुभूतिः नृप इव सुखं शेते ।

मुनि लोग परम वैभवशाली राजा-महाराजाओं की तरह धरती को ही शय्या, भुजा को ही अपना गुदगुदा तकिया, आकाश को ही चादर, अनुकूल पवन को ही अपना पंखा, चन्द्रमा को ही जलता हुआ प्रदीप मानकर, विरक्ति को हीअपनी स्त्री समझते हुए सुख से शयन करते हैं।

तात्पर्य — विषयों सें आसक्ति हटाने से ही परम सुख की प्राप्ति सम्भव है।

Ultimate Happiness through Renunciation Only

mahīśayyāśāyī vipulamupadhānaṁ bhujalatā
  vitānaṁ cākāśaṁ vyajanamanukūlo 'yamanilaḥ ।
sphuraddīpaścandro virativanitāsaṅgamuditaḥ
  sukhaṁ śāntaḥ śete muniratanubhūtirnṛpa iva ॥ 82 ॥

anvayaḥ — *mahīśayyāśāyī, bhujalatā vipulamupadhānaṁ, ākāśaṁ ca vitānaṁ, ayam anukūlaḥ anilaḥ vyajanaṁ, candraḥ sphuraddīpaḥ* । *virati-vanitāsaṅgamuditaḥ śāntaḥ muniḥ atanubhūtiḥ nṛpa iva sukhaṁ śete* ।

Like the most glorious kings and emperors, the sages, considering the earth as their bed, their arms as their cuddly

[154] मही रम्या शय्या — *JKM.1911*, महीशय्या पृथ्वी — *GAV.1954.*

[155] शरच्चन्द्रो दीपो — *GAV.1954.*

[156] सुखी — *GAV.1954.*

pillow, the sky as their bedsheet, the favourable wind as their fan, the moon as a burning lamp and detachment as their wife sleep happily.

Purport — Attainment of ultimate happiness is possible only by abating attachment to worldy pleasures.

ब्रह्मानन्द के सामने सांसारिक भोग की तुच्छता

त्रैलोक्याधिपतित्वमेव विरसं यस्मिन्महाशासने
तल्लब्ध्वाऽसमवस्त्र[157]मारघटने भोगे रतिं मा कृथाः
भोगः कोऽपि स एक एव सुभगो[158] नित्योदितो जृम्भते
यत्स्वादाद्विरसा भवन्ति विभवा[159]स्त्रैलोक्यराज्यादयः ॥ 83 ॥

अन्वय — यस्मिन् महाशासने त्रैलोक्याधिपतित्वं विरसम् एव, तल्लब्ध्वा असमवस्त्रमारघटने भोगे रतिं मा कृथाः। सः भोगः एव कोऽपि सुभगः नित्योदितः (सन्) जृम्भते, यत्स्वादात् त्रैलोक्यराज्यादयः विभवाः विरसाः भवन्ति।

हे आत्मा! अगर तुझे उस ब्रह्म का ज्ञान हो गया है, जिसके सामने तीनों लोक का राज्य तुच्छ मालूम होता है; तो तू तुच्छ वस्त्र आदि से शृंगार-रचना-रूपी भोगों की चाहना मत कर; क्योंकि वह ब्रह्मास्वाद का भोग सर्वश्रेष्ठ और नित्य है; उसके आस्वाद के सामने त्रिलोक के राज्य-प्रभृति वैभवों का सुख कुछ भी नहीं है।

तात्पर्य — वास्तविक सुख ब्रह्म-ज्ञान या आत्म-ज्ञान में है। उसके तुल्य आनन्द त्रिलोक के और किसी भोग में नहीं है। जो संसारी पदार्थों में सुख मानते हैं वे अज्ञानी हैं।

Insignificance of Worldly Pleasures in Front of the Knowledge of Supreme Bliss

trailokyādhipatitvameva virasaṁ yasminmahāśāsane
tallabdhvā 'samavastramāraghaṭane bhoge ratiṁ mā kṛthāḥ
bhogaḥ ko 'pi sa eka eva subhago nityodito jṛmbhate
yatsvādādvirasā bhavanti vibhavāstrailokyarājyādayaḥ ॥ 83 ॥

anvayaḥ — *yasmin mahāśāsane trailokyādhipatitvaṁ virasam eva, tallabdhvā asamavastramāraghaṭane bhoge ratiṁ mā kṛthāḥ*। *saḥ bhogaḥ eva ko 'pi*

[157] आसनवस्त्र — *JKM.1911.*

[158] परमो — *JKM.1911.*

[159] विषया — *JKM.1911.*

subhagaḥ nityoditaḥ (san) jṛmbhate, yatsvādāt trailokyarājyādayaḥ vibhavāḥ virasāḥ bhavanti ।

Oh soul! if you have got the knowledge of that *Brahman*, in front of the sovereignty over the three worlds seems insignificant; so do not crave for the pleasures of adorning yourself with trivial clothes, etc. Because that enjoyment of the taste of *Brahman* is the best and eternal; the pleasures and splendours of the kingdoms of the three worlds are nothing in comparison to that experience, such is the unique enjoyment of *Brahman*, eternal, supreme and immutable. Oh Pure One! indulge not in any pleasure that lasts no more than a moment.

Purport — Real happiness lies in the knowledge of Self (*Brahman*). There is no pleasure equal to it in any other pleasure of the world. Those who consider happiness in worldly enjoyments are ignorant.

ब्रह्मानन्द की स्वर्गसुख से भी श्रेष्ठता

किं वेदैः स्मृतिभिः पुराणपठनैः शास्त्रैर्महाविस्तरैः
स्वर्गग्रामकुटीनिवासफलदैः यज्ञक्रिया[160]विभ्रमैः ।
मुक्त्वैकं भवदुःखभाररचनाप्रध्वंसकालानलं[161]
स्वात्मानन्दपदं प्रवेशकठिनं[162] शेषैर्वणिग्वृत्तिभिः ॥ 84 ॥

अन्वय — एकं प्रवेशकठिनं भवदुःखभाररचनाप्रध्वंसकालानलं स्वात्मानन्दपदं मुक्त्वा वणिग्वृत्तिभिः स्वर्गग्रामकुटीनिवासफलदैः वेदैः स्मृतिभिः पुराणपठनैः महाविस्तरैः शास्त्रैः यज्ञक्रियाविभ्रमैः शेषैः किम्?

संसार बन्धनों के काटने में प्रलयाग्नि के समान दुष्प्राप्य ब्रह्मानन्द-रूपी गढ़ी में प्रवेश करने की चेष्टा के अलावा, व्यापारियों की तरह वेद, स्मृति, पुराण और बड़े-बड़े शास्त्रों के पढ़ने तथा भिन्न-भिन्न प्रकार के कर्मकाण्ड जैसे भ्रमित करने वाले कार्यों के करने से स्वर्ग में एक कुटिया की जगह प्राप्त करने के सिवा और क्या लाभ हो सकता है?

तात्पर्य — स्वर्गीय आनन्द भी परिमित एवं क्षणिक है। अतः मनुष्य को अपरिमित एवं अनन्त ब्रह्मानन्द की प्राप्ति हेतु प्रयास करना चाहिए।

---

160 कर्मक्रिया — *JKM.1911, GAV.1954.*

161 भवबन्धुदुःखरचनाविध्वंसकालानलं — *JKM.1911.*

162 स्वात्मानन्दपदप्रवेशकलनं — *JKM.1911, GAV.1954.*

Superiority of the Joy of Supreme Consciousness over Heavenly Bliss

kiṁ vedaiḥ smṛtibhiḥ purāṇapaṭhanaiḥ śāstrairmahāvistaraiḥ
svargagrāmakuṭīnivāsaphaladaiḥ yajñakriyāvibhramaiḥ ।
muktvaikaṁ bhavaduḥkhabhāraracanāpradhvaṁsakālānalaṁ
svātmānandapadaṁ praveśakaṭhinaṁ śeṣairvaṇigvṛttibhiḥ ॥ 84 ॥

anvayaḥ — *ekaṁ praveśakaṭhinaṁ bhavaduḥkhabhāraracanāpradhvaṁsa-kālānalaṁ svātmānandapadaṁ muktvā vaṇigvṛttibhiḥ svargagrāmakuṭīni-vāsaphaladaiḥ vedaiḥ smṛtibhiḥ purāṇapaṭhanaiḥ mahāvistaraiḥ śāstraiḥ yajñakriyāvibhramaiḥ śeṣaiḥ kim?*

Of what use is the study of Vedas, scriptures, mythology, the extensive codes and the bewildering labyrinth of rituals which promise just a passage to heaven, which is but a hamlet of hutments? The only way to destroy the burden of life's sorrows like the apocalyptic fire, is that which lets you enter the beatitude of self-realization. All else is but bartering for profit!

Purport — Heavenly joy is also finite and momentary. Therefore, man should strive to attain infinite and infinite *brahmānanda*.

ब्रह्म का चिन्तन ही मुक्ति का मार्ग

आयुः कल्लोललोलं कतिपयदिवसस्थायिनी यौवनश्री-
र्थाः संकल्पकल्पा घनसमयतडिद्विभ्रमा भोगभङ्ग्यः[163] ।
कण्ठाश्लेषोपभोग्यं[164] तदपि च न चिरं यत्प्रियाभिः प्रणीतं
ब्रह्मण्यासक्तचित्ता भवत भवभयाम्भोधिपारं तरीतुम् ॥ 85 ॥

अन्वय — आयुः कल्लोललोलं, कतिपयदिवसस्थायिनी यौवनश्रीः, अर्थाः संकल्पकल्पाः, घनसमयतडिद्विभ्रमाः भोगभङ्ग्यः। प्रियाभिः प्रणीतं यत् कण्ठाश्लेषोपभोग्यं तदपि च न चिरम्। (अतः) भवभयाम्भोधिपारं तरीतुं ब्रह्मण्यासक्तचित्ता भवत।

आयु जलतरंग के समान चञ्चल है, यौवन की शोभा कुछ ही दिनों के लिए रहा करती है, धन मानसिक कल्पना के समान अस्थिर है, वासना भी वर्षाकालीन विद्युद्विलास की तरह

163 भोगपूराः — *JKM.1911*, भोगपूगाः — *GAV.1954*.

164 कण्ठाश्लेषोपगूढं — *JKM.1911, GAV.1954*.

चञ्चल है, प्रियाओं से गले मिलकर दिया हुआ आलिंगन-रूप सुख भी चिरस्थायी नहीं है, इसलिए भव-भय-रूपी समुद्र से पार होने के लिए परमब्रह्म में मन लगाओ।

तात्पर्य — आयु, यौवन, धन, वासना, प्रियासंगम सुख सब कुछ अस्थिरता-रूपी भय के जनक हैं। संसार के इस अस्थिरता-रूपी भय से छुटकारा केवल परमब्रह्म के निदिध्यासन से ही सम्भव है।

Contemplation of Brahman Is the Path to Salvation

āyuḥ kallolalolaṁ katipayadivasasthāyinī yauvanaśrīrarthāḥ
saṅkalpakalpā ghanasamayataḍidvibhramā bhogabhaṅgyaḥ ।
kaṇṭhāśleṣopabhogyaṁ tadapi ca na ciraṁ yatpriyābhiḥ praṇītaṁ
brahmaṇyāsaktacittā bhavata bhavabhayāmbhodhipāraṁ
tarītum ॥ 85 ॥

anvayaḥ — *āyuḥ kallolalolaṁ, katipayadivasasthāyinī yauvanaśrīḥ, arthāḥ saṅkalpakalpāḥ, ghanasamayataḍidvibhramāḥ bhogabhaṅgyaḥ* । *priyābhiḥ praṇītaṁ yat kaṇṭhāśleṣopabhogyaṁ tadapi ca na ciram* । (*ataḥ*) *bhavabhayāmbhodhipāraṁ tarītuṁ brahmaṇyāsaktacittā bhavata* ।

Life undulates like a wave of water. Youthful beauty lasts a few days. Riches are as short-lived as thoughts. The lust is as fickle as lightning flashes of rainy days. The beloved's embrace round the neck lasts only a moment. Therefore, lovingly tie your mind to *Brahman* (eternal consciousness) to overcome the fear of crossing the ocean of cycles of births and deaths.

Purport — Age, youth, wealth, lust, sexual pleasures, everything is the source of fear of instability. Meditation on the Supreme *Brahman* is the only path to overcome this fear of instability.

मनस्वी की स्थिरता

ब्रह्माण्डमण्डलीमात्रं किं लोभाय मनस्विनः।
शफरीस्फुरितेनाब्धेः क्षुब्धता जातु जायते ॥ 86 ॥

अन्वय — मनस्विनः लोभाय ब्रह्माण्डमण्डलीमात्रं किम्। शफरीस्फुरितेन अब्धेः क्षुब्धता जातु जायते (वा)?

मनस्वी व्यक्ति को सम्पूर्ण ब्रह्माण्डमण्डल भी पर्याप्त नहीं जो उसे लुभा सके। मछली के उछलने से क्या समुद्र में क्षोभ उत्पन्न हो सकता है?

तात्पर्य — एक दृढ़-निश्चयी व्यक्ति किसी भी प्रलोभन से प्रलोभित नहीं होता।

Calmness of the Resolute Person

brahmāṇḍamaṇḍalīmātraṁ kiṁ lobhāya manasvinaḥ ।
śapharīsphuritenābdheḥ kṣubdhatā jātu jāyate ॥ 86 ॥

anvayaḥ — *manasvinaḥ lobhāya brahmāṇḍamaṇḍalīmātraṁ kim* । *śapharīsphuritena abdheḥ kṣubdhatā jātu jāyate* (*vā*)?

Even the entire universe is not enough for a resolute person to tempt him. Can the jumping of a fish cause disturbance in the sea?

Purport — A resolute person is never disturbed by any amount of dismaying factor.

कामान्धता से विवेकहीनता

यदासीदज्ञानं स्मरतिमिरसंस्कारजनितं
तदा दृष्टं नारीमयमिदमशेषं जगदिति[165] ।
इदानीमस्माकं पटुतरविवेकाञ्जनजुषां
समीभूता दृष्टिस्त्रिभुवनमपि ब्रह्म मनुते ॥ 87 ॥

अन्वय — स्मरतिमिरसंस्कारजनितं यदा अज्ञानम् आसीत् तदा इदम् अशेषं जगत् नारीमयम् इति दृष्टम्। इदानीं पटुतरविवेकाञ्जनजुषाम् अस्माकं समीभूता दृष्टिः त्रिभुवनम् अपि ब्रह्म मनुते।

जब तक हमें काम-भाव-रूप अन्धकार से उत्पन्न अज्ञान था, तब तक हमें सम्पूर्ण जगत् स्त्री-रूप ही दिखता था। अब विवेक-रूपी अञ्जन से समत्वभाव से पूर्ण हमारी दृष्टि को तीनों भुवन भी ब्रह्म-रूप दिखाई देते हैं।

तात्पर्य — कामान्धता से व्यक्ति विवेक-भ्रष्ट हो जाता है। अतः काम से उत्पन्न अज्ञान को त्यागने कर विवेक-रूपी प्रकाश से ब्रह्म-साक्षात्कार हेतु यत्न करना चाहिए।

---

[165] जगदपि — *JKM.1911.*

Lust Causes Indiscretion

yadāsīdajñānaṁ smaratimirasaṁskārajanitaṁ
tadā dṛṣṭaṁ nārīmayamidamaśeṣaṁ jagaditi ।
idānīmasmākaṁ paṭutaravivekāñjanajuṣāṁ
samībhūtā dṛṣṭistribhuvanamapi brahma manute ॥ 87 ॥

anvayaḥ — *smaratimirasaṁskārajanitaṁ yadā ajñānam āsīt tadā idam aśeṣaṁ jagat nārīmayam iti dṛṣṭam* । *idānīṁ paṭutaravivekāñjanajuṣām asmākaṁ samībhūtā dṛṣṭiḥ tribhuvanam api brahma manute* ।

When there was ignorance produced by the infection of the "blindness" caused due to lust, then the entire world was appeared as filled with women. Now as we have applied the excellent ointment of discretion, the sight has gained equal vision and sees only *Brahman* everywhere in all the three worlds.

Purport — Lust annihilates one's conscience. Therefore, one should give up the ignorance arising from lust and strive to realize *Brahman* in the light of wisdom.

भौतिक सुख-साधनों की अनित्यता

रम्याश्चन्द्रमरीचयस्तृणवती रम्या वनान्तस्थली
रम्यं साधुसभासमागमसुखं[166] रम्याः कवीनां गिरः[167] ।
कोपोपाहितबाष्पबिन्दुतरलं रम्यं प्रियाया मुखं
सर्वं रम्यमनित्यतामुपगते चित्ते न किञ्चित्पुनः ॥ 88 ॥

अन्वय — चन्द्रमरीचयः रम्याः, तृणवती वनान्तस्थली रम्या, साधुसभासमागमसुखं रम्यं, कवीनां गिरः रम्या, कोपोपाहितबाष्पबिन्दुतरलं प्रियाया मुखं रम्यं, सर्वं रम्यम्, (परन्तु) अनित्यतामुपगते चित्ते पुनः किञ्चिद् (अपि) न (रम्यम्) ।

चन्द्रमा की किरणें, हरित एवं शीतल उपवन, सज्जनों की सभाओं के समागम का सुख, कवियों के रसपूर्ण काव्य, प्रणय-कोप से अश्रुपूर्ण प्रिया का चञ्चल मुख — पहले ये सब हमें रमणीय प्रतीत होते थे; किन्तु जब से हमें संसार की अनित्यता का बोध हुआ, तब से हमें इनमें से कुछ भी अच्छा नहीं लगता।

---

166 साधुसमागमागतसुखं काव्येषु रम्याः कथाः — *GAV.1954.*

167 काव्येषु रम्याः कथाः — *JKM.1911.*

तात्पर्य — भौतिक सुख के सभी साधन अनित्य हैं, एवं आपाततः रमणीय प्रतीत होते हैं। अतः इन पर आसक्त होकर अपने जीवन को व्यर्थ व्यतीत नहीं करना चाहिए।

Ephemerality of the Material Means of Happiness

ramyāścandramarīcayastr̥ṇavatī ramyā vanāntasthalī
ramyaṁ sādhusabhāsamāgamasukhaṁ ramyāḥ kavīnāṁ giraḥ ।
kopopāhitabāṣpabindutaralaṁ ramyaṁ priyāyā mukhaṁ
sarvaṁ ramyamanityatāmupagate citte na kiñcitpunaḥ ॥ 88 ॥

anvayaḥ — *candramarīcayaḥ ramyāḥ, tr̥ṇavatī vanāntasthalī ramyā, sādhusabhāsamāgamasukhaṁ ramyaṁ, kavīnāṁ giraḥ ramyā, kopopāhitabāṣpabindutaralaṁ priyāyā mukhaṁ ramyaṁ, sarvaṁ ramyam,* (*parantu*) *anityatāmupagate citte punaḥ kiñcid* (*api*) *na* (*ramyam*) ।

Enchanting are the moonbeams and the verdant outskirts of the forest; delightful is the company of the wise and the compositions of poets; charming is the beloved's face gleaming in tears of indignation; all is fascinating, except when the mind realizes the transience of it all.

Purport — All means of material happiness are impermanent and delightful at first sight, but produce disgust at the end. Therefore, one should not spend one's life in vain by getting attached to them.

तपस्वी का प्रकृष्ट लक्षण

भिक्षाशी जनमध्यसङ्गरहितः स्वायत्तचेष्टः सदा
हानादानविविक्तमार्गरहितः[168] कश्चित्तपस्वी स्थितः ।
रथ्याकीर्णविशीर्णजीर्णवसनः[169] संस्यूतकन्थाधरो[170]
निर्मानो निरहंकृतिः शमसुधाभोगैक[171]बद्धस्पृहः ॥ 89 ॥

अन्वय — भिक्षाशी जनमध्यसङ्गरहितः स्वायत्तचेष्टः सदा हानादानविविक्तमार्गरहितः रथ्याकीर्णविशीर्णजीर्णवसनः संस्यूतकन्थाधरो निर्मानो निरहंकृतिः शमसुधाभोगैकबद्धस्पृहः कश्चित् (विरल एव) तपस्वी स्थितः ।

---

168 दानादानविरक्तमार्गनिरतः — *JKM.1911*, हादानादानविरक्तमार्गनिरतः — *GAV.1954*.

169 वसनैः — *Ms ORLS-3*.

170 सम्प्राप्तकन्थासनः — *GAV.1954*.

171 शमसुखाभोगैकबद्धस्पृहः — *GAV.1954*.

ऐसा तपस्वी विरल ही होता है, जो भीख माँगकर खाता है, जो अपने लोगों में रहकर भी उनमें मोह नहीं रखता, जो स्वाधीनतापूर्वक अपना जीवन निर्वाह करता है, जिसने लेने और देने का व्यवहार छोड़ दिया है, जो रास्ते में पड़े हुए जीर्ण वस्त्रों को ही धारण करता है, जो चीथड़ों की गुदड़ी लेकर घूमता है, जिसे मान का ख्याल नहीं है, जिसमें अभिमान नहीं है और जो शान्ति के सुख को ही सुख मानता है।

तात्पर्य — भैतिक वस्तु एवं सुख-साधनों का सम्पूर्ण त्याग ही वास्तविक संन्यास है।

Characteristic of a True Ascetic

bhikṣāśī janamadhyasaṅgarahitaḥ svāyattaceṣṭaḥ sadā
hānādānaviviktamārgarahitaḥ kaścittapasvī sthitaḥ ।
rathyākīrṇaviśīrṇajīrṇavasanaḥ saṁsyūtakanthādharo
nirmāno nirahaṁkṛtiḥ śamasudhābhogaikabaddhaspṛhaḥ ॥ 89 ॥

anvayaḥ — *bhikṣāśī janamadhyasaṅgarahitaḥ svāyattaceṣṭaḥ sadā hānādānaviviktamārgarahitaḥ rathyākīrṇaviśīrṇajīrṇavasanaḥ saṁsyūta-kanthādharo nirmāno nirahaṁkṛtiḥ śamasudhābhogaikabaddhaspṛhaḥ kaścit (virala eva) tapasvī sthitaḥ* ।

Such an individual living on alms, unattached to the company of people, ever acting with total freedom, devoted to the path of dispassion towards the exchange of wealth, wearing worn-out rags thrown in the streets, using a blanket received by chance for a seat, without pride or selfishness, wishing solely for the joy of quiescence is a true ascetic.

Purport — Complete impassiveness towards material objects and comforts is real renunciation.

ब्रह्मलीनता

मातर्मेदिनि तातमारुत सखे ज्योतिः[172] सुबन्धो जल
भ्रातर्व्योम निबद्ध एष भवतामग्रप्रणामाञ्जलिः[173] ।

---

172 तेजः — *JKM.1911, GAV.1954.*

173 अन्त्यः प्रणामाञ्जलिः — *JKM.1911, GAV.1954.*

युष्मत्सङ्गसखो[174]पजातसुकृतोद्रेकस्फुरन्निर्मल-
ज्वालापास्त[175]समस्तमोहमहिमा लीये परंब्रह्मणि ॥ 90 ॥

अन्वय — मातः मेदिनि! तात मारुत! सखे ज्योतिः! सुबन्धो जल! भ्रातः व्योम! भवताम् एष अग्रप्रणामाञ्जलिः निबद्धः। युष्मत्सङ्गसखोपजातसुकृतोद्रेकस्फुरन्निर्मलज्वालापास्तसमस्तमोहमहिमा (अहं) परंब्रह्मणि लीये।

हे माता पृथ्वी! पिता वायु! मित्र ज्योतिः! बन्धु जल! भाई आकाश! अब मैं आपको अन्तिम विदाई का प्रणाम करता हूँ। आपकी संगति से मैंने पुण्य कर्म किए और पुण्यों के फलस्वरूप मुझे आत्म-ज्ञान हुआ, जिसने मेरे संसारी मोह का नाश कर दिया। अब मैं परम ब्रह्म में लीन होता हूँ।

तात्पर्य — पञ्च तत्त्वों से छूटकर ब्रह्म में लीन हो जाना ही मनुष्य जीवन का अन्तिम लक्ष्य है।

Unification with Supreme Consciousness

mātarmedini tātamāruta sakhe jyotiḥ subandho jala
bhrātarvyoma nibaddha eṣa bhavatāmagrapraṇāmāñjaliḥ ।
yuṣmatsaṅgasakhopajātasukṛtodrekasphurannirmala-
jvālāpāstasamastamohamahimā līye paraṁbrahmaṇi ॥ 90 ॥

anvayaḥ — *mātaḥ medini! tāta māruta! sakhe jyotiḥ! subandho jala! bhrātaḥ vyoma! bhavatām eṣa agrapraṇāmāñjaliḥ nibaddhaḥ* । *yuṣmatsaṅgasakhopajātasukṛtodrekasphurannirmalajvālāpāstasamastamohamahimā (ahaṁ) paraṁbrahmaṇi līye* ।

Oh Mother Earth! Oh Wind, my Father! Oh Fire, my friend! Oh Water, my good relative! Oh Sky, my Brother! With clasped hands this is my concluding salutations to you! My association with you all resulted in an accumulation of scintillating merits, culminating in abundance of pure knowledge, which helped me overcome the marvellous sway of Unreality! May I now unite with the Transcendent Truth!

Purport — The ultimate goal of human life is to become free from the five elements and merge into *Brahman*.

---

174 युष्मत्सङ्गसुख — *Ms ORLS-3*, युष्मत्सङ्गवश — *JKM.1911, GAV.1954.*

175 ज्ञानापास्त — *JKM.1911, GAV.1954.*

आध्यात्मिक साधना के लिए समयानुकूल प्रयास की सार्थकता

यावत्स्वस्थमिदं शरीरमरुजं यावज्जरा दूरतो
यावच्चेन्द्रियशक्तिरप्रतिहता यावत्क्षयो नायुषः।
आत्मश्रेयसि तावदेव विदुषा[176] कार्यः प्रयत्नो महान्
संदीप्ते भवने तु कूपखननं प्रत्युद्यमः[177] कीदृशः ॥ 91 ॥

अन्वय — यावत् इदं शरीरं स्वस्थम् अरुजं च, यावत् जरा दूरतः, यावत् च इन्द्रियशक्तिः अप्रतिहता, यावत् आयुषः क्षयो न, तावत् एव विदुषा आत्मश्रेयसि महान् प्रयत्नः कार्यः, संदीप्ते भवने तु कूपखननं कीदृशः प्रत्युद्यमः?

जब तक यह शरीर स्वस्थ एवं निरोग हो, जब तक वृद्धावस्था दूर हो, और जब तक इन्द्रियों की शक्ति अबाधित हो, जब तक आयु बची हो, तब तक बुद्धिमान को आत्म-कल्याण हेतु प्रयत्न करना चाहिए जिससे कि परम पुरुषार्थ प्राप्ति हो सके। घर को आग लगने पर कुआँ खोदने का उद्यम आरम्भ करना क्या उचित होगा?

तात्पर्य — मनुष्य जीवन सीमित काल के लिए है। अतः समय रहते ही परम पुरुषार्थ प्राप्ति हेतु प्रयास करना चाहिए। अन्तिम समय पर आत्म-कल्याण हेतु किया हुआ आरम्भ घर जलने पर कुआँ खोदने के तुल्य निष्फल है।

Timely Efforts for Spiritual Attainment

yāvatsvasthamidaṁ śarīramarujaṁ yāvajjarā dūrato
yāvaccendriyaśaktirapratihatā yāvatkṣayo nāyuṣaḥ ।
ātmaśreyasi tāvadeva viduṣā kāryaḥ prayatno mahān
saṅdīpte bhavane tu kūpakhananaṁ pratyudyamaḥ kīdṛśaḥ ॥ 91 ॥

anvayaḥ — *yāvat idaṁ śarīraṁ svastham arujaṁ ca, yāvat jarā dūrataḥ, yāvat ca indriyaśaktiḥ apratihatā yāvat āyuṣaḥ kṣayo na, tāvat eva viduṣā ātmaśreyasi mahān prayatnaḥ kāryaḥ, saṅdīpte bhavane tu kūpakhananaṁ kīdṛśaḥ pratyudyamaḥ?*

As long as this body is healthy and free of infirmity, as long as senility is distant, as long as the faculties have not lost their vigour, as long as the life is not enfeebled, till then should the

---

176 सुधिया — *Ms ORLS-3.*

177 प्रत्युद्गमः — *Ms eG-1.*

wise ones make great efforts to reach the supreme goal of life. What is the use of setting out to dig a well when the house is on fire?

Purport — Human life is for a limited period. Therefore, as soon as there is time, efforts should be made for spiritual realization. An initiative taken at the end of life for self-welfare is as fruitless as digging a well for water when the house is burning down.

पुरुषार्थ-प्राप्ति के बिना जीवन की निष्फलता

नाभ्यस्ता भुवि वादिदर्पदलनी[178] विद्या विनीतोचिता
खड्गाग्रैः करिकुम्भदन्तदलनै[179]र्नाकं न नीतं यशः ।
कान्ताकोमलपल्लवाधररसः पीतो न चन्द्रोदये
तारुण्यं गतमेव निष्फलतया शून्यालये दीपवत् ॥ 92 ॥

अन्वय — भुवि वादिदर्पदलनी विनीतोचिता विद्या न अभ्यस्ता, खड्गाग्रैः करिकुम्भदन्तदलनैः यशः नाकं न नीतं, चन्द्रोदये कान्ताकोमलपल्लवाधररसः न पीतः, शून्यालये दीपवत् तारुण्यं निष्फलतया एव गतम् ।

हमने इस जगत् में नम्रों को सन्तुष्ट करने वाली और वादियों की मान-भञ्जन करने वाली विद्या नहीं पढ़ी, तलवार की धार से हाथी के मस्तक और दाँत काटकर अपना यश स्वर्ग तक नहीं पहुँचाया; चाँदनी रात में सुन्दरी के कोमल अधर-पल्लव (निचले ओठ) का रस भी नहीं पिया। हाय! हमारी जवानी सूने घर में जलने वाले दीपक की तरह यूँ ही नष्ट हो गई!

तात्पर्य — पुरुषार्थ-प्राप्ति ही जीवन का श्रेष्ठ प्रयोजन है, जिसके बिना मनुष्य-जीवन निरर्थक है।

Futility of Life without the Pursuit of Puruṣārtha

nābhyastā bhuvi vādidarpadalanī vidyā vinītocitā
khaḍgāgraiḥ karikumbhadantadalanairnākaṁ na nītaṁ yaśaḥ ।
kāntākomalapallavādhararasaḥ pīto na candrodaye
tāruṇyaṁ gatameva niṣphalatayā śūnyālaye dīpavat ॥ 92 ॥

anvayaḥ — *bhuvi vādidarpadalanī vinītocitā vidyā na abhyastā, khaḍgāgraiḥ karikumbhadantadalanaiḥ yaśaḥ nākaṁ na nītaṁ, candrodaye kāntākomalapallavādhararasaḥ na pītaḥ, śūnyālaye dīpavat tāruṇyaṁ niṣphalatayā eva gatam* ।

---

178 वादिदर्पशमनी — *Ms ORLS-3*, वादिवृन्ददलनी — *JKM.1911, GAV.1954.*

179 पीठदलनैः — *JKM.1911, GAV.1954.*

Neither studied and acquired adequate knowledge to defeat scholarly debaters; nor gained heaven-high fame by wielding the sword strongly enough to knock down an elephant's head and teeth; nor kissed at moonrise the tender lips of a woman! Alas! Entire youthhood has slipped out in vain, like a lamp in a deserted house.

Purport — Attainment of *puruṣārtha* is the best purpose of life, without which human life is meaningless.

परमात्मा की भक्ति ही परम लक्ष्य

जीर्णा एव मनोरथाः स्वहृदये[180] यातं च तद्यौवनं
हन्ताङ्गेषु गुणाश्च वन्ध्यफलतां याता गुणज्ञैर्विना ।
किं युक्तं सहसाभ्युपैति बलवान्कालः कृतान्तोऽक्षमी
न ज्ञातं मधुसूदनाङ्घ्रियुगलं[181] मुक्त्वास्ति नान्या गतिः ॥ 93 ॥

अन्वय — हन्त! मनोरथाः स्वहृदये जीर्णा एव, अङ्गेषु तद् यौवनं च यातं, गुणाश्च गुणज्ञैः विना वन्ध्यफलतां याताः। कृतान्तः अक्षमी बलवान् कालः सहसा अभ्युपैति, किं युक्तं न ज्ञातम्। (अतः) मधुसूदनाङ्घ्रियुगलं मुक्त्वा अन्या गतिः न अस्ति।

हमारी इच्छाएं हमारे हृदय में ही जीर्ण हो गईं, शरीर का यौवन भी चला गया, हमारे अच्छे-अच्छे गुण भी गुणों के महत्त्व को समझने वालों के न होने से निष्फल हो गए, शक्तिमान् सर्वनाशक मृत्यु का स्वामी यमराज भी शीघ्र हमारे पास आ रहा है; इसलिए अब हमारी समझ में भगवान् विष्णु के चरणों को छोड़कर हमारी अन्य कहीं गति नहीं है।

तात्पर्य — नश्वर एवं क्षणभंगुर संसार में भगवद्भक्ति ही शाश्वत मार्ग है।

Devotion to God Is the Ultimate Goal

jīrṇā eva manorathāḥ svahṛdaye yātaṁ ca tadyauvanaṁ
hantāṅgeṣu guṇāśca vandhyaphalatāṁ yātā guṇajñairvinā ।
kiṁ yuktaṁ sahasābhyupaiti balavānkālaḥ kṛtānto 'kṣamī
na jñātaṁ madhusūdanāṅghriyugalaṁ muktvāsti nānyā gatiḥ ॥ 93 ॥

---

180 मनोरथाश्च हृदये — *Ms ORLS-3, GAV.1954.*

181 हा ज्ञातं स्मरशासनाङ्घ्रियुगलं — *JKM.1911*, मदनान्तकाङ्घ्रियुगलं — *GAV.1954.*

anvayaḥ — *hanta! manorathāḥ svahṛdaye jīrṇā eva, aṅgeṣu tad yauvanaṁ ca yātaṁ, guṇāśca guṇajñaiḥ vinā vandhyaphalatāṁ yātāḥ। kṛtāntaḥ akṣamī balavān kālaḥ sahasā abhyupaiti, kiṁ yuktaṁ na jñātam। (ataḥ) madhusūdanāṅghriyugalaṁ muktvā anyā gatiḥ na asti।*

Desires have worn away in the own heart; that youthfulness of the body is gone away. Alas! The virtues in our limbs have become fruitless due to lack of admirers. The mighty, unforgiving Yama, is causing the end, approaching suddenly. What is proper now? Ah, it is known (to me) — there is no other refuge, except the twin-feet of Viṣṇu, the Lord who punished the demon Madhu.

Purport — Devotion to God is the eternal path in this mortal and transitory world.

ज्ञान के सदुपयोग से ही मुक्ति

ज्ञानं सतां मानमदादिवारणं[182]
केषाञ्चिदन्तर्मद[183]मानकारणम्।
स्थानं विविक्तं यमिनां विमुक्तये
कामातुराणामपि कामकारणम्॥ 94॥

अन्वय — ज्ञानं सतां मानमदादिवारणं, (परं तदेव) केषांचित् अन्तर्मदमानकारणम्। विविक्तं स्थानं यमिनां विमुक्तये, (परं तदेव) कामातुराणाम् अपि कामकारणं (भवति)।

जो ज्ञान सज्जनों के मान मद आदि का नाश करता है और वही दुर्जन के मद और मान को बढ़ाता है। वही ज्ञान योगी पुरुषों की मुक्ति का एकान्त स्थानरूप साधन है परन्तु वही ज्ञान कामी पुरुषों के काम को बढ़ाने वाला है।

तात्पर्य — मनुष्य अपने ज्ञान के कारण ही सन्मार्ग या कुमार्ग में प्रवृत्त होता है, अतः अपने ज्ञान का सदुपयोग करके सन्मार्गोन्मुखी होना चाहिए जिससे उसे पश्चात्ताप न करना पड़े।

Proper Use of Knowledge only Leads to Salvation

jñānaṁ satāṁ mānamadādivāraṇaṁ
keṣāñcidantarmadamānakāraṇam।

---

[182] नाशनं — *JKM.1911.*

[183] एतन्मद — *JKM.1911.*

sthānaṁ viviktaṁ yamināṁ vimuktaye
kāmāturāṇāmapi kāmakāraṇam ॥ 94 ॥

anvayaḥ — *jñānaṁ satāṁ mānamadādivāraṇaṁ, (paraṁ tadeva) keṣāñcit antarmadamānakāraṇam* । *viviktaṁ sthānaṁ yamināṁ vimuktaye, (paraṁ tadeva) kāmāturāṇām api kāmakāraṇaṁ (bhavati)* ।

The knowledge, which destroys the pride and arrogance of good people, increases the pride and arrogance of the wicked ones. The same knowledge is the only means of liberation for *yogī*s, but it is erogenous for lustful people.

Purport — It is only because of his knowledge that a human being is inclined towards the right path or the wrong path. Therefore, one should make good use of one's knowledge and be oriented towards the right path so that one does not have to repent.

सुख का भ्रम

तृषाशुष्यत्यास्ये पिबति सलिलं शीत[184]सुरभि
क्षुधार्तः [185]शच्छालीन्कवलयति सांस्पाकवलितान्[186] ।
प्रदीप्ते रागाग्नौ[187] घननिविड[188]माश्लिष्यति वधूं
प्रतीकारे[189] व्याधेः सुखमिति विपर्यस्यति जनः ॥ 95 ॥

अन्वय — जनः तृषाशुष्यति आस्ये शीतसुरभि सलिलं पिबति, क्षुधार्तः सांस्पाकवलितान् शच्छालीन् कवलयति। रागाग्नौ प्रदीप्ते वधूं घननिविडम् आश्लिष्यति, (एवं प्रकारेण) व्याधेः प्रतीकारे (जनः) सुखम् इति विपर्यस्यति।

जब मनुष्य का कण्ठ प्यास से सूखने लगता है, तब वह शीतल जल पीता है; जब उसे भूख लगती है, तब वह साग और कढ़ी प्रभृति के संग चावल आदि अन्न खाता है; जब

---

184 स्वादु सुरभि — *JKM.1911*, शीतमधुरं — *GAV.1954.*

185 सञ्शालीन् — *JKM.1911*, शाल्यन्नं — *GAV.1954.*

186 शाकादिवलितान् — *JKM.1911.*

187 कामाग्नौ — *GAV.1954.*

188 सुदृढतरम् — *JKM.1911, GAV.1954.*

189 प्रतीकारो — *JKM.1911*, प्रतिकारं — *GAV.1954.*

उसकी कामाग्नि तेज़ होती है तब वह स्त्री को ज़ोर से गले लगाता है; विचार करके देखने से मालूम होता है, कि ये सब बीमारियों की एक-एक दवा है; परन्तु लोग इन्हें भूल से सुख समान मानते हैं।

तात्पर्य — सांसारिक सुख उन सभी बीमारियों के लिए एक अस्थायी इलाज़ है, जिनसे सांसारिक जीवन घिरा हुआ है। जब खुशी की यह सापेक्ष और अस्थायी प्रकृति हमारे सामने स्पष्ट हो जाती है, तो हमें इसके पीछे भागना छोड़ देना चाहिए एवं त्याग के माध्यम से स्थायी शान्ति की तलाश करनी चाहिए।

Delusion of Happiness

tṛṣāśuṣyatyāsye pibati salilaṁ śītasurabhi
kṣudhārtaḥ śacchālīnkavalayati sāṁspākavalitān ।
pradīpte rāgāgnau ghananiviḍamāśliṣyati vadhūṁ
pratīkāre vyādheḥ sukhamiti viparyasyati janaḥ ॥ 95 ॥

anvayaḥ — *janaḥ tṛṣāśuṣyati āsye śītasurabhi salilaṁ pibati, kṣudhārtaḥ sāṁspākavalitān śacchālīn kavalayati* । *rāgāgnau pradīpte vadhūṁ ghananiviḍam āśliṣyati, (evaṁ prakāreṇa) vyādheḥ pratīkāre (janaḥ) sukham iti viparyasyati* ।

When the mouth is parched with thirst, an individual drinks cool and sweet water; when smitten with hunger he eats rice, flavoured with juicy vegetables; when afire with passion, he embraces his beloved wife with a tight hug; thus, joy is the remedying of these diseases (thirst, hunger, lust) and yet people mistakenly take these remedies as happiness!

Purport — Worldly happiness is but the temporary remedy we constantly seek for all the diseases with which our worldly life is beset. When this relative and fugitive nature of happiness becomes apparent to us, we should give up running after it, to seek permanent peace by renunciation.

समाधि से ही शाश्वत सुख

भो मर्त्याः शृणुत स्फुटाक्षरमिदं वाक्यं शिवावाप्तये
भक्ताः क्रीडितुमिन्द्रियैः सुखलवावाप्त्यर्थमभ्युद्यताः ।

संसारे तृणभङ्गभङ्गुरतरे लभ्यं न चाऽऽत्यन्तिकं[190]
स्वात्मन्यस्ति समाधिनिर्मलसुखं यत्तत्स्वयं चिन्त्यताम् ॥ 96 ॥

अन्वय — भोः सुखलवावाप्त्यर्थम् इन्द्रियैः क्रीडितुम् अभ्युद्यताः मर्त्याः भक्ताः! शिवावाप्तये इदं स्फुटाक्षरं वाक्यं शृणुत। तृणभङ्गभङ्गुरतरे संसारे आत्यन्तिकं समाधिनिर्मलसुखं च न लभ्यं, यत् स्वात्मनि अस्ति तत् स्वयं चिन्त्यताम्।

थोड़े से सुख पाने के लिए इन्द्रियों के साथ खेलने को उद्यत मानव भक्त! आत्म-कल्याण हेतु यह स्पष्ट अर्थ वाला वाक्य सुनें। तिनके की तरह क्षणभंगुर इस भौतिक संसार में समाधि से ही प्राप्त होने वाले शाश्वत सुख नहीं मिल सकता। अतः सांसारिक विषयों से बुद्धि को हटाकर आत्म-निदिध्यासन में जो सुख है वही चिन्ता करें।

तात्पर्य — क्षणभंगुर भौतिक संसार में शाश्वत सुख की प्राप्ति सम्भव नहीं। अतः आत्म-निदिध्यासन में ही शाश्वत सुख की खोज करें।

Infinite Bliss Attains through Abstract Meditation Only

bho martyāḥ śṛṇuta sphuṭākṣaramidaṁ vākyaṁ śivāvāptaye
bhaktāḥ krīḍitumindriyaiḥ sukhalavāvāptyarthamabhyudyatāḥ ।
saṁsāre tṛṇabhaṅgabhaṅguratare labhyaṁ na cā ''tyantikaṁ
svātmanyasti samādhinirmalasukhaṁ yattatsvayaṁ
cintyatām ॥ 96 ॥

anvayaḥ — *bhoḥ sukhalavāvāptyartham indriyaiḥ krīḍitum abhyudyatāḥ martyāḥ bhaktāḥ! śivāvāptaye idaṁ sphuṭākṣaraṁ vākyaṁ śṛṇuta* । *tṛṇabhaṅgabhaṅguratare saṁsāre ātyantikaṁ samādhinirmalasukhaṁ ca na labhyaṁ, yat svātmani asti tat svayaṁ cintyatām* ।

Oh human devotees willing to play with the senses to get a little happiness! Listen to this sentence with clear meaning for your self-welfare. In this material world, which is temporary like a straw, one cannot get eternal happiness that can be attained only by *samādhi* (abstract meditation). Therefore, divert your mind from worldly matters and concentrate only on the happiness you find in self-reflection.

Purport — Eternal happiness cannot be achieved in the fleeting material world. It is only self-meditation that by which one can experience supreme and endless pleasure.

---

190 क्षणभङ्गभङ्गुरतराण्येतानि चाऽऽत्यन्तिकं — *Ms ORLS-3.*

तप साधन द्वारा सांसारिक दुःखों से मुक्ति

स्नात्वा गाङ्गैः पयोभिः शुचिकुसुमफलै[191]रर्चयित्वा प्रभो त्वां
ध्येयं ध्याने निवेश्य[192] क्षितिधरकुहरग्रावमूले निषण्णः[193]।
आत्मारामः फलाशी गुरुवचनरतस्त्वत्प्रसादात्स्मरारे
दुःखं मोक्ष्ये कदाहं समकरचरणे पुंसि सेवासमुत्थम् ॥ 97 ॥

अन्वय — हे प्रभो स्मरारे! गाङ्गैः पयोभिः स्नात्वा, शुचिकुसुमफलैः त्वाम् अर्चयित्वा, ध्येयं ध्याने निवेश्य, क्षितिधरकुहरग्रावमूले निषण्णः फलाशी आत्मारामः गुरुवचनरतः त्वत्प्रसादात् समकरचरणे पुंसि सेवासमुत्थम् दुःखम् अहं कदा मोक्ष्ये?

हे शिव! हे कामारि! गंगाजल से स्नान करके, पवित्र फल-फूलों से आपकी अर्चना करते हुए, ध्येय को ध्यान में रखकर, पर्वत की गुफ़ा में शिला पर बैठा हुआ, वन के ही फल खाता हुआ, अपनी ही आत्मा में मग्न होता हुआ, गुरु के उपदेशों का पालन करते हुए, आप के प्रसाद से, समान कर एवं चरणों वाले पुरुष का ध्यान करता हुआ कब मैं इन संसारी दुःखों से छुटकारा पाऊँगा?

तात्पर्य — जब तक सांसारिक सुखों से आसक्ति नहीं छूटती तब तक परमात्मा का सान्निध्य सम्भव नहीं ।

Austerity: The Way to Free from Worldly Sufferings

snātvā gāṅgaiḥ payobhiḥ śucikusumaphalairarcayitvā prabho tvāṁ
dhyeyaṁ dhyāne niveśya kṣitidharakuharagrāvamūle niṣaṇṇaḥ ।
ātmārāmaḥ phalāśī guruvacanaratastvatprasādātsmarāre
duḥkhaṁ mokṣye kadāhaṁ samakaracaraṇe puṁsi
sevāsamuttham ॥ 97 ॥

anvayaḥ — *he prabho smarāre! gāṅgaiḥ payobhiḥ snātvā, śucikusumaphalaiḥ tvām arcayitvā, dhyeyaṁ dhyāne niveśya, kṣitidharakuharagrāvamūle niṣaṇṇaḥ phalāśī ātmārāmaḥ guruvacanarataḥ tvatprasādāt samakaracaraṇe puṁsi sevāsamuttham duḥkham ahaṁ kadā mokṣye?*

After bathing in the waters of the Gaṅgā, worshipping you with the choicest fruits and flowers, with my mind meditating on you,

---

191 शुचिकुसुमजलै — *Ms ORLS-3.*

192 ध्येये ध्यानं नियोज्य — *JKM.1911*, ध्येये ध्यानं निवेश्य — *GAV.1954.*

193 ग्रावपर्यङ्कमूले — *JKM.1911.*

seated on a bed of stone in a mountain-cave, enjoying the bliss of the Self, surviving on fruits, joyfully engrossed in the spiritual preceptor's instructions, Oh Cupid's enemy! when will you free me with your grace from the sorrow of having served the rich?

Purport — Unless one renounces his attachment to worldly pleasures, unification with God is not possible.

शिवाराधन की श्रेष्ठता

महेश्वरे वा जगतामधीश्वरे जनार्दने वा जगदन्तरात्मनि।
न भेदभावप्रतिपत्ति[194]रस्ति मे तथापि भक्तिस्तरुणेन्दुशेखरे ॥ 98 ॥

अन्वय — जगताम् अधीश्वरे महेश्वरे वा, जगदन्तरात्मनि जनार्दने वा, मे भेदभावप्रतिपत्तिः नास्ति। तथापि तरुणेन्दुशेखरे (मे) भक्तिः अस्ति।

यद्यपि मुझे विश्वेश्वर शिव और जगत् की अन्तरात्मा विष्णु में कोई भेद नहीं दिखता; तथापि मेरा मन उन्हीं की ओर झुकता है, जिनके मस्तक में तरुण चन्द्रमा विराजमान है; अर्थात् मैं शिव को ही चाहता हूँ।

तात्पर्य — शिव ही वैराग्य के प्रतीक देव हैं, और वैराग्य ही परम सुख का कन्द है। अतः शिव-सायुज्य ही सर्वतोपेक्षा प्रार्थनीय है।

The Superiority of Devotion to Śiva

maheśvare vā jagatāmadhīśvare janārdane vā jagadantarātmani ।
na bhedabhāvapratipattirasti me tathāpi bhaktistaruṇendu-
śekhare ॥ 98 ॥

anvayaḥ — *jagatām adhīśvare maheśvare vā, jagadantarātmani janārdane vā, me bhedabhāvapratipattiḥ nāsti* । *tathāpi taruṇenduśekhare (me) bhaktiḥ asti* ।

Between the great Lord of the universe, Śiva, and the innermost Self of the universe, Viṣṇu, there is no difference for me. However, my devotion is to Śiva, holding the crescent moon on His head.

Purport — Śiva is the symbol of renunciation, and renunciation is the tuber of Supreme Bliss. Therefore, union with Śiva is the most desirable.

---

[194] तयोर्नभेदप्रतिपत्ति — *JKM.1911*, न वस्तुभेदप्रतिपत्ति — *GAV.1954*.

शिव-भक्ति से कामविकारहीनता

किं कंदर्प करं कदर्थयसि भोः कोदण्डटङ्कारवैः
रे रे कोकिल कोमलं त्यज रुतं किं त्वं वृथा वल्गसि[195]।
अग्रे[196] स्निग्धविदग्धमुग्धमधुरैर्लोलैः कटाक्षैरलं
चेतः सम्प्रति चन्द्रचूडचरणध्यानामृतं सेवते ॥ 99 ॥

अन्वय — भोः कंदर्प! कोदण्डटङ्कारवैः करं किं कदर्थयसि? रे रे कोकिल! कोमलं रुतं त्यज, किं त्वं वृथा वल्गसि? अग्रे स्निग्धविदग्धमुग्धमधुरैः लोलैः कटाक्षैः अलम्। सम्प्रति चेतः चन्द्रचूडचरणध्यानामृतं सेवते।

हे कामदेव! धनुष के टंकारों से अपने हाथ को क्यों कष्ट दे रहे हो, अरे कोयल! कोमल स्वर से कूजना अब बन्द करो; मेरे सामने अपने सुन्दर, चतुर और चञ्चल कटाक्षों से क्या लाभ? क्योंकि मेरा मन अब चन्द्रशेखर भगवान् के चरणों के ध्यान-रूपी अमृत में मग्न है।

तात्पर्य — कामादि वासना से स्वयं को दूर रखने के लिए शिव के प्रति भक्ति एवं तन्मयता अपेक्षित है।

Devotion to Śiva Confiscates Lust

kiṁ kaṅdarpa karaṁ kadarthayasi bhoḥ kodaṇḍaṭaṅkāravaiḥ
re re kokila komalaṁ tyaja rutaṁ kiṁ tvaṁ vṛthā valgasi ।
agre snigdhavidagdhamugdhamadhurairlolaiḥ kaṭākṣairalaṁ
cetaḥ samprati candracūḍacaraṇadhyānāmṛtaṁ sevate ॥ 99 ॥

anvayaḥ — *bhoḥ kaṅdarpa! kodaṇḍaṭaṅkāravaiḥ karaṁ kiṁ kadarthayasi? re re kokila! komalaṁ rutaṁ tyaja, kiṁ tvaṁ vṛthā valgasi? agre snigdhavidagdhamugdhamadhuraiḥ lolaiḥ kaṭākṣaiḥ alam* । *samprati cetaḥ candracūḍacaraṇadhyānāmṛtaṁ sevate* ।

Oh Lord Cupid! why are you troubling your hand with the strokes of the bow, oh cuckoo! now stop cooing softly; what is the benefit of beautiful, clever and playful sarcasm of a lady in front of me? Because my mind is now engrossed in the nectar of meditation at the feet of Lord Śiva.

Purport — Devotion to Śiva confiscates lust and other desires.

---

195 जल्पसि — *JKM.1911.*

196 मुग्धे — *JKM.1911.*

योगी के लिए संसार की असारता

कौपीनं शतखण्डजर्जरतरं कन्था पुनस्तादृशी
निश्चिन्तं[197] निरपेक्षभैक्षमशनं[198] निद्रा[199] श्मशाने वने।
ब्रह्माण्डोदरमन्दिरं सुविपुलं भक्तिश्च गुर्वी शिवे[200]
योगाभ्यासरतिर्महोत्सवसुखं त्रैलोक्यराज्येन किम्[201] ॥ 100 ॥

अन्वय — शतखण्डजर्जरतरं कौपीनं, कन्था पुनः तादृशी, निरपेक्षभैक्षं निश्चिन्तम् अशनं, श्मशाने वने (वा) निद्रा, ब्रह्माण्डोदरमन्दिरं सुविपुलं, गुर्वी शिवे च भक्तिः, योगाभ्यासरतिः महोत्सवसुखं, त्रैलोक्यराज्येन किम्?

जिनका कौपीन (लंगोटी) जीर्ण होकर टुकड़े-टुकड़े हो गया है और कथरी भी इसी तरह हो गई और जो स्वयं निश्चिन्त है, भोजन के लिए चिन्तारहित होकर जो भिक्षान्न की अपेक्षा भी नहीं करता हो, जिसकी निद्रा श्मशान में अथवा वन में हुआ करती है, विस्तृत ब्रह्माण्ड ही जिसका वासस्थान है, शिवजी में जिसकी प्रगाढ़ भक्ति हो, योगाभ्यास का प्रेम ही जिसके लिए महोत्सव जैसा सुख हो, उसके लिए त्रैलोक्यरूपी राज्य का क्या प्रयोजन?

तात्पर्य — योगी-जनों के लिए त्रिभुवन का वैभव अत्यन्त तुच्छ है।

Futility of the World for an Ascetic

kaupīnaṁ śatakhaṇḍajarjarataraṁ kanthā punastādṛśī
niścintaṁ nirapekṣabhaikṣamaśanaṁ nidrā śmaśāne vane ।
brahmāṇḍodaramandiraṁ suvipulaṁ bhaktiśca gurvī śive
yogābhyāsaratirmahotsavasukhaṁ trailokyarājyena kim ॥ 100 ॥

anvayaḥ — *śatakhaṇḍajarjarataraṁ kaupīnaṁ, kanthā punaḥ tādṛśī, nirapekṣabhaikṣaṁ niścintam aśanaṁ, śmaśāne vane (vā) nidrā, brahmāṇḍodaramandiraṁ suvipulaṁ, gurvī śive ca bhaktiḥ, yogābhyāsaratiḥ mahotsavasukhaṁ, trailokyarājyena kim?*

---

197 नैश्चिन्त्यं — *GAV.1954.*

198 सुखसाध्यभैक्ष्यमशनं — *JKM.1911.*

199 शय्या — *JKM.1911.*

200 मित्रामित्रसमानता पशुपतेश्चिन्ताऽथ शून्यालये — *JKM.1911*, स्वातन्त्र्येण निरङ्कुशं स्वान्तं प्रशान्तं सदा — *GAV.1954.*

201 ध्वस्ताशेषमदप्रमादमुदितो योगी सुखं तिष्ठति — *JKM.1911*, स्थैर्यं योगमहोत्सवेऽपि च यदि त्रैलोक्यराज्येन किम् — *GAV.1954.*

The Way of Life of a Self-Realized Ascetic: Wearing a loincloth worn-out and tattered into a hundred rags, with a wrap-around in similar condition, eating food from alms begged without any expectations, sleeping in a forest or a cremation-ground, whose abode is the vast universe, who has deep devotion to Lord Śiva, for whom love of Yogic practice brings happiness like a festival, for such a one even sovereignty of the three worlds is beneath comparison.

Purport — For a celibate even sovereignty of the three worlds is beneath comparison.

सांसारिक सुखों से मन को हटाना

भोगा भङ्गुरवृत्तयो बहुविधास्तैरेव चायं भव-
स्तत्कस्येह कृते परिभ्रमत रे लोकाः कृतं चेष्टितैः ।
आशापाशशतोपशान्तिविशदं चेतः समाधीयतां
क्वाप्यात्यन्तिकसौख्यधामनि[202] यदि श्रद्धेयमस्मद्वचः ॥ 101 ॥

अन्वय — रे लोकाः! भोगा बहुविधाः भङ्गुरवृत्तयः, तैः एव च अयं भवः, तत् कस्य कृते इह परिभ्रमत? चेष्टितैः कृतम्। यदि अस्मद्वचः श्रद्धेयं (तदा) आशापाशशतोपशान्तिविशदं चेतः क्वापि आत्यन्तिकसौख्यधामनि समाधीयताम्।

नाना प्रकार के विषय-भोग नाशमान और संसार-बन्धन के कारण हैं, इस बात को जानकर भी हे मनुष्यों! किसके लिए इस संसार में फंसे हो? इन सांसारिक चेष्टाओं से क्या लाभ होगा? यदि आपको हमारी बात का विश्वास हो, तो आप अनेक प्रकार के आशा-जाल के टूटने से शुद्ध हुए चित्त को किसी शाश्वत सुख के धाम (परमात्मा) में लगाओ।

तात्पर्य — सांसारिक सुखों की क्षणभंगुर प्रकृति को जानकर शाश्वत सुख के निवास में ध्यान केन्द्रित करना चाहिए।

Diverging the Mind from Worldly Pleasures

bhogā bhaṅguravṛttayo bahuvidhāstaireva cāyaṁ bhava-
statkasyeha kṛte paribhramata re lokāḥ kṛtaṁ ceṣṭitaiḥ ।
āśāpāśaśatopaśāntiviśadaṁ cetaḥ samādhīyatāṁ
kvāpyātyantikasaukhyadhāmani yadi śraddheyamasmadvacaḥ ॥ 101 ॥

[202] कामोच्छित्तिवशे स्वधामनि — *JKM.1911*, कामोत्पत्तिवशत् — *GAV.1954*.

***anvayaḥ** — re lokāḥ! bhogā bahuvidhāḥ bhaṅguravṛttayaḥ, taiḥ eva ca ayaṁ bhavaḥ, tat kasya kṛte iha paribhramata? ceṣṭitaiḥ kṛtam। yadi asmadvacaḥ śraddheyaṁ (tadā) āśāpāśaśatopaśāntiviśadaṁ cetaḥ kvāpi ātyantikasaukhyadhāmani samādhīyatām।*

Varied and transient pleasures are the cause of worldly bondage. Then why do you wander here exerting yourself incessantly? If you trust on what we say, thus, concentrate your mind, purified by breaking bonds of hope arising from desires, with their hundreds of strings, in the abode of eternal happiness (God).

Purport — Knowing the transient nature of the worldly pleasures, one should concentrate on the abode of eternal happiness.

नश्वर इच्छाओं से निरर्थक क्षीयमाण जीवन

धन्यानां गिरिकन्दरेषु वसतां ज्योतिः परं ध्यायता-
मानन्दाश्रुजलं पिबन्ति शकुना निःशङ्कमङ्केशयाः।
अन्येषां तु[203] मनोरथैः परिचित[204]प्रासादवापीतट-
क्रीडाकाननकेलिकौतुकजुषामायुः परं क्षीयते ॥ 102 ॥

अन्वयः — गिरिकन्दरेषु वसतां, परं ज्योतिः ध्यायतां (च) धन्यानाम् अङ्केशयाः शकुनाः निःशङ्कम् आनन्दाश्रुजलं पिबन्ति । अन्येषां तु परिचितप्रासादवापीतटक्रीडाकाननकेलिकौतुकजुषां मनोरथैः आयुः परं क्षीयते।

वे धन्य हैं, जो पर्वतीय कन्दराओं में निवास करते हैं और परम ब्रह्म की ज्योति का ध्यान करते हैं, जिनके आनन्दजनित आँसुओं का पक्षीगण उनकी ही गोद में बैठकर निःशंक पान किया करते हैं। महलों में बने हुए तालाब के तट के क्रीडोद्यान में विलास करने वाले लोगों की आयु तो यूँ ही कल्पनाओं में रमण करने की अनेक नश्वर इच्छाओं के कारण दूसरों के तो जीवन छोटे होते जा रहे हैं।

तात्पर्य — नश्वर इच्छाओं एवं सांसारिक मोह से मनुष्य जीवन की सार्थकता नष्ट हो जाती है।

Vanity of Life by Mortal Desires

dhanyānāṁ girikandareṣu vasatāṁ jyotiḥ paraṁ dhyāyatā-
mānandāśrujalaṁ pibanti śakunā niḥśaṅkamaṅkeśayāḥ।

---

[203] अस्माकं तु — *JKM.1911, GAV.1954.*

[204] मनोरथोपरचित — *JKM.1911, GAV.1954.*

*anyeṣāṁ tu manorathaiḥ paricitaprāsādavāpītaṭa-
krīḍākānanakelikautukajuṣāmāyuḥ paraṁ kṣīyate* ॥ 102 ॥

anvayaḥ — *girikandareṣu vasatāṁ, paraṁ jyotiḥ dhyāyatāṁ (ca) dhanyānām aṅkeśayāḥ śakunāḥ niḥśaṅkam ānandāśrujalaṁ pibanti* । *anyeṣāṁ tu paricitaprāsādavāpītaṭakrīḍākānanakelikautukajuṣāṁ manorathaiḥ āyuḥ paraṁ kṣīyate* ।

Blessed are they who live in mountain-caves, meditating on the Supreme Light, with the birds fearlessly sitting on their laps drinking the tears of joy. Whereas for others, those who enjoy living in the playgrounds built in palaces on the banks of ponds, their lives are getting shortened due to many mortal desires of revelling in fantasies.

Purport — The significance of human life gets spoiled by mortal desires and worldly attachment.

प्रत्येक पार्थिव वस्तु को नाश का भय

आघ्रातं[205] मरणेन जन्म जरया विद्युच्चलं जीवितं[206]
सन्तोषो धनलिप्सया शमसुखं प्रौढाङ्गनाविभ्रमैः ।
लोकैर्मत्सरिभिर्गुणा वनभुवो व्यालैर्नृपा दुर्जनै-
रस्थैर्येण विभूतिरप्युपहता ग्रस्तं न किं केन वा ॥ 103 ॥

अन्वय — मरणेन जन्म आघ्रातं, जरया विद्युच्चलं जीवितं (आघ्रातं), धनलिप्सया सन्तोषः (आघ्रातः), प्रौढाङ्गनाविभ्रमैः शमसुखम् (आघ्रातं), मत्सरिभिः लोकैः गुणाः (आघ्राताः), व्यालैः वनभुवः (आघ्राताः), नृपाः दुर्जनैः (आघ्राताः), अस्थैर्येण विभूतिः अपि उपहता, किं केन वा न ग्रस्तम्?

मृत्यु ने जन्म को ग्रस्त कर रखा है, वृद्धावस्था ने बिजली के समान चञ्चल जीवन को ग्रस्त कर रखा है, धन की इच्छा ने सन्तोष को ग्रस्त कर रखा है, शान्ति के सुख को प्रौढ़ स्त्रियों के विभ्रमों ने ग्रस्त कर रखा है, जलने वालों लोगों ने गुणों को ग्रस्त कर रखा है, सर्प और जंगली जानवरों ने वन को ग्रस्त कर रखा है, दुष्टों ने राजाओं को ग्रस्त कर रखा है, अस्थिरता या चञ्चलता ने धनैश्वर्य को ग्रस्त कर रखा है; तब ऐसी कौन सी वस्तु है, जो किसी दूसरे से ग्रस्त नहीं है?

---

205 आक्रान्तं — *GAV.1954.*

206 यौवनं — *JKM.1911, GAV.1954.*

तात्पर्य — संसार की सभी वस्तुओं को नाश या मृत्यु का भय है; तथापि अज्ञानी मनुष्य, मोहवश, अपना हानि-लाभ नहीं देखता; नाशशील संसार की झूठी माया में फँसा रहता है।

Every Worldly Matter Has Fear of Destruction

āghrātaṁ maraṇena janma jarayā vidyuccalaṁ jīvitaṁ
santoṣo dhanalipsayā śamasukhaṁ prauḍhāṅganāvibhramaiḥ ।
lokairmatsaribhirguṇā vanabhuvo vyālairnṛpā durjanai-
rasthairyeṇa vibhūtirapyupahatā grastaṁ na kiṁ kena vā ॥ 103 ॥

anvayaḥ — *maraṇena janma āghrātaṁ, jarayā vidyuccalaṁ jīvitaṁ (āghrātaṁ), dhanalipsayā santoṣaḥ (āghrātaḥ), prauḍhāṅganāvibhramaiḥ śamasukham (āghrātaṁ), matsaribhiḥ lokaiḥ guṇāḥ (āghrātāḥ), vyālaiḥ vanabhuvaḥ (āghrātāḥ), nṛpāḥ durjanaiḥ (āghrātāḥ), asthairyeṇa vibhūtiḥ api upahatā, kiṁ kena vā na grastam?*

Birth is attacked by death and fickle life by old age; contentment by greed for wealth; tranquillity by the illusions of beautiful women; virtues by the envy of others; forests by beasts of prey; kings by the unscrupulous persons; and even opulence by transitoriness. Is there anything on the earth that is not afflicted by something?

Purport — Every worldly object faces the terror of destruction; nevertheless, the ignorant man, out of delusion, does not see his own profit or loss; he remains trapped in the false illusion of the perishable world.

जीवनकाल की अत्यल्प सीमा

आयुर्वर्षशतं नृणां परिमितं रात्र्या ततोऽर्धं हृतं[207]
तस्यार्धस्य परस्य चार्धमपरं बाल्यत्व[208]वृद्धत्वयोः ।
शेषं व्याधिवियोगदुःखशरणैर्भूपालसेवारसै[209]-
र्जीवे वारितरङ्गबुद्बुद(ध)समे[210] सौख्यं कुतः प्राणिनाम् ॥ 104 ॥

---

[207] रात्रौ तदर्धं गतम् — *JKM.1911, GAV.1954.*

[208] बालत्व — *JKM.1911, GAV.1954.*

[209] व्याधिवियोगदुःखसहितं सेवादिभिर्नीयते — *JKM.1911, GAV.1954.*

[210] तरङ्गचञ्चलतरे — *JKM.1911, GAV.1954.*

अन्वय — नृणाम् आयुर्वर्षशतं परिमितं, रात्र्या ततः अर्धं हृतं, तस्यार्धस्य परस्य अपरं च अर्धं बाल्यत्ववृद्धत्वयोः (गतम्)। शेषं व्याधिवियोगदुःखशरणैः भूपालसेवारसैः (गतम्)। वारितरङ्गबुद्बुदसमे जीवे प्राणिनां सौख्यं कुतः?

मनुष्य की पूर्ण आयु की सीमा एक सौ वर्ष की है, उसमें से आधी आयु 50 वर्ष की रात्रि ने हर ली, बाकी बचे 50 में से 25 वर्ष की बाल्यावस्था और वृद्धावस्था में बीत गई, इसमें से भी बचे 25 वर्ष रोग, वियोग आदि दुःख में तथा अपनी आजीविका के लिए भू-पालकों की सेवा आदि में बीत गई, तो अब जलतरंग के बुलबुलों के समान चञ्चल इस जीवन में प्राणी को सुख कैसे मिल सकता है?

तात्पर्य — वृद्धावस्था, व्याधि, वियोग आदि से निरन्तर ग्रस्त मनुष्य के जीवन में वास्तविक सुख का अभाव।

Margins of Lifespan

āyurvarṣaśataṁ nṛṇāṁ parimitaṁ rātryā tato 'rdhaṁ hṛtaṁ
tasyārdhasya parasya cārdhamaparaṁ bālyatvavṛddhatvayoḥ ।
śeṣaṁ vyādhiviyogaduḥkhaśaraṇairbhūpālasevārasai-
rjīve vāritaraṅgabudbuda(dha)same saukhyaṁ kutaḥ
prāṇinām ॥ 104 ॥

anvayaḥ — *nṛṇām āyurvarṣaśataṁ parimitaṁ, rātryā tataḥ ardhaṁ hṛtaṁ, tasyārdhasya parasya aparaṁ ca ardhaṁ bālyatvavṛddhatvayoḥ (gatam)*। *śeṣaṁ vyādhiviyogaduḥkhaśaraṇaiḥ bhūpālasevārasaiḥ (gatam)*। *vāritaraṅgabudbudasame jīve prāṇināṁ saukhyaṁ kutaḥ?*

Man's lifespan is limited to a hundred years; half of it is spent in the darkness of nights; half of the remaining half is spent in childhood and old age; and the rest is passed with illnesses, bereavements and vexatious service to earn livelihood. Where is the happiness for individuals whose life is as fickle as the ripples of water?

Purport — Suffering from old age, disease, separation, etc. shrinks real happiness in an individual's life.

व्याधि-मृत्यु द्वारा प्राणियों की आक्रान्तता

आधिव्याधिशतैर्नरस्य विविधैरारोग्यमुन्मूल्यते
लक्ष्मीर्यत्र पतन्ति तत्र विवृतद्वारा इव व्यापदः।

जातं जातमवश्यमार्तिविवशं[211] मृत्युः करोत्यात्मसात्
तत्किं नाम निरङ्कुशेन विधिना यन्निर्मितं सुस्थिरम्[212] ॥ 105 ॥

अन्वय — विविधैः आधिव्याधिशतैः नरस्य आरोग्यम् उन्मूल्यते, यत्र लक्ष्मीः तत्र विवृतद्वारा इव व्यापदः पतन्ति। मृत्युः जातं जातम् आर्तिविवशम् अवश्यम् आत्मसात् करोति। तत् निरङ्कुशेन विधिना किं नाम सुस्थिरं निर्मितम्?

अनेक प्रकार की मानसिक चिन्ताएं तथा शारीरिक व्याधियाँ मनुष्य के स्वास्थ्य को नष्ट कर देती हैं, जहाँ लक्ष्मी का वास रहता है वहाँ आपत्तियों की भी भरमार रहा करती है; जन्म लेते ही पीड़ाओं से विवश प्राणी को मृत्यु अवश्य ही अपने वश में कर लेती है। इस परिस्थिति में कौन सी वस्तु है, जिसको विधाता ने स्थिर बनाया है?

तात्पर्य — प्रत्येक प्राणी रोग, विपत्ति एवं मृत्यु से विवश है, अतः जीवन की नश्वरता को नहीं भूलना चाहिए।

Entity's Subjugation by Disease and Death

ādhivyādhiśatairnarasya vividhairārogyamunmūlyate
lakṣmīryatra patanti tatra vivṛtadvārā iva vyāpadaḥ ।
jātaṁ jātamavaśyamārtivivaśaṁ mṛtyuḥ karotyātmasāt
tatkiṁ nāma niraṅkuśena vidhinā yannirmitaṁ susthiram ॥ 105 ॥

anvayaḥ — *vividhaiḥ ādhivyādhiśataiḥ narasya ārogyam unmūlyate, yatra lakṣmīḥ tatra vivṛtadvārā iva vyāpadaḥ patanti* । *mṛtyuḥ jātaṁ jātam ārtivivaśam avaśyam ātmasāt karoti* । *tat niraṅkuśena vidhinā kiṁ nāma susthiraṁ nirmitam?*

Hundreds of varieties of illness root out the health of people. Adversities find an open door wherever Lakṣmī, Goddess of Wealth, is present. As soon as an entity is born, it is forced by pain and bound to be captured by death. Then what has the Creator made that can be regarded as stable?

Purport — Every living being is afflicted by disease, calamity and death, hence the impermanence of life should not be forgotten.

---

211 आशु विवशं — *JKM.1911, GAV.1954.*

212 सुस्थितम् — *JKM.1911.*

मनुष्य-जीवन की दुःखमयता

कृच्छ्रेणामेध्यमध्ये नियमिततनुभिः स्थीयते गर्भवासे
[213]कान्ताविश्लेषदुःखव्यतिकरविषमे यौवने विप्रयोगः[214]।
नारीणामप्यवज्ञावलिविकृतमुखे[215] वृद्धभावेऽप्यसाधु[216]
संसारेऽस्मिन् मनुष्या[217] वदत यदि सुखं स्वल्पमप्यस्ति किञ्चित्॥ 106॥

अन्वय — अमेध्यमध्ये गर्भवासे नियमिततनुभिः कृच्छ्रेण स्थीयते, कान्ताविश्लेषदुःखव्यतिकरविषमे यौवने विप्रयोगः। वृद्धभावे अपि नारीणाम् अवज्ञावलिविकृतमुखे असाधु, हे मनुष्याः! वदत यदि अस्मिन् संसारे स्वल्पम् अपि किञ्चित् सुखम् अस्ति?

गर्भवास में अपने शरीर को संकुचित करके अपवित्र मलमूत्र में किसी तरह रहना पड़ता है, यौवन में विषय-सुख प्रिया के वियोग दुःख से अत्यन्त कष्टप्रद है, वृद्धावस्था में भी इन्द्रियों के शिथिल हो जाने के कारण स्त्रियों के तिरस्कार एवं परिहास का पात्र बनना पड़ता है, तो हे मनुष्यों! आप ही कहो, क्या इस संसार में तनिक भी सुख है?

तात्पर्य — मनुष्य का जीवन गर्भ से लेकर वृद्धावस्थापर्यन्त कष्ट, तिरस्कार एवं निराशा से ही भरा है, अतः उससे मुक्त होने के लिए सांसारिक आसक्ति को छोड़कर परम ब्रह्म का ध्यान करना चाहिए।

Despondency of Human Life

kṛcchreṇāmedhyamadhye niyamitatanubhiḥ sthīyate garbhavāse
kāntāviśleṣaduḥkhavyatikaraviṣame yauvane viprayogaḥ ।
nārīṇāmapyavajñāvalivikṛtamukhe vṛddhabhāve 'pyasādhu
saṁsāre 'smin manuṣyā vadata yadi sukhaṁ svalpamapyasti kiñcit ॥ 106 ॥

anvayaḥ — *amedhyamadhye garbhavāse niyamitatanubhiḥ kṛcchreṇa sthīyate, kāntāviśleṣaduḥkhavyatikaraviṣame yauvane viprayogaḥ*। *vṛddhabhāve api nārīṇām avajñāvalivikṛtamukhe asādhu, he manuṣyāḥ! vadata yadi asmin saṁsāre svalpam api kiñcit sukham asti?*

---

213 वामाक्षीणामवज्ञाविहसितवसति — *GAV.1954.*

214 विषमो यौवने चोपभोगः — *GAV.1954.*

215 विलसति नियतं — *JKM.1911.*

216 वृद्धभावेऽप्यसाधुः — *Ms ORLS-3*, वृद्धभावोऽप्यसाधुः — *JKM.1911, GAV.1954.*

217 संसारे रे मनुष्या — *Ms ORLS-3.*

Life in the womb involves lying in discomfort amidst unclean surroundings, with the limbs confined. Enjoyments in youth are vitiated by intense sorrow when separated from the beloved. Even old age incurs contempt and derision of women. Oh, men! say, is there even a trace of happiness in such a life?

Purport — Human life is full of suffering, contempt and disappointment from the womb till old age, hence to be free from it, one should leave worldly attachment and meditate on the Supreme God.

अतितृष्णा की परित्याज्यता

ब्रह्मज्ञानविवेकिनोऽमलधियः कुर्वन्त्यहो दुष्करं
यन्मुञ्चन्त्युपभोगभाञ्ज्यपि[218] धनान्येकान्ततो निःस्पृहाः।
न प्राप्तानि पुरा न सम्प्रति न च प्राप्तो पुनःप्रत्यये[219]
वाञ्छामात्रपरिग्रहाण्यपि परं त्यक्तुं न शक्ता वयम्॥ 107॥

अन्वय — अहो! अमलधियः ब्रह्मज्ञानविवेकिनः दुष्करं कुर्वन्ति, यत् निःस्पृहाः (ते) उपभोगभाञ्जि धनानि अपि एकान्ततः मुञ्चन्ति। वयं (तु) न पुरा प्राप्तानि, न सम्प्रति (प्राप्तानि), न प्राप्तः (अपि) पुनःप्रत्यये च, वाञ्छामात्रपरिग्रहाणि अपि परं त्यक्तुं न शक्ताः।

यह अत्यन्त आश्चर्य की बात है कि निर्मल बुद्धि वाले ब्रह्मज्ञानी विवेकी लोग अत्यन्त दुष्कर कर्म करते हैं; जैसे कि वे निरासक्त होकर उपभोग के लिए युक्त धन-सम्पत्ति का भी सर्वथा परित्याग कर देते हैं। परन्तु हमारे जैसे संसारासक्त व्यक्ति न तो पहले प्राप्त की हुई वस्तु को, न अभी प्राप्त की हुई वस्तु को, और न ही अप्राप्त की पुनः प्राप्ति के विश्वास से, लेश मात्र अपनी सम्पत्ति को छोड़ने हेतु समर्थ होते हैं।

तात्पर्य — मनुष्य को अत्यधिक तृष्णा पर विजय करके विषयों का त्याग करना चाहिए।

Desertion of Excessive Acquisitiveness

brahmajñānavivekino 'maladhiyaḥ kurvantyaho duṣkaraṁ
yanmuñcantyupabhogabhāñjyapi dhanānyekāntato niḥspṛhāḥ।
na prāptāni purā na samprati na ca prāpto punaḥpratyaye
vāñchāmātraparigrahāṇyapi paraṁ tyaktuṁ na śaktā vayam॥ 107॥

---

218 उपभोगवन्त्यपि — *JKM.1911.*

219 दृढप्रत्ययो — *JKM.1911, GAV.1954.*

anvayaḥ — *aho! amaladhiyaḥ brahmajñānavivekinaḥ duṣkaraṁ kurvanti, yat niḥspṛhāḥ (te) upabhogabhāñji dhanāni api ekāntataḥ muñcanti। vayaṁ (tu) na purā prāptāni, na samprati (prāptāni), na prāptḥ (api) punaḥpratyaye ca, vāñchāmātraparigrahāṇi api paraṁ tyaktuṁ na śaktāḥ।*

Ah! knowledge of Reality gained by discrimination through purified intellect must be difficult. As they become impassive and they absolutely renounce their desires for wealth that enabled them to enjoy. But worldly people like us are not capable of giving up even a little bit of our share, neither with the things we have achieved before, nor with the things we have yet to achieve with the faith of getting back.

Purport — Individuals should overcome excessive craving and give up objects of worldly happiness.

आध्यात्मिक प्राप्ति के प्रति अजागरूकता

व्याघ्रीव तिष्ठति जरा परितर्जयन्ती
रोगाश्च दस्यव[220] इव प्रहरन्ति गात्रे[221] ।
आयुः परिस्रवति भिन्नघटादिवाम्भो
लोको न चात्महितमाचरतीति कष्टम्[222] ॥ 108 ॥

अन्वय — जरा परितर्जयन्ती व्याघ्रीव तिष्ठति, रोगाश्च दस्यव इव गात्रे प्रहरन्ति। भिन्नघटात् अम्भः इव आयुः परिस्रवति, (तथापि) लोकः च आत्महितं न आचरति इति कष्टम्।

कितने आश्चर्य की बात है कि जब बुढ़ापा सामने खड़ी बाघिन की भाँति भयभीत करता है, रोग दस्युओं की भाँति शरीर पर आक्रमण करते हैं, टूटे हुए घड़े से पानी की भाँति आयु बह जाती है, तब भी लोग अपने लिए हित नहीं करते!

तात्पर्य — भावी अनर्थ को जानते हुए भी लोग सांसारिक विषय-सुखों के प्रति आसक्त होते हुए आध्यात्मिक हित के लिए यत्न नहीं करते।

---

220 शत्रव — *JKM.1911, GAV.1954.*

221 देहम् — *JKM.1911, GAV.1954.*

222 लोकस्तथाप्यहितमाचरतीति चित्रम् — *JKM.1911, GAV.1954.*

Unawareness of Spiritual Attainment

vyāghrīva tiṣṭhati jarā paritarjayantī
rogāśca dasyava iva praharanti gātre ।
āyuḥ parisravati bhinnaghaṭādivāmbho
loko na cātmahitamācaratīti kaṣṭam ॥ 108 ॥

anvayaḥ — *jarā paritarjayantī vyāghrīva tiṣṭhati, rogāśca dasyava iva gātre praharanti* । *bhinnaghaṭāt ambhaḥ iva āyuḥ parisravati, (tathāpi) lokaḥ ca ātmahitaṁ na ācarati iti kaṣṭam* ।

What a wonder it is that even when old age frightens like a tigress waiting in front, diseases attack (torment) the body like robbers, life flows out like water from a broken pitcher, people still do not practise welfare to themselves!

Purport — Despite the awareness of future disaster, people become attached to worldly pleasures and do not initiate for spiritual attainment.

संसार की सम्पूर्ण अस्थिरता

भोगास्तुङ्गतरङ्गचञ्चलतराः प्राणाः क्षणध्वंसिनः
स्तोकान्येव दिनानि यौवनसुखं प्रीतिः प्रियेष्वस्थिरा[223] ।
जातं जातमवश्यमार्तिविवशं मृत्युः करोत्यात्मसात्
तत्किं नाम निरङ्कुशेन विधिना यन्निर्मितं सुस्थिरम्[224] ॥ 109 ॥

अन्वय — भोगाः तुङ्गतरङ्गचञ्चलतराः, प्राणाः क्षणध्वंसिनः, यौवनसुखं स्तोकानि दिनानि एव (यावत्), प्रियेषु प्रीतिः अस्थिरा। मृत्युः जातं जातम् आर्तिविवशम् अवश्यम् आत्मसात् करोति। तत् निरङ्कुशेन विधिना किं नाम सुस्थिरं निर्मितम्?

इन्द्रिय सुख ऊँची लहरों के समान क्षणिक होते हैं, जीवन एक क्षण में समाप्त हो सकता है, मोह में यौवन का उत्साह कुछ ही दिनों तक रहता है, प्रियजनों के साथ प्रेम भी क्षणिक होता है। जैसे ही कोई प्राणी जन्म लेता है, वह पीड़ा से विवश हो जाता है और मृत्यु द्वारा आत्मसात् कर लिया जाता है। फिर विधाता ने ऐसा क्या बनाया है जिसे स्थिर माना जा सके?

---

223 स्फूर्तिः प्रियासु स्थिता — *GAV.1954.*

224 तत्संसारमशरमेव निखिलं बुध्वा बिधा बोधका लोकानुग्रहपेशलेन मनसा यत्नः समाधीयताम् — *GAV.1954.*

तात्पर्य — मनुष्य के लिए संसार की अस्थिरता को समझते हुए उससे मोह का त्याग करके परमात्मा में ध्यान लगाना ही श्रेय है।

Absolute Instability of the World

bhogāstuṅgataraṅgacañcalatarāḥ prāṇāḥ kṣaṇadhvaṁsinaḥ
stokānyeva dināni yauvanasukhaṁ prītiḥ priyeṣvasthirā ।
jātaṁ jātamavaśyamārtivivaśaṁ mṛtyuḥ karotyātmasāt
tatkiṁ nāma niraṅkuśena vidhinā yannirmitaṁ susthiram ॥ 109 ॥

anvayaḥ — *bhogāḥ tuṅgataraṅgacañcalatarāḥ, prāṇāḥ kṣaṇadhvaṁsinaḥ, yauvanasukhaṁ stokāni dināni eva (yāvat), priyeṣu prītiḥ asthirā । mṛtyuḥ jātaṁ jātam ārtivivaśam avaśyam ātmasāt karoti । tat niraṅkuśena vidhinā kiṁ nāma susthiraṁ nirmitam?*

Sensual pleasures are transient like the breaking of high waves, life can end in a moment, youthful cheerfulness in infatuation lasts only a few days, love with beloved ones is also momentary. As soon as an entity is born, it is forced by pain and bound to be captured by death. Then what has the creator made that can be regarded as stable?

Purport — There is only way to welfare for an individual to give up his attachment to the instable world and concentrate on God.

गुणों की भी अस्थिरता

सृजति तावदशेषगुणाकरं पुरुषरत्नमलङ्करणं भुवः।
तदपि तत्क्षणभङ्गि करोति चेदहह कष्टमपण्डितता विधेः ॥ 110 ॥

अन्वय — (विधिः) भुवः अलङ्करणम् अशेषगुणाकरं पुरुषरत्नं तावत् सृजति। तदपि तत्क्षणभङ्गि करोति चेत् अहह विधेः अपण्डितता कष्टम्।

विधाता ने संसार के अलंकार के रूप में मनुष्य को अनेक गुणों के साथ उत्पन्न किया है। परन्तु यह चिन्ता का विषय है कि गुणी व्यक्ति को भी क्षणभंगुर बनाता है यही विधि का अपाण्डित्य है।

तात्पर्य — चाहे मनुष्य कितना भी गुणवान हो, उसकी मृत्यु भी सुनिश्चित है। अतः गुणों के साथ-साथ वैराग्य एवं ईश्वर-भक्ति अपेक्षित है।

Attributes Are also Instable

sṛjati tāvadaśeṣaguṇākaraṁ puruṣa-
ratnamalaṅkaraṇaṁ bhuvaḥ ।
tadapi tatkṣaṇabhaṅgi karoti cedahaha
kaṣṭamapaṇḍitatā vidheḥ ॥ 110 ॥

anvayaḥ — *(vidhiḥ) bhuvaḥ alaṅkaraṇam aśeṣaguṇākaraṁ puruṣaratnaṁ tāvat sṛjati* । *tadapi tatkṣaṇabhaṅgi karoti cet ahaha vidheḥ apaṇḍitatā kaṣṭam* ।

The Creator has created man with many qualities as an ornament of the world. But it is a matter of concern that it is the lack of erudition of the Creator that makes a virtuous person fleeting.

Purport — No matter how virtuous a person is, he/she cannot avoid death. Therefore, along with virtues, renunciation and devotion to God are also indispensable.

संसार में मृत्यु की अवश्यम्भाविता

क्षणं बालो भूत्वा क्षणमपि युवा कामरसिकः
क्षणं वित्तैर्हीनः क्षणमपि च सम्पूर्णविभवः ।
जराजीर्णैरङ्गैर्नट इव वलीमण्डिततनुः
नरः संसाराङ्के[225] विशति यमधानीजवनिकाम् ॥ 111 ॥

अन्वय — क्षणं बालो भूत्वा, क्षणम् अपि कामरसिकः युवा, क्षणं वित्तैः हीनः, क्षणम् अपि च सम्पूर्णविभवः । संसाराङ्के जराजीर्णैः अङ्गैः वलीमण्डिततनुः नरः नट इव यमधानीजवनिकां विशति ।

एक पल के लिए एक बच्चे की तरह, दूसरे पल के लिए एक कामुक युवा की तरह; एक क्षण में धनहीन, दूसरे क्षण में वैभववान् ; जीवन के अन्त में, उम्र के कारण शरीर जर्जर हो जाता है और झुर्रियों से ढक जाता है, इसी तरह मनुष्य एक अभिनेता की तरह संसार-रूपी नाट्य के मञ्च से निकलकर यमपुरी-रूपी यवनिका में प्रवेश कर जाता है ।

तात्पर्य — क्षण-क्षण में परिवर्तनशील इस संसार में मृत्यु को टाला नहीं जा सकता । अतः शाश्वत-सत्य की खोज में निरन्तर लगे रहना चाहिए ।

---

225 संसारान्ते — *JKM.1911, GAV.1954.*

Inevitability of Death in the World

kṣaṇaṁ bālo bhūtvā kṣaṇamapi yuvā kāmarasikaḥ
kṣaṇaṁ vittairhīnaḥ kṣaṇamapi ca sampūrṇavibhavaḥ ।
jarājīrṇairaṅgairnaṭa iva valīmaṇḍitatanuḥ
naraḥ saṁsārāṅke viśati yamadhānījavanikām ॥ 111 ॥

anvayaḥ — *kṣaṇaṁ bālo bhūtvā, kṣaṇam api kāmarasikaḥ yuvā, kṣaṇaṁ vittaiḥ hīnaḥ, kṣaṇam api ca sampūrṇavibhavaḥ* । *saṁsārāṅke jarājīrṇaiḥ aṅgaiḥ valīmaṇḍitatanuḥ naraḥ naṭa iva yamadhānījavanikāṁ viśati* ।

For a moment like a child, for another moment a lascivious youth; one moment a pauper, another a wealthy person; at the end of life, the body worn out by age and covered with wrinkles, man enters the abode of death like an actor exiting the stage and enters behind the screen.

Purport — Death cannot be avoided in this ever-changing world. Therefore, one should constantly be engaged in the search for eternal truth.

॥ इति श्री तत्रभगवद्भर्तृहरिविरचितं वैराग्यशतकं समाप्तम् ॥

॥ *iti śrītatrabhagavadbhartṛhariviracitaṁ vairāgyaśatakaṁ samāptam* ॥

3

Notes on Variations between the Text of Śāradā Manuscript and that of Other Available Editions

वैराग्यशतकस्य इतरसंस्करणेषु उपलब्धपाठेभ्यः शारदापाठस्य वैशिष्ट्यमधिकृत्य टिप्पण्यः

1. यां चिन्तयाम्यनुदिनं[1] मयि सा विरक्ता
 साऽप्यन्यमिच्छति नरं स नरोऽन्यसक्तः।
 अस्मत्कृतेऽपि परितुष्यति[2] काचिदन्या
 धिक्तां च तं च कुसुमेषु[3]मिमां च मां च ॥ 2 ॥

अत्र *JKM.1911* इत्यस्मिन् संस्करणे **सततं, परिशुष्यति, मदनम्** इति पाठान्तराणिं लभ्यन्ते। प्रिययोः विप्रयोगावस्थायामेव सततचिन्तनं भवतीति सततपदप्रयोगेण विप्रयोगोऽभिव्यज्यते। शारदापाठे तु अनुदिनम् इति लभ्यते। अत्र आसक्तिमात्र एव कवेस्तात्पर्यम्। सा च अनुदिनस्मरणेन सिद्ध्यति। तथैव परिशुष्यति नाम प्रियस्य विप्रयोगेन कार्श्यं गच्छति। एवं परिशुष्यति इति पाठेऽपि परस्परमेलनाभावात् कार्श्यतापत्तिरूपः परिशोषः विप्रयोगमेवाभिव्यनक्ति। सा च प्रकृतार्थविरुद्धा। शारदापाठे तु परितुष्यति इति लभ्यते। परितुष्यति नाम प्रियं प्रति प्रियायाः परितोषः

---

1 सततं — *JKM.1911.*

2 परिशुष्यति — *JKM.1911.*

3 मदनं — *JKM.1911.*

अर्थात् प्रसन्नता। परितोषेण आसक्तेरभिव्यक्तिर्भवति। एवञ्च मदनमिति पदं सामान्यतः कामवाचकम्। तथैव शारदापाठगतेन "कुसुमेषु" इति पदेन आसक्ति-क्रियानिष्ठकार्यतानिरूपितकारणताया अभिव्यक्तिर्भवति। सा च कारणता अत्र कामबाणप्रयोगव्यापाररूपा। अर्थात् आसक्तिजनकं कुषुमेषुं धिगिति। *JKM.911* इति संस्करणलब्धात् मदनपदात्तु न तादृशकारणतानिष्ठव्यापारः प्रतीयते। अत एव अत्र शारदापाठ एव कवेरभिप्रेतमभिव्यनक्तीति, तस्य मौलिकत्वं सिद्ध्यति।

Here in this verse available readings in the *JKM.1911* edition are: **सततं, परिशुष्यति** and **मदनम्**. However, the use of the term **सततं** expresses separation, since constant thought occurs only in the state of separation from the beloved one. Similarly, **परिशुष्यति** expresses emaciation out of the separation from one's beloved one. Thus, expression of separation is not the intended meaning in this context. But the poet never intends to express separation rather than attachment. Here in the Śāradā manuscript, the available readings are: अनुदिनं, परितुष्यति and "कुसुमेषु". The word अनुदिनं leads to imply daily remembrance and expresses attachment to the beloved one. Similarly, परितुष्यति renders satisfaction out of love for the beloved one, that finally leading to express attachment. The use of the word "कुसुमेषु" also expresses the action resulting in promoting attachment. Therefore, the readings available in Śāradā manuscripts appear to be primary and original, which sufficiently meet to the context.

2. बोद्धारो मत्सरग्रस्ता विभवः[4] स्मयदूषिताः।
अबोधोपहताश्चान्ये जीर्णमङ्गे सुभाषितम्॥ 3॥

पद्येऽस्मिन् *JKM.1911* इत्यस्मिन् संस्करणे "विभवः" इत्यस्य स्थाने "प्रभवः" इति पाठान्तरं लभ्यते। सुभाषितानि उपदेशार्हाणां जनसामान्यानां कृते उद्दिष्टानि सन्ति। जनसामान्येष्वेव वैभवशालिनो भवन्ति। ते च विभवः वैभवयुक्तत्वात् प्रायः स्मयदूषिता भवन्तीति तात्पर्यम्। अपरपक्षे प्रभुर्नाम स्वामी भगवान् वा, स

[4] प्रभवः — *JKM.1911.*

च सामान्यतया उपदेशानाम् अभाजनमिति सुभाषितैः प्रभवः अप्रयोज्याः। अतः विभूनां सुभाषितैः प्रयोज्यत्वादत्र विभव इति शारदापाठ एव मूलानुगामी।

Here in the *JKM.1911* edition, a variant reading "प्रभवः" is available in the place of "विभवः". The meaning here is: *subhāṣitā*s (proverbs) are intended for the common people, including opulent and powerful individuals, to be advised with moral values. The opulent and powerful individuals are often slurred with jealousy. On the other hand, *prabhu* means a lord, and he is generally not the recipient of the precepts. Therefore, the reading "विभवः", that is found in the Śāradā manuscripts, follows the context and retains the primary source.

3. भ्रान्त्वा[5] देशमनेकदुर्गविषमं प्राप्तं न किञ्चित्फलं
त्यक्त्वा जातिकुलाभिमानमुचितं सेवा कृता निष्फला
भुक्तं मानविवर्जितं परगृहे साशङ्कमाः[6] काकवत्
तृष्णे जृम्भसि पापकर्मपिशुने नाद्यापि विश्राम्यसि[7] ॥ 4 ॥

पद्येऽस्मिन् *JKM.1911* तथा *GAV.1954* इत्यनयोः संस्करणयोः "भ्रान्तं देशम्" इति पाठो लभ्यते, यत्र कर्मणि प्रयोगः प्रामादिकः, कर्मणोऽनुक्तत्वात्, देशपदस्य पुंस्येव प्रयोगनिर्देशाच्च। "अभिहिते तु कर्मणि प्रातिपदिकार्थमात्र इति प्रथमैव। अभिधानं च प्रायेण तिङ्कृत्तद्धितसमासैः" इति सिद्धान्तकौमुदीगतदर्शनादत्र कृताऽभिहितत्वेन देशपदे प्रथमाप्रयोगोऽपेक्ष्यते। अतः शारदापाठगतः 'भ्रान्त्वा' इति प्रयोगः साधुतां मौलोकतां च भजते। अन्यच्च तृतीयचरणे *JKM.1911* तथा *GAV.1954* इत्यनयोः संस्करणयोः "परगृहेष्वाशङ्कया" इति पाठो लभ्यते, परं तत्र शारदामातृकासु "साशङ्कमाः" इति पठितम्। अत्राऽयं विवेको यत् शारदापाठगतम् आः इत्यव्ययपदं खेदं पीडा वाऽभिव्यञ्जयतीति शारदापाठ एव मौलिकतां बिभर्ति। अथच चतुर्थचरणे तृष्णाया जृम्भनं यथा विश्रान्तेरभावं प्रकाशयति न तथा सन्तोषस्याभावमिति *JKM.1911* तथा *GAV.1954* इत्यनयोः संस्करणयोः

---

5 भ्रान्तं — *JKM.1911, GAV.1954.*

6 परगृहेष्वाशङ्कया — *JKM.1911, GAV.1954.*

7 सन्तुष्यसि — *JKM.1911, GAV.1954.*

लभ्यमानस्य सन्तुष्यसि इति पाठस्यापेक्षया शारदापाठलब्धस्य विश्राम्यसि इति पाठस्य मूलानुगामिता प्रतीयते।

Here, a variant reading "भ्रान्तं देशम्" is available in the *JKM.1911* and *GAV.1954* editions, that is grammatically inaccurate, because the *karma*-relation is not specified by the verb, etc. and the word देश takes masculine gender only. As there is a rule *abhihite tu karmaṇi prātipadikārthamātra iti prathamaiva, abhidhānaṁ ca prāyeṇa tiṅkṛttaddhitasamāsaiḥ* (if the *karma*-relation is specified by the verb, etc. then the word will take the affix of the first case (*prathamā*)). The force of a case affix is generally denoted either by first, the conjugal affixes तिङ्, second, by the primary affixes कृत्, third, by the secondary affixes तद्धित, or lastly, by the compounds समास. Hence, the word "भ्रान्तं" is denoted by the primary affix कृत्, so the first-case-affix must be applied to the word *deśa*. Therefore, the reading "भ्रान्त्वा" available in the Śāradā manuscripts is correct and justified. Another variant reading "परगृहेष्वाशङ्कया", available in the *JKM.1911* and *GAV.1954* editions, is inconsiderably missing the sense of grief and pain expressed by the indeclinable आः, in the Śāradā reading as "साशङ्कमाः". In the fourth quarter of the verse, just as the bursting upon of desire expresses the absence of rest, not so the absence of satisfaction. Therefore, the reading "विश्राम्यसि" found in the Śāradā manuscripts retains the primary source, rather than the reading "सन्तुष्यसि" available in the *JKM.1911* and *GAV.1954* editions.

4. खलोल्लापाः सोढाः कथमपि तदाराधनपरैः
निगृह्यान्तर्बाष्पं हसितमपि शून्येन मनसा।
कृतो वित्तस्तम्भप्रणिहितधियामञ्जलिरपि[8]
त्वमाशे मोघाशे [9]किमपरमतो नर्तयसि माम्॥ 6॥

---

[8] कृतो चित्तस्तम्भप्रतिहतधियामञ्जलिरपि — *JKM.1911.*

[9] किमुपर — *JKM.1911.*

अत्र *JKM.1911* इत्यस्मिन् संस्करणे "चित्तस्तम्भप्रतिहतधियाम्" इति पाठात् प्रार्थनीयपदार्थस्य गम्यता स्पष्टं न प्रतीयते, परं "वित्तस्तम्भप्रणिहितधियाम्" इति शारदामातृकालब्धे पाठे वित्तेन धनेन यस्तम्भो जडीभावः तं प्राप्ता धीर्येषां तेषामित्यर्थलब्धस्य धनस्य प्रार्थनीयता स्पष्टं गम्यत इति शारदापाठस्य तात्पर्यगर्भता द्योतत इति मौलिकता वरीवर्ति।

The *JKM.1911* edition reads here "चित्तस्तम्भप्रतिहतधियाम्", where the object of desire is not clear, but वित्तस्तम्भप्रणिहितधियाम्, the text of Śāradā manuscripts clearly denotes "वित्त (wealth)" as the object of desire. Hence, वित्तस्तम्भप्रणिहितधियाम्, mentioned in the Śāradā manuscript appears to be the text of primary source, as it explicitly exposes the intention of the poet.

5. दीनां दीनमुखैः सहैव शिशुकैराकृष्टजीर्णाम्बरां
   क्रोशद्भिर्विधुरैः क्षुधातिविधुरां पश्येन्न चेद्गेहिनीम्[10]।
   याच्ञाभङ्गभयेन गद्गदगलत्त्रुट्यद्विलीनाक्षरं
   को देहीति वदेत्स्वदग्धजठरस्यार्थे मनस्वी जनः ॥ 8 ॥

JKM.1911 इत्यस्मिन् संस्करणेऽस्य पद्यस्य पूर्वार्द्धे गतपाठे "दीना दीनमुखैः सहैव शिशुकैराकृष्टजीर्णाम्बरा क्रोशद्भिः क्षुधितैर्नरैर्न विधुरा दृश्येत चेद्गेहिनी" इति कर्मणि प्रयोगो लभ्यते यश्च उत्तरार्द्धगतेन कर्तरि प्रयोगेन सह अन्वितिं न लभते। अत एव शारदापाठगते सम्पूर्णपद्ये कर्तरि प्रयोगः अन्वितिं भजत इति प्रमादराहित्यं मौलिकतां च बिभर्ति।

Here in the *JKM.1911* edition, in the first half of the verse, the text is available as "दीना दीनमुखैः सहैव शिशुकैराकृष्टजीर्णाम्बरा क्रोशद्भिः क्षुधितैर्नरैर्न विधुरा दृश्येत चेद्गेहिनी" that is in passive voice, where the *karma*-relation is specified by the verb दृश्येत; which does not follow the later half of the verse, where the syntax is based on active voice. Therefore, the available reading in the text of Śāradā manuscript, where the syntax of the full verse, is based on active voice and, hence, is faultless as well as primary.

10 दीना दीनमुखैः सहैव शिशुकैराकृष्टजीर्णाम्बरा क्रोशाद्भिः क्षुधितैर्नरैर्न विधुरा दृश्येत चेद्गेहिनी। — *JKM.1911.*

6. निवृत्ता भोगेच्छा पुरुषबहुमानो विगलितः
समानाः स्वर्याताः सपदि सुहृदो जीवितसमाः ।
शनैर्यष्ट्युत्थानं घनतिमिररुद्धे च नयने
अहो भ्रष्टः[11] कायस्तदपि मरणापायचकितः ॥ 10 ॥

अस्मिन् पद्ये पूर्ववाक्यैः कायस्य भ्रष्टताऽभिहितेति "भ्रष्टः" इति शारदामातृकालभ्यः पाठः याथार्थ्यमन्वेति। *JKM.1911* इत्यस्मिन् संस्करणे उपलब्धेन "धृष्टः" इति पाठेन सह पूर्ववाक्यानां नान्वयः, न च *GAV.1954* इत्यस्मिन् संस्करणे उपलब्धेन "मूढः" इति पाठेन सह पूर्ववाक्यानां नान्वयः। ननु मरणापायचकितः इत्युत्तरवाक्येन सहान्वयापेक्षायां धृष्टत्वमूढत्वयोरन्वयः संगच्छत इति, तदोच्यते कायस्य चकितत्वमसम्भवमिति, तन्न साधु। अत एव भ्रष्टः इति शारदापाठ एव कवेरभिप्रायमभिव्यनक्तीति, तस्य मौलिकत्वं सिद्ध्यति।

In this verse, the previous sentences indicate the decaying nature of the body. Therefore, the word भ्रष्टः available in the Śāradā manuscript is meaningful in the context. As there is no correlation of the preceding sentences with the text "धृष्टः" available in the *JKM.1911* edition, nor with the text "मूढः" available in the *GAV.1954* edition. If, indeed, धृष्टता (arrogance) and मूढता (foolishness) have their correlation with the following sentence that is "shocked by death", then we can say that it is impossible for the body to be shocked. That is why it is the Śāradā text, which expresses the poet's intention sufficiently, and hence its originality is justified.

7. हिंसाशून्यमयत्नलभ्यमशनं धात्रा मरुत्कल्पितं
व्यालानां पशवस्तृणाङ्कुरभुजः सृष्टा[12] [13]महीशायिनः ।
संसारार्णवलङ्घनक्षमधियां वृत्तिः कृता सा नृणां
यामन्वेषयतां प्रयान्ति सहसा सर्वे समाप्तिं गुणाः ॥ 11 ॥

---

[11] धृष्टः — *JKM.1911*, मूढः — *GAV.1954*.

[12] तुष्टाः — *GAV.1954*.

[13] स्थली — *JKM.1911, GAV.1954*.

अत्र द्वितीयचरणे "महीशायिनः" इत्यस्य शारदापाठस्य स्थाने "स्थलीशायिनः" इति पाठः *JKM.1911* तथा *GAV.1954* इत्यनयोः मुद्रितसंस्करणयोः लभ्यते। स्थलेतरेषु जलादिष्वपि शायिनः पशवो भवन्तीति "महीशायिनः" इति शारदापाठस्य औचित्यं वरीवर्ति। अपरञ्च व्यालानामिव पशूनामपि सृष्टिः कल्पिता न तु तुष्टिरिति *GAV.1954* इत्येतत्संस्करणलब्धस्य "तुष्टाः" इति पाठस्यापेक्षया "सृष्टा" इति शारदापाठः मौलिकतां प्रकाशयति।

Here, in the second quarter, the text as "स्थलीशायिनः" is found in the printed editions of *JKM.1911* and *GAV.1954*, in the place of "महीशायिनः" available in the Śāradā text. The justification of the Śāradā text is that there are animals also who rest in the places other than the land, i.e. water, etc. As the creation of animals is made by Brahmā, but never their contentment. Therefore, the Śāradā text justifies primariness of its source than that of the *GAV.1954* edition.

8. स्तनौ मांसग्रन्थी कनककलशावित्युपमितौ
   मुखं श्लेष्मागारं तदपि च शशाङ्केन तुलितम्।
   स्रवन्मूत्रक्लिन्नं करिवरकरस्पर्धि जघनं
   मुहुर्निन्द्यं रूपं कविवर[14]विशेषैर्गुरुकृतम्॥ 20॥

स्त्रीणां रूपं निन्द्यं सदपि न कविसामान्यैरपि तु कविश्रेष्ठैः तदुदात्तीकृतमिति भावं द्योतयितुमत्र शारदामातृकालभ्यस्य "कविवर" इत्यस्य पाठस्य मौलिकता भाति, नतु *JKM.1911* तथा *GAV.1954* इत्यनयोः मुद्रितसंस्करणयोः लब्धस्य "कविजन" इत्यस्य पाठस्य।

A variant reading "कविजन" is found in the *JKM.1911* and *GAV.1954* editions, in place of "कविवर" found in the Śāradā manuscript. The reading of the Śāradā text, "कविवर", seems to be primary here, to denote that the form of women, although disgusting, has been embellished by the poets of extraordinary merits, but not by the ordinary poets.

---

[14] कविजन — *JKM.1911, GAV.1954.*

9. अजानन्माहात्म्यं पतति[15] शलभस्तीव्रदहने
स मीनोऽविज्ञानाद्बडिशयुतमश्नाति[16] पिशितम्।
विजानन्तोऽप्येवं वयमिह विपज्जालजटिला-
न्न मुञ्चामः कामानहह गहनो मोहमहिमा ॥ 21 ॥

अत्र पद्ये *JKM.1911* तथा *GAV.1954* इत्यनयोः मुद्रितसंस्करणयोः "पतति" इत्यस्य स्थाने "पततु" इति तथा च "अश्नाति" इत्यस्य स्थाने "अश्नातु" इति भिन्नौ पाठौ लभ्येते। इदमत्रविचारणीयं कयोः पाठयोः सन्दर्भानुगुणता इति। शलभस्य अग्नौ पतनं, तथा मीनस्य वडिशयुतपिशिताशनं सामान्यतथ्यरूपेण कविना प्रस्तुतमिति लट्-लकारप्रयोग एव युक्तो भाति। "पततु" इति "अश्नातु" चेति पाठयोस्तु लोट्-लकारप्रयोगो विहितोऽस्ति। "विधिनिमन्त्रणामन्त्रणाधीष्टसंप्रश्न-प्रार्थनेषु लिङ्" (*अष्टाध्यायी* ३.३.१६१) इति, "लोट् च" (*अष्टाध्यायी* ३.३.१६२) चेति सूत्रबलात् नात्र विध्यादिष्वन्यतरस्य अर्थस्य प्रवृत्तिरिति लोटि प्रयोगो न सान्दर्भिकः। अत एव शारदापाठगतः लटि प्रयोग एव मौलिक इति भाति।

Here in this verse, the printed editions of *JKM.1911* and *GAV.1954* have two different texts, "पततु" instead of "पतति" and "अश्नातु" instead of "अश्नाति". It is worth considering here that which of the two readings are contextual as well as primary? It seems appropriate to use the लट्-लकार, employing present indefinite, as the poet presents the "fall of the locust into the fire" and the "eating of the hooked flesh by the fish" as a general fact. Instead, the लोट्-लकार has been applied in the printed editions of *JKM.1911* and *GAV.1954* as "पततु" and "अश्नातु". By virtue of the *sūtra*s "विधिनिमन्त्रणामन्त्रणाधीष्टसंप्रश्नप्रार्थनेषु लिङ्" (*अष्टाध्यायी* 3.3.161) and "लोट् च" (*अष्टाध्यायी* 3.3.162). It must be noted here that the use of लोट् is not relevant here, since there is no such meaning like command, invite, permit, a wish, enquiry or a pray. Rather, it is just a affirmative statement. Therefore, the use of the लट्-लकार (present indefinite), available in the Śāradā manuscript, seems to be the primary.

[15] पततु — *JKM.1911, GAV.1954.*

[16] अश्नातु — *JKM.1911, GAV.1954.*

10. फलमलमशनाय स्वादु पानाय तोयं
शयनमवनिपृष्ठे[17] वाससी वल्कले च।
[18]धनलवमधुपानभ्रान्तसर्वेन्द्रियाणा-
मभिनयमनुमन्तुं नोत्सहे दुर्जनानाम्॥ 22॥

श्लोकेस्मिन् द्वितीयचरणे *JKM.1911* इत्यस्मिन् संस्करणे उपलब्धं पाठान्तरमित्थ-मस्ति — शयनम् अवनिपृष्ठम् इति। परन्तु शयनस्य अधिकरणम् अवनिपृष्ठं, न तु आधार इति, कर्मत्वविवक्षाभावात् अत्र शयनमवनिपृष्ठे इति शारदामातृकालभ्यं वाचनमेव प्रामाण्यं मौलिकतां च धत्ते। अथ च *JKM.1911* तथा *GAV.1954* इत्यनयोः मुद्रितसंस्करणयोः नवधन-इन्द्रियभ्रमयोः अविरुद्धत्वात् नात्र तात्पर्या-नुगुणमिति, धनलव-इन्द्रियभ्रमयोः विरोधः एव साधीयानिति धनलव इति शारदापाठ एव मौलिकः।

The reading available in the *JKM.1911* edition, in the second quarter of this verse, is शयनम् अवनिपृष्ठम् since the earth is the substratum for sleeping, but not an object. Therefore, the available reading in the Śāradā manuscript शयनमवनिपृष्ठे has its authority over the other. In the third quarter of this verse, the poet wants to express antithesis between little wealth and arrogance by mentioning धनलवमधुपानभ्रान्तसर्वेन्द्रियाणाम्, which is not expressible by the reading नवधनमधुपान, found in the *JKM.1911* edition, as there is no any such antithesis between new wealth and arrogance. Thus, the available reading in the Śāradā manuscript is apt to the context.

11. अभुक्तायां यस्यां क्षणमपि न जातं नृपशतै-
र्भुवस्तस्या लाभे क इव बहुमानः क्षितिभुजाम्[19]।
तदंशस्याप्यंशे तदवयवलेशेऽपि पतयो
विषादे कर्तव्ये विदधति जडाः प्रत्युत मुदम्॥ 25॥

---

17 अवनिपृष्ठं — *JKM.1911.*

18 नवधनमधुपान — *JKM.1911, GAV.1954.*

19 क्षितिभृताम् — *GAV.1954.*

पद्येऽस्मिन् द्वितीयचरणे शारदापाण्डुलिप्यां "क्षितिभुजाम्" इति पाठो लभ्यते। अत्र कवेराशयो भवति यत् या पृथ्वी पूर्वं नृपशतैः भुक्तपूर्वा तस्या पुनः भोगे को लाभ इति √भुज् अभ्यवहारे = उपभोगे इत्यस्माद् धातोः प्रयोगोऽस्ति। परन्तु *GAV.1954* इत्यस्मिन् संस्करणे "क्षितिभृताम्" इति पाठान्तरं दृश्यते। "क्षितिभृताम्" इति पाठे √डुभृञ् — धारणपोषणयोः इति धातोः प्रयोगः भिन्नार्थकत्वं व्यञ्जयति, तेन च "पूर्वमुभुक्तायाः पृथ्व्या अधुना पालनं पोषणञ्च भवती"ति पूर्वापेक्षया वरमिति कवेरभिप्रेतस्य विरुद्धार्थं गमयतीति अयुक्तः। अतः "क्षितिभुजाम्" इति शारदापाण्डुलिपिगतः पाठ एव मौलिकः भाति।

In the second stanza of this verse, the reading "क्षितिभुजाम्" is found in the Śāradā manuscript, where of the verb "√भुज् अभ्यवहारे = to enjoy" has been applied. Here the poet's intention is that what is the use of enjoying the earth, which has already been enjoyed by hundreds of kings earlier? However, in the *GAV.1954* edition, the text changes to "क्षितिभृताम्", where the use of the verb √डुभृञ्-धारणपोषणयोः = to protect and nourish, which expresses a completely different and opposite meaning than that of the poet's intention as "the earth previously enjoyed is now nourished and protected". Therefore, the text "क्षितिभुजाम्" in the Śāradā manuscript seems to be the original.

12. अर्थानामीशिषे त्वं वयमपि च गिरामीश्महे यावदिच्छं
शूरस्त्वं वादिदर्पव्युपशमनविधावक्षयं पाटवं नः ।
सेवन्ते त्वां धनान्धा[20] मतिमलहतये मामपि श्रोतुकामा
मय्यस्त्यास्था न चेत्ते त्वयि मम सुतरामेष राजन् गतोऽस्मि ॥ 32 ॥

अत्र राज्ञः धनाढ्यैः सेवमानत्वकथनापेक्षया धनान्धैः सेवमानत्वकथनं राजविदुषोः वैषम्यं स्पष्टतरमभिव्यज्यते। अतः *JKM.1911* तथा *GAV.1954* इति संस्करणोक्तात् "धनाढ्या" इत्यस्माद् वाचनात् शारदामातृकोक्तस्य "धनान्धा" इत्यस्य वाचनस्य सन्दर्भानुकूलत्वम्।

The distinction between a king and a scholar is clearly expressed by the word धनान्धा than by धनाढ्या. Therefore,

---

[20] धनाढ्या — *JKM.1911, GAV.1954.*

the reading धनान्धा of the Śāradā manuscript is more appropriate than "धनाढ्या" found in the editions *JKM.1911* and *GAV.1954*.

13. परेषां चेतांसि प्रतिदिवसमाराध्य बहुधा
प्रसादं किं नेतुं विशसि हृदयक्लेशकलिलम्।
प्रसन्ने त्वय्येव स्वयमुदितचिन्तामणिगुणो
विविक्तः[21] संकल्पः किमभिलषितं पुष्यति न ते ॥ 35 ॥

अत्र संकल्पस्य विविक्तत्वं यथा अभिलाषपोषणरूपं प्रकृतार्थमुपकरोति विमुक्तत्वं न तथेति *JKM.1911* संस्करणलब्धस्य "विमुक्तः" इत्यस्य वाचनस्यापेक्षस्या शारदामातृकालब्धस्य "विविक्त" इत्यस्य पाठस्य मूलानुगामिता वर्तते।

As the "purity of resolution" boosts up one's goodwill, not so the "liberation from resolution". So the text of Śāradā manuscript, विविक्तः, retains its originality, than that available in *JKM.1911* edition, i.e. "विमुक्तः".

14. स्फुरत्स्फारज्यौत्स्नि धवलिततले क्वापि पुलिने
सुखासीनाः शान्तध्वनिषु रजनीषु द्युसरितः।
भवाभोगोद्विग्नाः शिव शिव शिवेत्यात्तवचसः
कदा स्यामो[22] हर्षोद्गतबहलबाष्पाकुलदृशः ॥ 44 ॥

पद्येऽस्मिन् चतुर्थचरणे "स्यामो" इत्यस्य शारदापाठस्य स्थाने *JKM.1911* संस्करणे "स्याम" इति (अस्-धातोः विधिलिङ्लकारे मस्-प्रत्यये रूपं) तथा *GAV.1954* संस्करणे "यास्याम" इति याधातोः लृट्लकारे मस्-प्रत्यये रूपं) पाठान्तरत्वेन लभ्येते। एवं प्रतीयते यत् अत्र पाठसम्पादकैः "स्यामो" इति पाठः सत्तावाचकस्य √अस्-भुवि इति धातोः विधिलिङ्लकारे मस्-प्रत्यये भवतीति मत्वा प्रमादजन्यत्वेन गृहीतः। वस्तुतस्तु दिवादिगणे √सो - षो अन्तकर्मणि — इति धातोः लट्लकारे मस्-प्रत्यये रूपं भवति, यस्यार्थः पञ्चत्वं प्राप्नुमः इति। अतः

---

21 विमुक्तः — *JKM.1911.*

22 स्यामानन्दोद्गतबहुलबाष्पाप्लुतदृशः — *JKM.1911*, यास्यामोन्तर्गतबहुलबाष्पाकुलदशाम् — *GAV.1954.*

"स्यामो" इति पाठमशुद्धं मत्वा पाठान्तरकल्पनमयुक्तं कवेराशयनाशकं च। एवं "स्यामो" इत्यस्य शारदापाठस्य सन्दर्भानुकूलता प्राचीनता, मौलिकता च प्रमाणिता भवन्ति।

In the fourth stanza of the verse, the Śāradā text of "स्यामो" is replaced by "स्याम" in the *JKM.1911* edition (the form of the root "अस्" with the suffix "मस्" in the potential mood) and the *GAV.1954* version of "यास्याम" (in the form of the root "या" with the suffix "मस्" in the future tense). It seems that the text-editors, due to their laxity and ignorance, have considered "स्यामो" as grammatically incorrect. In fact, in the word "स्यामो" is derived from the root √सो — to bring into an end with the suffix "मस्" in present tense, which means "to die". Therefore, considering the text "स्यामो" to be incorrect is inappropriate and hence the altered text "स्याम" destroys the poet's intention. Thus, the contextual appropriateness, antiquity and originality of the Śāradā text "स्यामो" here are justified.

15. आशा नाम नदी मनोरथजला तृष्णातरङ्गाकुला
रागग्राहवती वितर्कविहगा धैर्यद्रुमध्वंसिनी।
मोहावर्तसुदुस्तरातिगहना प्रोत्तुङ्गचिन्तातटा
तस्याः पारगता विशुद्धमनसो नृत्यन्ति[23] योगीश्वराः ॥ 48 ॥

अत्र "नृत्यन्ति" इति शारदापाठस्थाने "नन्दन्ति" इति पाठः *JKM.1911* तथा *GAV.1954* इत्यनयोः संस्करणयोः लभ्यते। परं "नन्दन्ति" इति वाच्येन कथनापेक्षया तदनुभावमुखेन "नृत्यन्ति" इति पदेन तत्प्रकाशनं समुचितं काव्यशास्त्रसिद्धान्तानुरूपं चास्ति।

Here, the reading "नन्दन्ति" is found in both the *JKM.1911* and *GAV.1954* editions in place of the Śāradā text "नृत्यन्ति". It is more appropriate and in accordance with the theory of poetics to express an emotion, by its ensuent, i.e. to dance, than directly mentioning it by the term, i.e. "to rejoice".

[23] नन्दन्ति — *JKM.1911, GAV.1954.*

16. वयमिह परितुष्टा वल्कलैस्त्वं च लक्ष्म्या[24]
सम इह परितोषो निर्विशेषोऽपि शेषः ।
स तु भवतु दरिद्रो यस्य तृष्णा विशाला
मनसि तु परितुष्टे कोऽर्थवान्को दरिद्रः ॥ 54 ॥

अत्र वल्कलपदं न परिधानार्थमपि तु तुच्छवस्तुनिमित्तं प्रयुक्तमिति लक्ष्म्या तद्विपरीतार्थता प्रतीयते। अत एव *JKM.1911* तथा *GAV.1954* इत्यनयोः संस्करणलब्धस्य "दुकूलैः" इति पाठस्य प्रकृतार्थानुगुणता न सिद्ध्यति इति लक्ष्म्या इति शारदापाठस्य मूलानुगापिता सिद्ध्यति।

Here "वल्कलैः" (with the barks) is used not for clothing but for insignificant things, and the word "लक्ष्म्या" has its opposite meaning. The text "दुकूलैः" found in the editions of *JKM.1911* and *GAV.1954* does not prove to be consistent with the context; hence, it is justified to say that the reading available in the Śāradā manuscripts is primary.

17. भोगा मेघवितानमध्यविलसत्सौदामिनीचञ्चला
आयुर्वायुविघट्टिताब्ज[25]पटलीलीनाम्बुवद्भङ्गुरम् ।
लोला यौवनलालनास्तनुभृतामित्याकलय्य द्रुतं
योगे ध्येयसमाधिसिद्धिसुभगे बुद्धिं विदध्वं बुधाः ॥ 59 ॥

पद्येऽस्मिन् द्वितीयचरणे "आयुर्वायुविघट्टि<u>ताब्ज</u>पटलीलीनाम्बुवद्भङ्गुरम्" इत्यत्र शारदामातृकागतस्य "अब्ज" इत्यस्य स्थाने *JKM.1911* तथा *GAV.1954* इत्यनयोः संस्करणयोः "अभ्र" इति पाठो लभ्यते। यदि "अभ्र" इति पाठः स्वीक्रियते तदा मेघे लीनस्य जलस्य भङ्गुरत्वं न सिद्ध्यतीत्यतः कमलपत्रे लीनस्य जलस्य इव आयुषः भङ्गुरत्वमित्यर्थः संगच्छते।

In the second stanza of this verse, *āyurvāyuvighaṭṭitābjapaṭalīlīnāmbuvadbhaṅguram,* the word "अभ्र" is seen in both the *JKM.1911* and *GAV.1954* editions in the place of "अब्ज" found in the Śāradā manuscripts. If the text "अभ्र" meaning "cloud" is accepted, then the fragility of water

---

24 दुकूलैः — *JKM.1911, GAV.1954.*

25 अभ्र — *JKM.1911.*

stuck on a cloud is not meaningful, so the meaning "the life is as fragile as the water put on a lotus leaf" becomes consistent with the context. Therefore, "अब्ज", the reading in the Śāradā manuscript, is primary.

18. गङ्गातरङ्गभरशीकर[26]शीतलानि
विद्याधराध्युषितधामशिलातलानि।
स्थानानि किं हिमवतो विलये गतानि
येनावमानपरपिण्डरता मनुष्याः ॥ 74 ॥

पद्येऽस्मिन् "गङ्गातरङ्गभरशीकरशीतलानि" इति शारदापाठगतस्य "भर" इत्यस्य स्थाने *JKM.1911* इत्यस्मिन् संस्करणे "हिम" इति प्राप्यते। अत्र शीतलत्वरूपसाधर्म्यस्य प्रतियोगित्वेन उपमानभूताः गङ्गातरङ्गा उक्तास्तदा पुनः हिमेत्यस्य पमानान्तरकल्पनं व्यर्थतामायाति। अतः "गङ्गातरङ्गभरशीकरशीतलानि" इति शारदापाठ एव मौलिको भाति।

In this verse, in the Śāradā text "गङ्गातरङ्गभरशीकरशीतलानि" instead of "भर", "हिम" is found in the *JKM.1911* edition. Here, when the waves of the Gaṅgā are mentioned as standard of comparison, then again the assumption of snow becomes irrelevant. Therefore, the Śāradā text "गङ्गातरङ्गभरशीकरशीतलानि" seems to meet the original source.

19. मोहं [27]मार्जयतामुपार्जय रतिं चन्द्रार्द्धचूडामणौ
चेतः स्वर्गतरङ्गिणीतटभुवामासङ्गमङ्गीकुरु।
को वा वीचिषु बुद्बुदेषु च तडिल्लेखासु च स्त्रीषु[28] च
ज्वालाग्रेषु च पन्नगेषु च सरिद्वर्गेषु[29] च प्रत्ययः ॥ 64 ॥

पद्येऽस्मिन् "मार्जयतामुपार्जय" इत्यस्य शरदापाठस्य स्थाने *JKM.1911* तथा *GAV.1954* इत्यनयोः संस्करणयोः "मार्जय ताम् उपार्जय" इति

---

26 हिमशीकर — *JKM.1911*, कणशीकर — *GAV.1954*.

27 मार्जय तां — *JKM.1911, GAV.1954*.

28 श्रीषु — *GAV.1954*.

29 सरिद्वर्गेषु — *Ms ORLS.3*, सरिद्वेगेषु — *JKM.1911, GAV.1954*.

पदभङ्गपूर्वकतया पाठः कल्पितः। परं *JKM.1911* तथा *GAV.1954* इत्यनयोः संस्करणयोः समुपलब्धे पाठे तामित्यस्य पदस्य आनर्थक्यं प्रतीयते। यतो हि चन्द्रार्धचूडामणौ तां रतिम् इति कथनेन कीदृशीं रतिमिति साकांक्षता भवति, तेन च वाक्यगतसाकांक्षतादोषो जायते। शारदापाठे तु स्वर्गतरङ्गिणीतटभुवां मोहमार्जनशीलतेत्यर्थः कवेरभिप्रेतं प्रत्याययति। अतः शारदापाठगतः "मार्जयतामुपार्जय" इत्यभङ्गः पाठ एव साधुतां मौलिकतां च प्रमाणयति।

In this verse, the Śāradā text "मार्जयतामुपार्जय/मार्जयताम् उमुपार्जय" is replaced by the text "मार्जय ताम् उपार्जय" in both the *JKM.1911* and *GAV.1954* editions. However, in both these editions, the word "तां" seems to be meaningless, because the word "तां" is an adjective to "रतिं", arising a question to which रति, and finally leads to a fault named want of correlation (साकांक्षता). As per the Śāradā text, however, the meaning of the poet's intention is to wipe away the earthly delusion on the banks of the River Gaṅgā. Therefore, the reading "मार्जयतामुपार्जय" in the Śāradā text is apparently primary and original.

सन्दर्भ-ग्रन्थ सूची (Bibliography)

Bhartṛhari, 1916, *Vairagyaśatakam*, Almora: Advaita Ashrama.

Gopalachariar, A.V. (ed.), 1954, *Bhartrihari's Sringara Sataka and Vairagya Sataka*, Madras: V. Ramaswamy Satrulu & Sons.

Gopinath, P., 2023, *Bhartrihari's Three Shatakam*, New Delhi: Central Sanskrit University.

Jayamaṅgalā of the Bhaṭṭikāvya, the commentary Nirnayasagar Press, Bombay, 1920.

Joglekar, K.M. (ed.), 1911, *Bhartrihari's Niti and Vairagya Shatak*, Bombay: Oriental Publishing Company.

Kale, M.R. and M.B. Gurjar (eds), 1898, *Nîtiśataka and Vairāgyaśataka*, Bombay: Gopal Narayan & Company.

Kennedy, J.M. (ed.), 1913, *The Satakas of Bhartrihari*, 1st edn, Clifford's Inn: T. Werner Laurie.

Kosambi, D.D. (ed.), 1948, *Epigrams Attributed to Bhartrhari*, 1st edn, Shinghi Jain Shastra Shiksha Pitha, vol. 23, Bomboy: Bharatiya Vidya Bhavan.

Mishra, Narasimha (ed.), 2014, *Bhartriharishatakatrayi*, 1st edn, Bhubaneswar: Saraswati Prakashani.

Panda, Bhagavan (ed.), 1989, *Vairagyashataka*, 1st edn, Cuttack: Granthamandira.

Scott, Dixon, 1941, *Bhartrihari Says*, 2nd edn, London: Frederic Muller.

Telang, K.T. (ed.), 1874, *Nitishataka and Vairagyashataka of Bhartrihari*, Bombay: Government Central Book Depot.

Tripathi, Ram Sagar (ed.) 1963a, *Dhvanyālokaḥ* (1st edn), Delhi: Motilal Banarsidass.

Tripathi, Ram Sagar (ed.) 1963b, *Locana of Dhvanyālokaḥ* (1st edn), Delhi: Motilal Banarsidass.

Wortham, B.H. (ed.), 1886, *Bhartrihari's Niti and Vairagya Shatak*, London: B Hale. Trubner & Co. https://doi.org/10.2307/2718169

श्लोकानुक्रमणिका

Ślokānukramaṇikā

Manuscript in Śārada Lipi

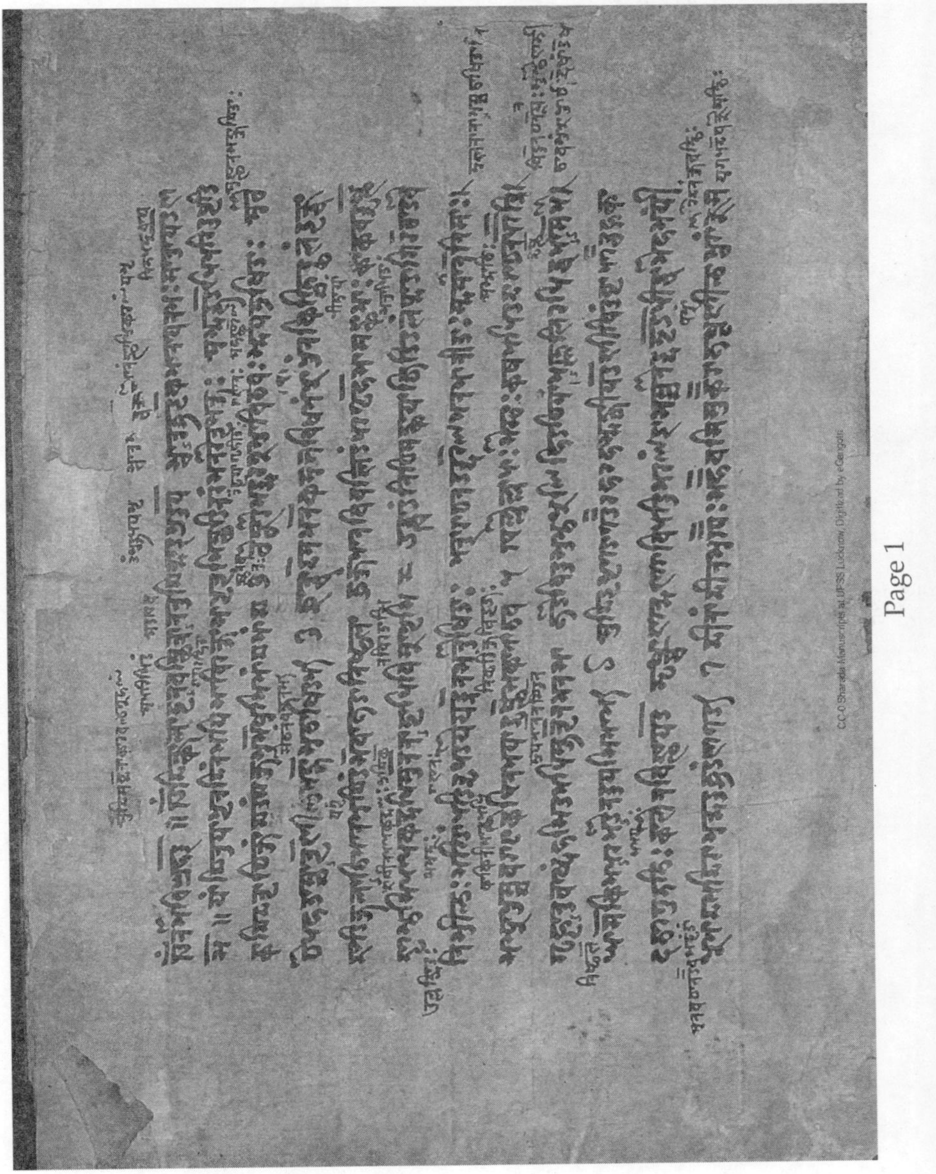

Page 1

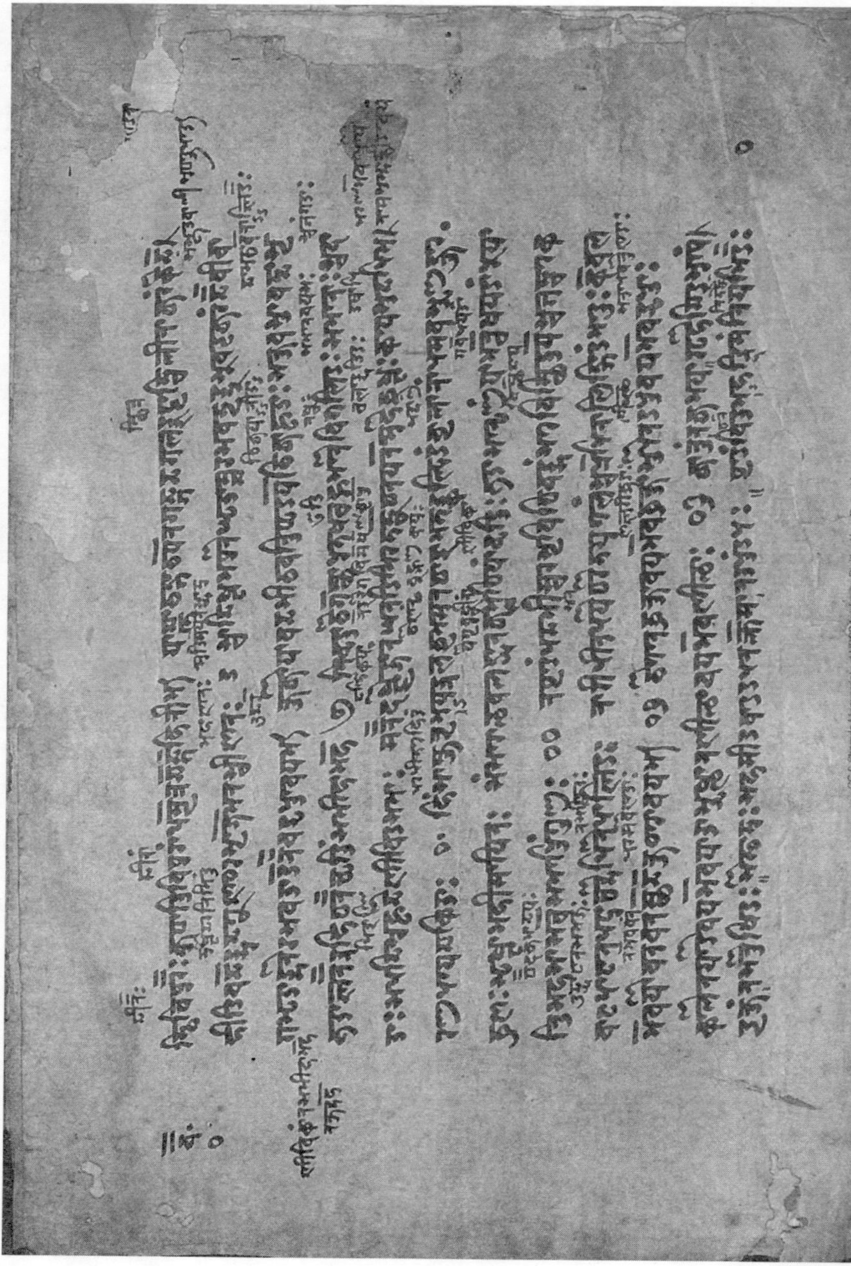

Page 2

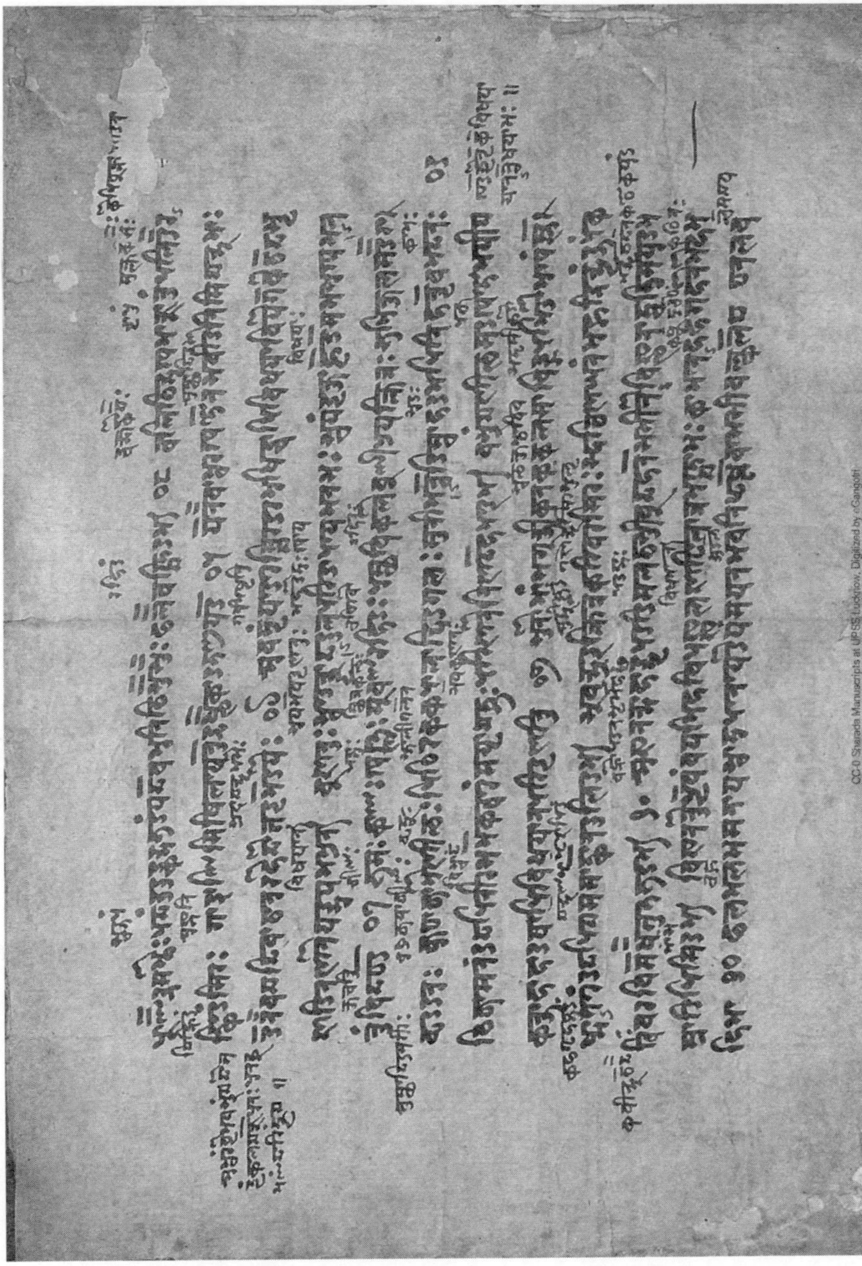

Page 3

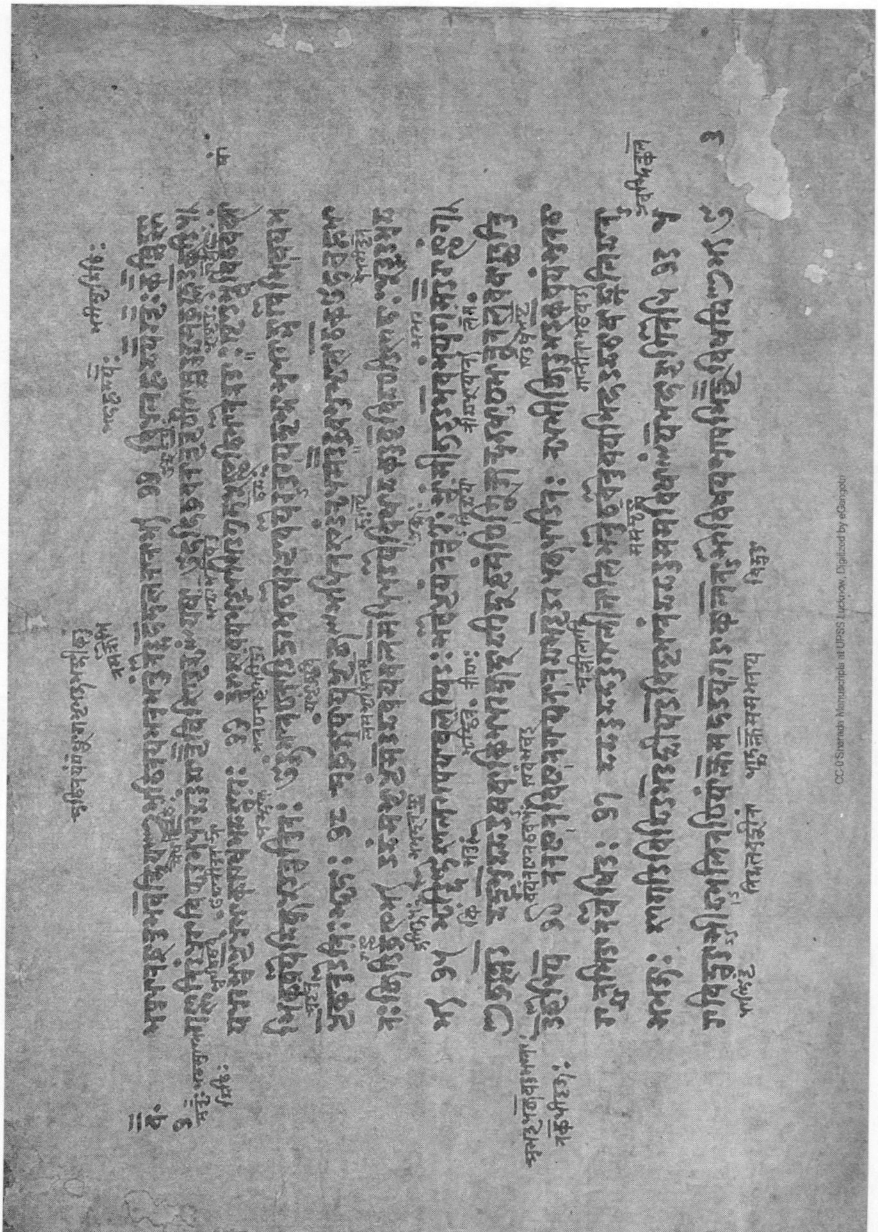

Page 4

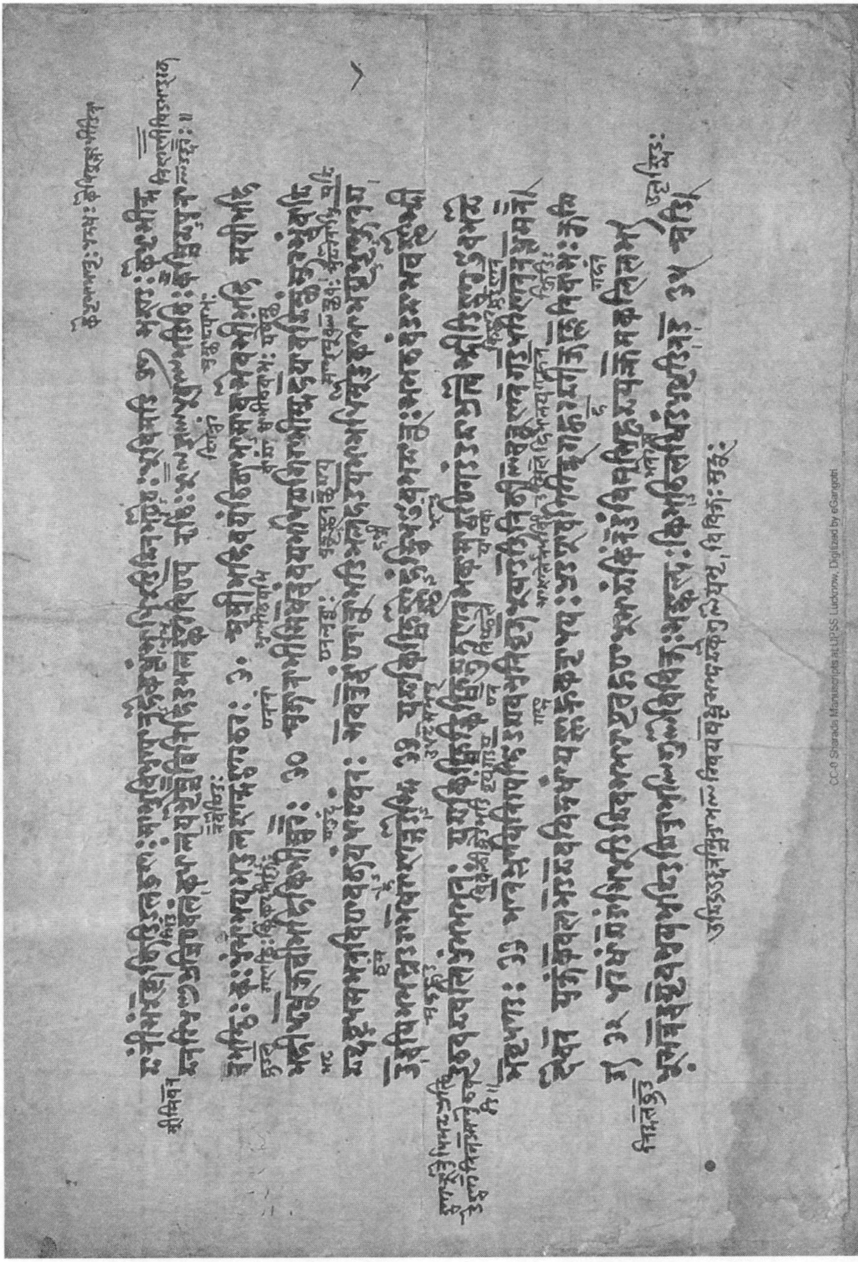

Page 5

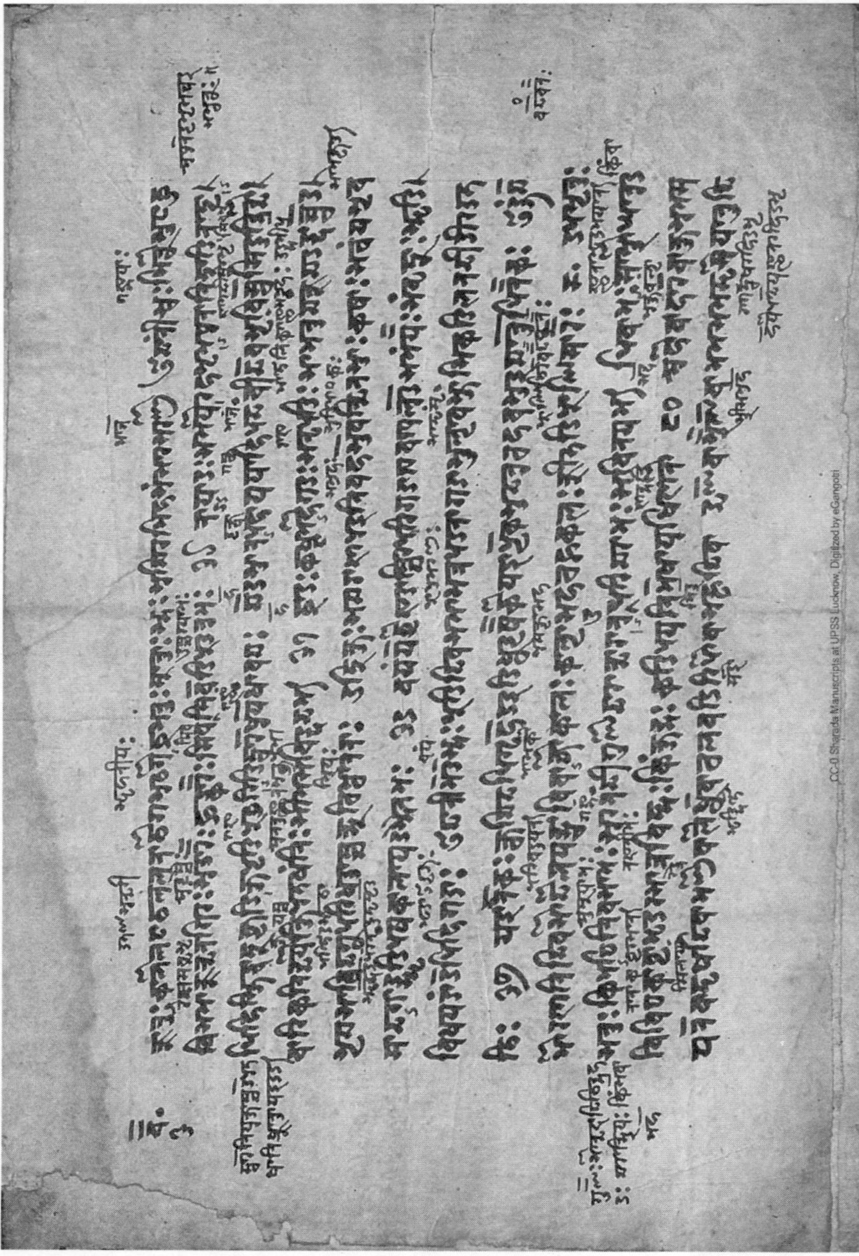

Page 6

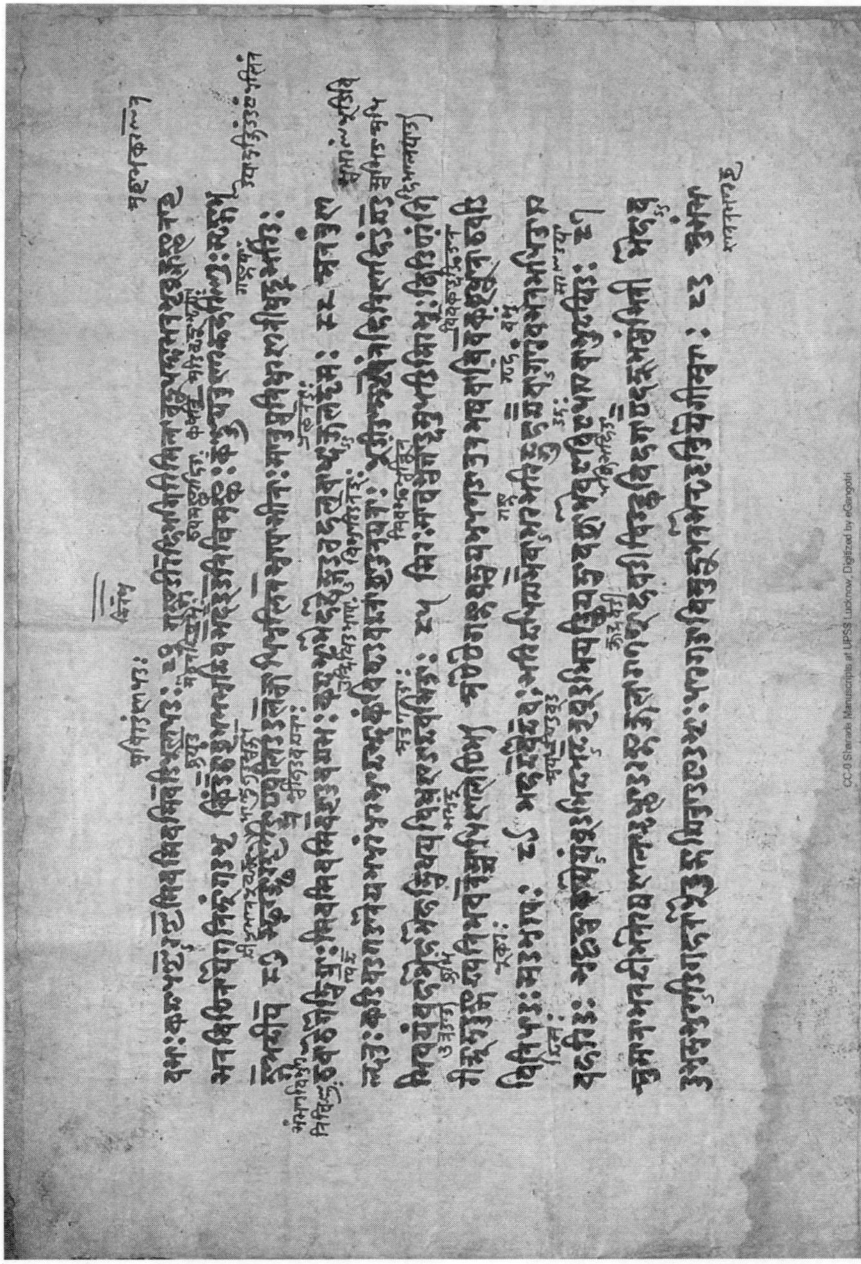

Page 7

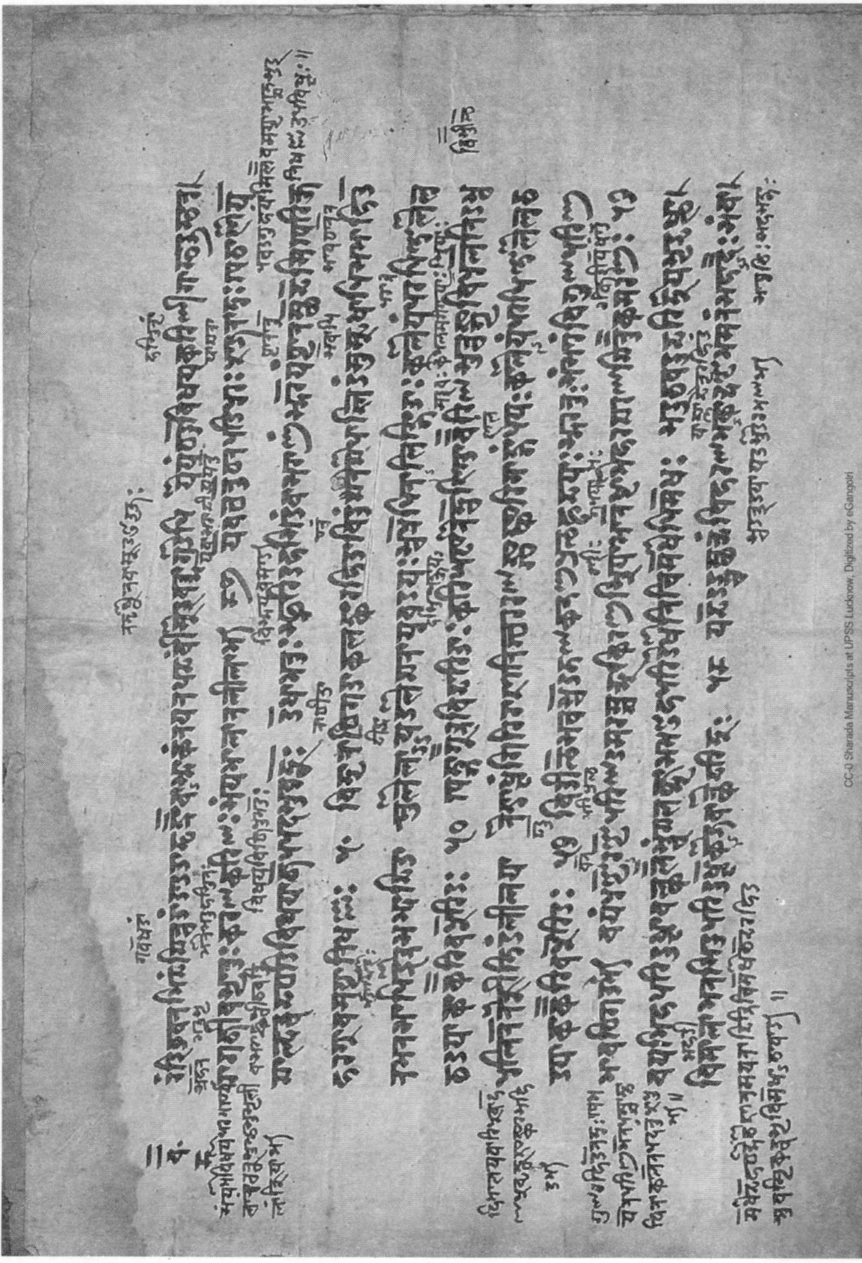

Page 8

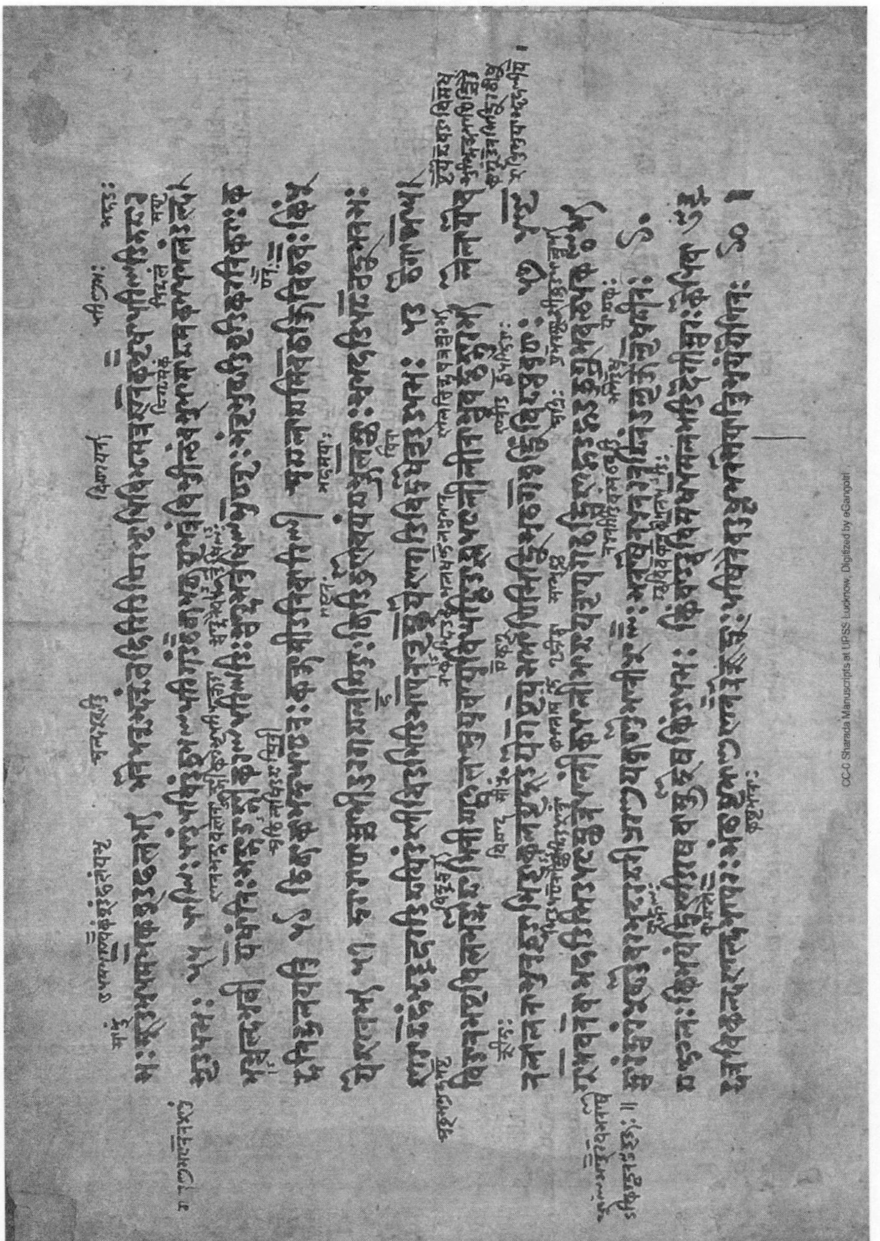

Page 9

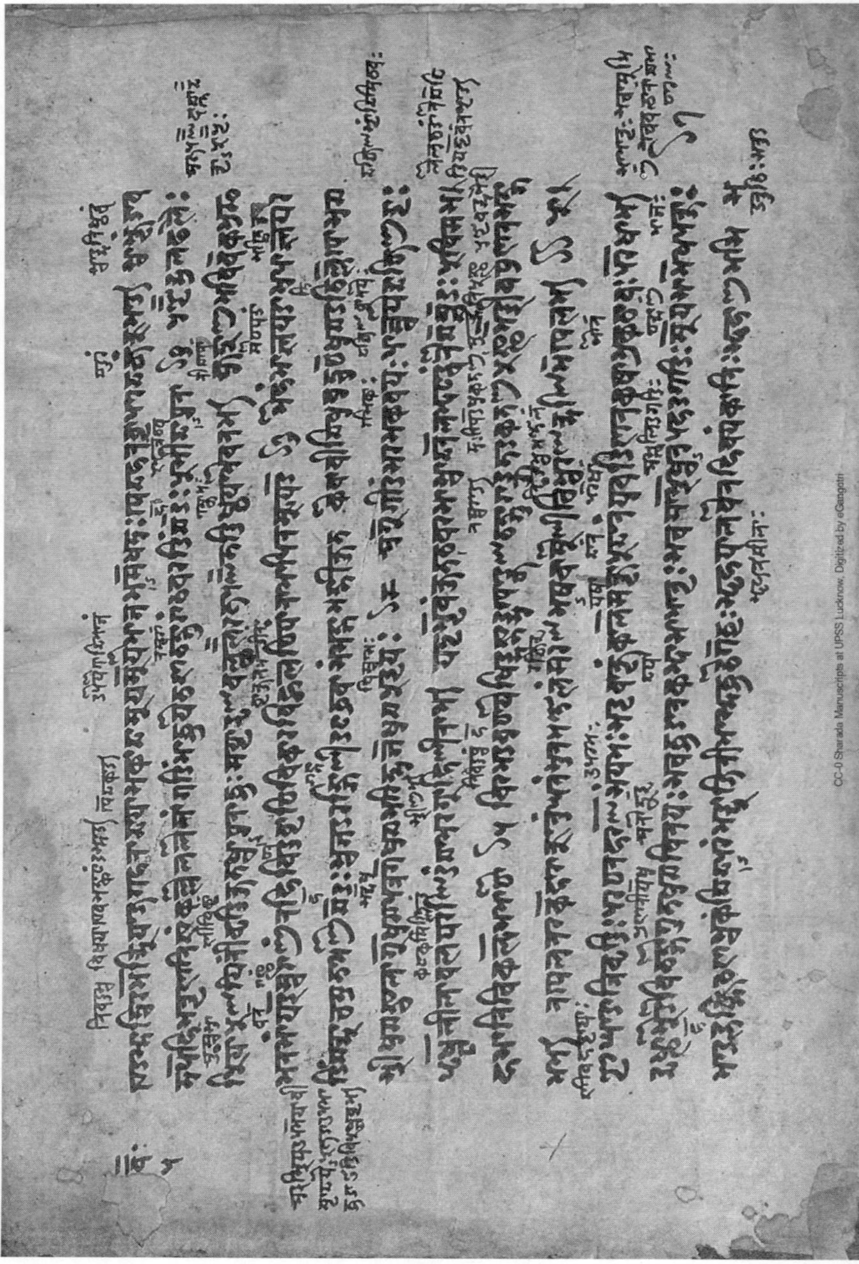

Page 10

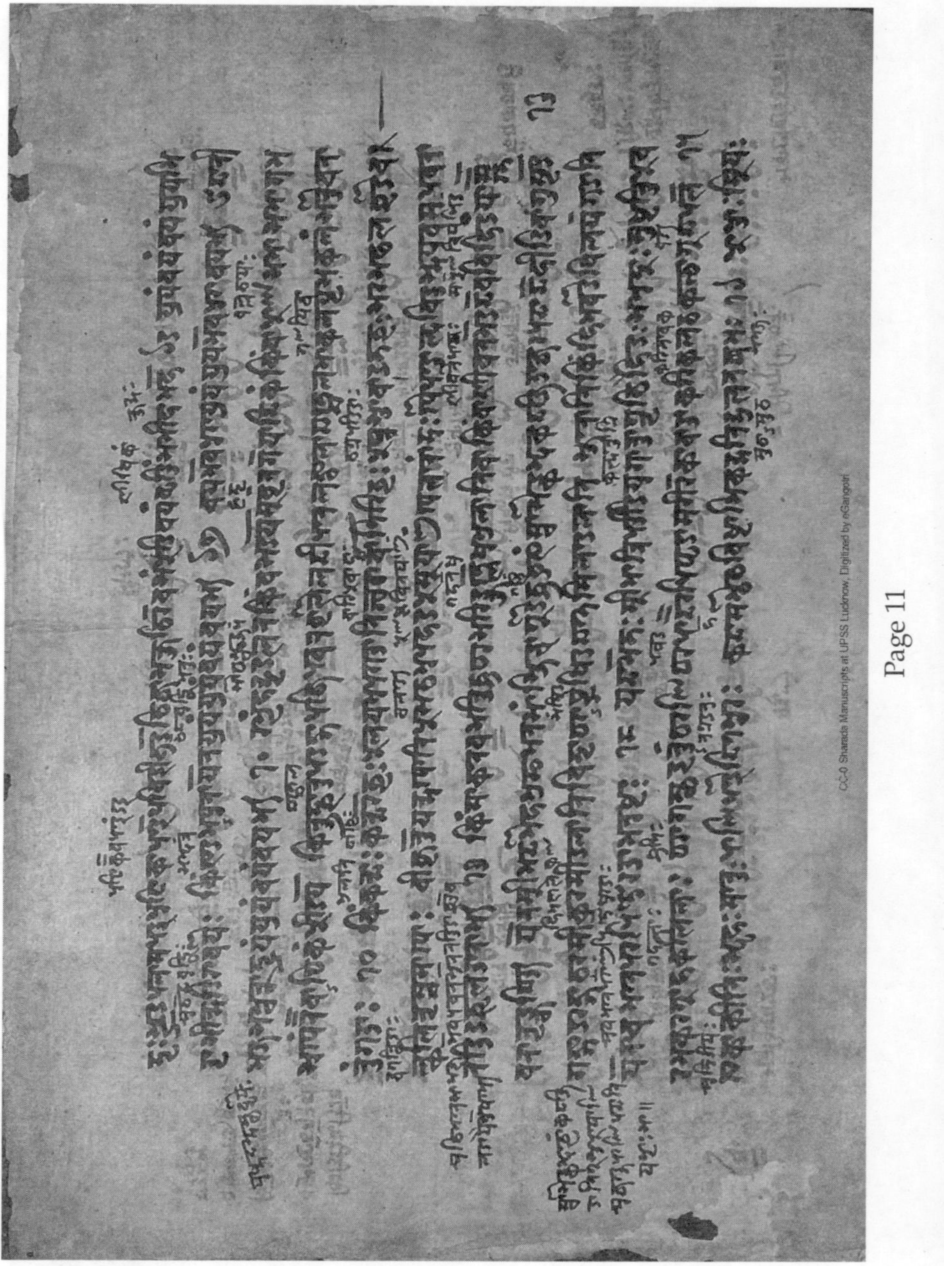

Page 11

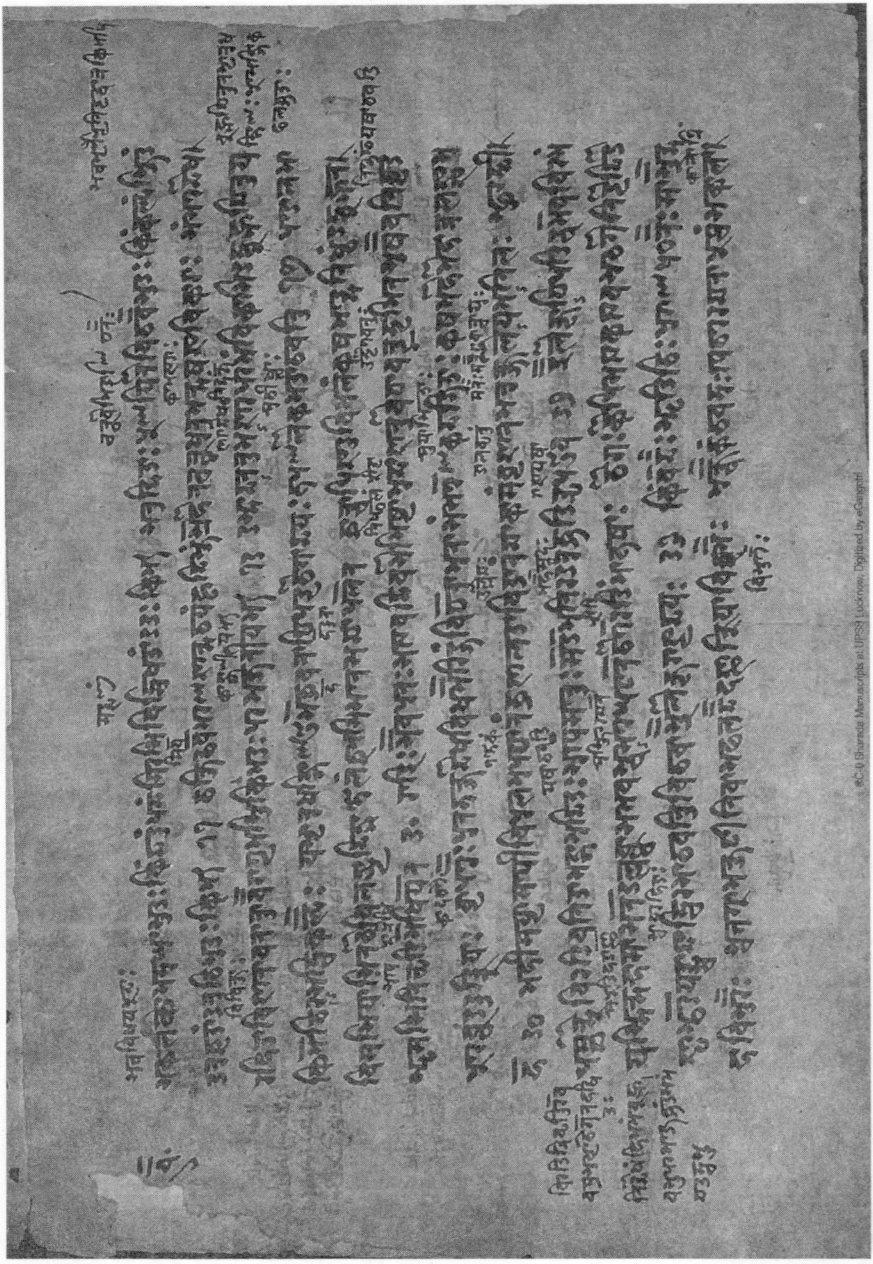

Page 12

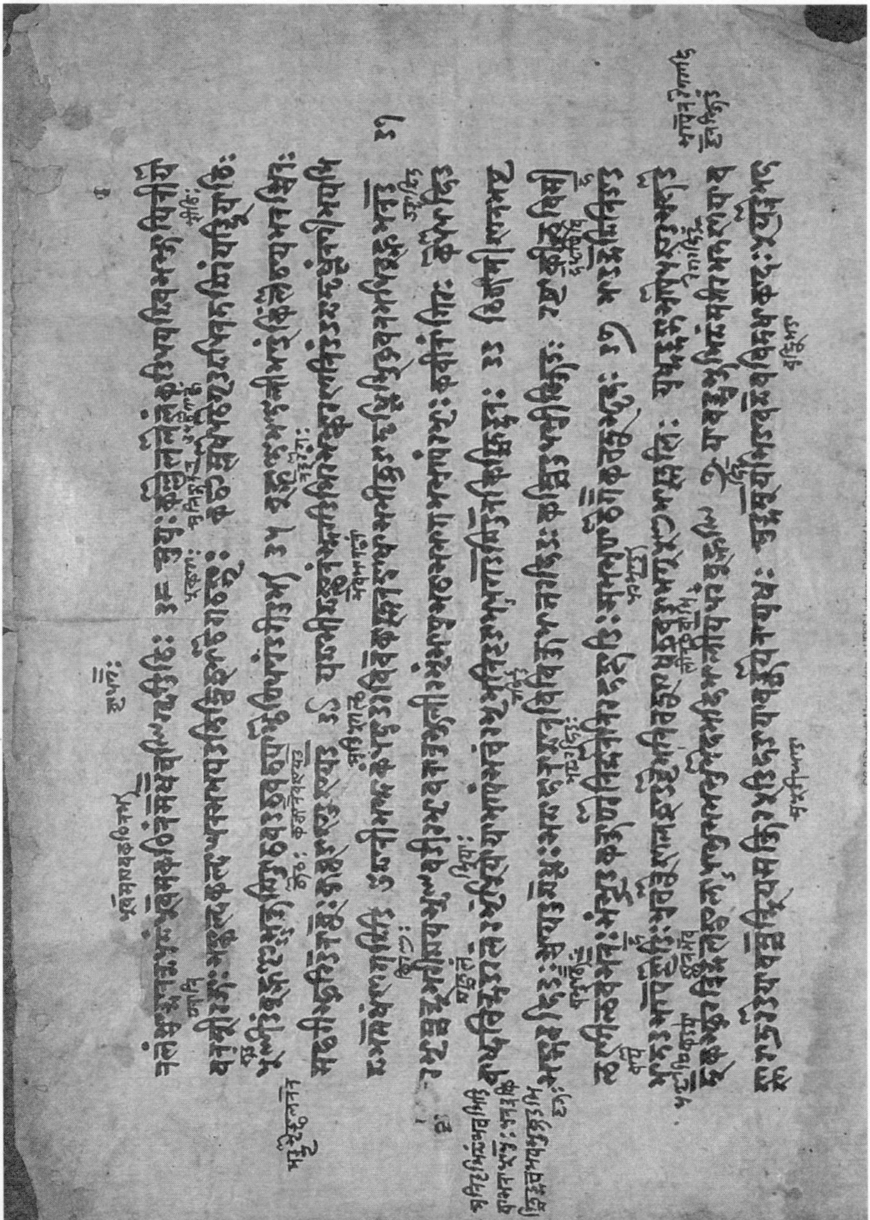

Page 13

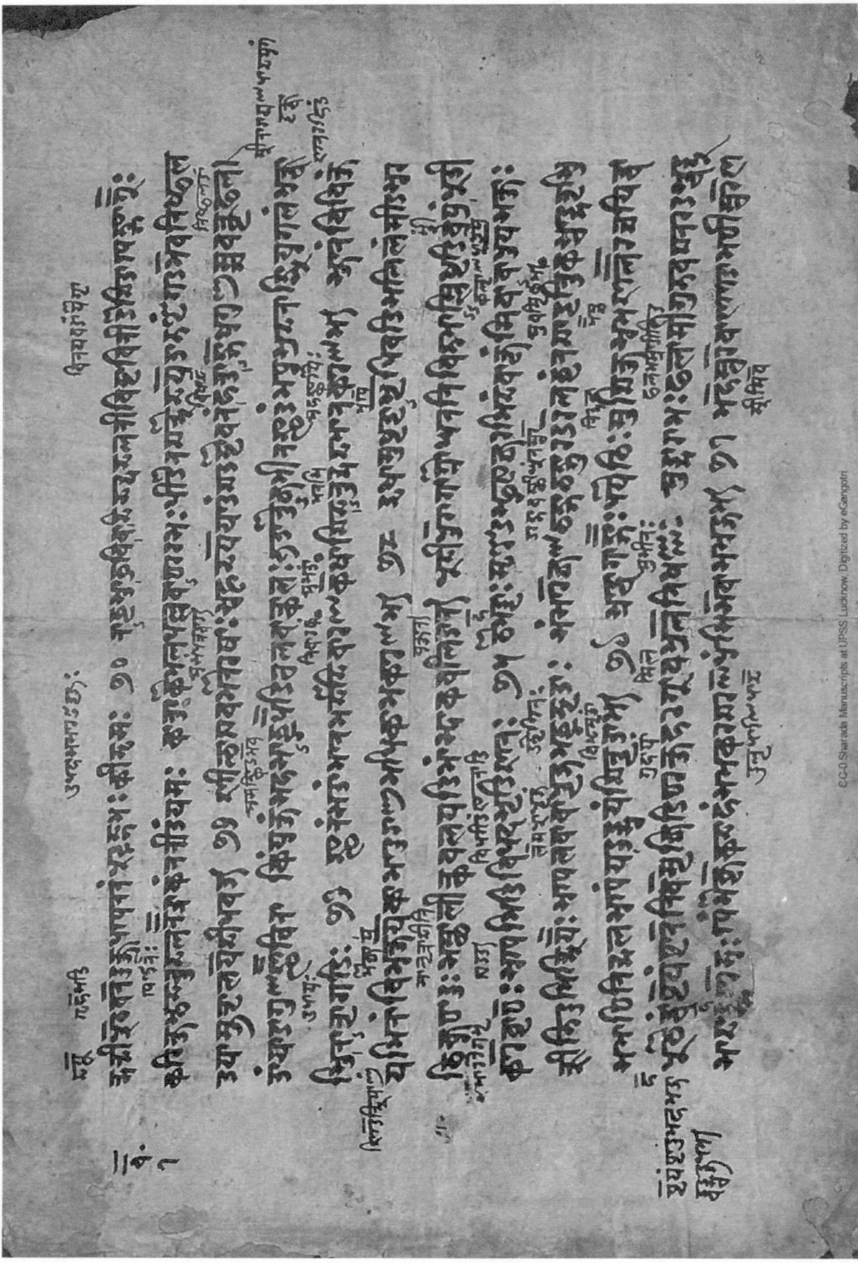

Page 14

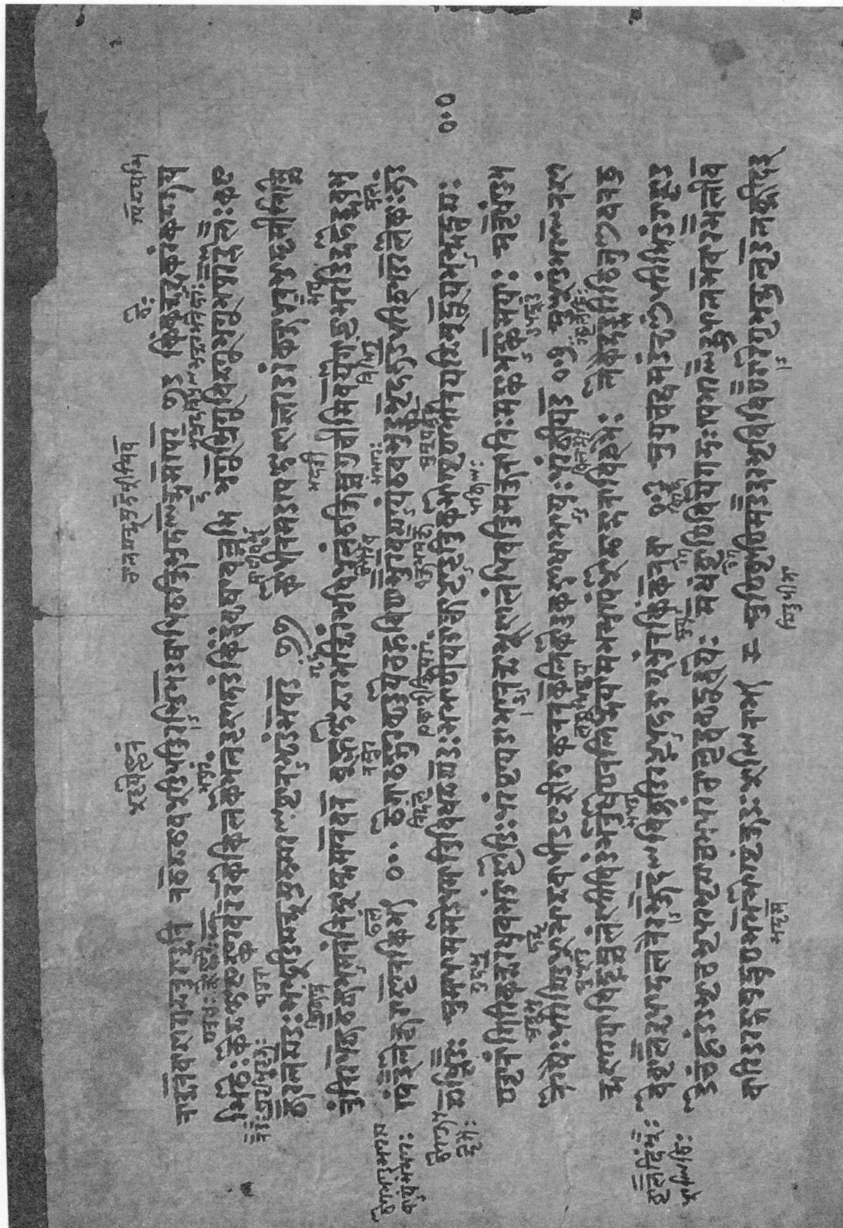

Page 15

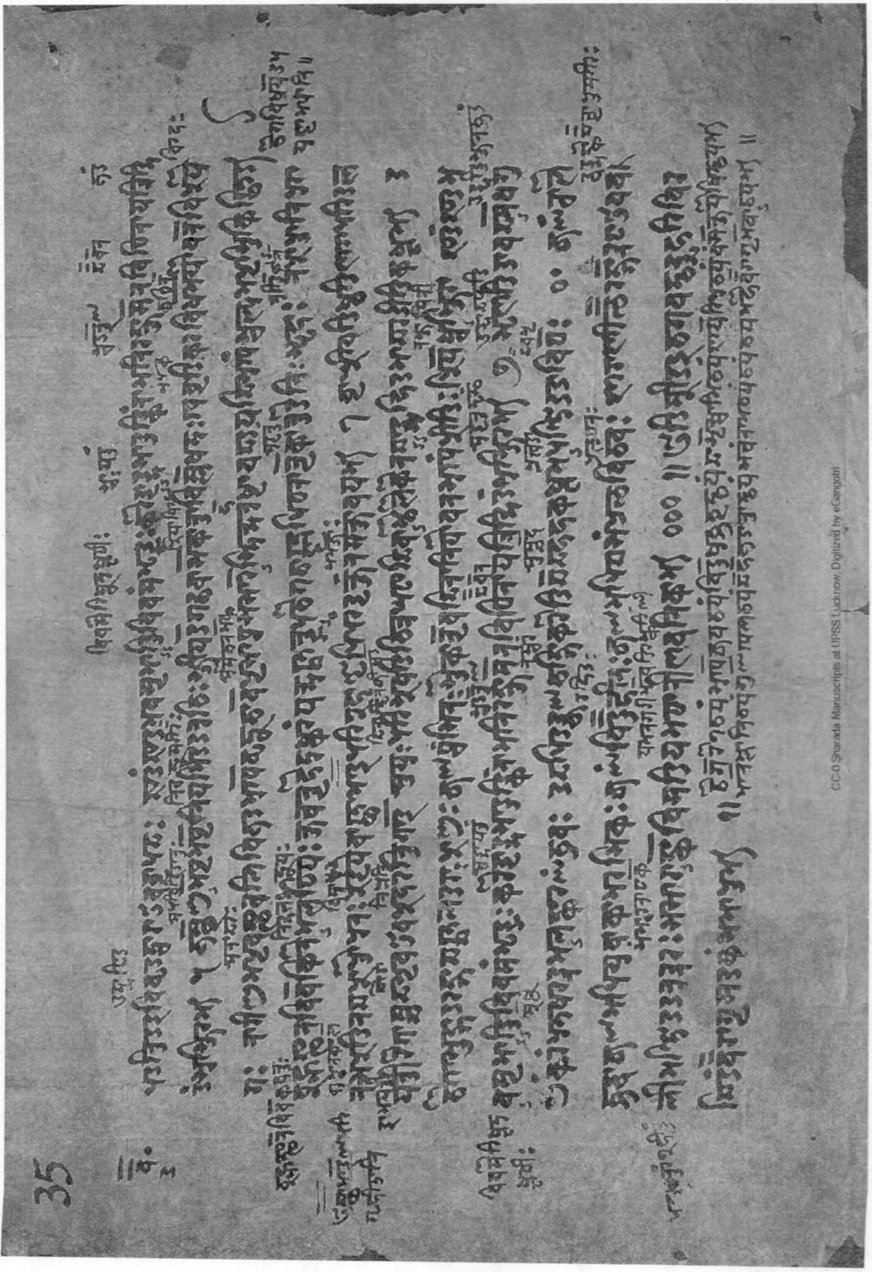

Page 16